Contents

Contents

Disaffection and Diversity
Overcoming Barriers for Adult Learners

Edited by

Judith Calder

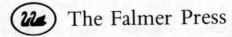 The Falmer Press

(A member of the Taylor & Francis Group)
London • Washington, D.C.

UK   The Falmer Press, 4 John St, London WC1N 2ET
USA   The Falmer Press, Taylor & Francis Inc., 1900 Frost Road, Suite 101,
         Bristol, PA 19007

First published 1993

**A catalogue record of this publication is available from the British
Library**

ISBN 0 75070 117 X cased
ISBN 0 75070 148 8 paperback

**Library of Congress Cataloging-in-Publication Data are available
on request**

Jacket design by Caroline Archer

Typeset in 9.5/11 pt Bembo by
Graphicraft Typesetters Ltd., Hong Kong

*Printed in Great Britain by Burgess Science Press, Basingstoke
on paper which has a specified pH value on final paper
manufacture of not less than 7.5 and is therefore 'acid free'.*

Introduction

A quiet but profound revolution in the design and delivery of learning opportunities for adults and in the accreditation of learning outcomes is taking place. Higher education is expanding at a rate which exceeds even that of the Robbins era; alternative routes for adults into further and higher education and into training are being introduced through the use of Access courses, and through the recognition of competencies acquired in a whole variety of different ways. The structure of the courses and training which adults can now undertake, the methods of teaching those courses and the types of qualifications which are beginning to be awarded reflect the accelerating social, technological and economic changes in the UK. Unfortunately, previous learning experiences which were unsatisfactory may act as major barriers to people's participation in and progress with organised learning.

The objectives of this book are to identify the major new developments in the provision of education and training for adults, and to examine the ideas, developments and strategies currently being developed and used in the light of the particular needs of disaffected adult learners. Disaffection in this context is taken to refer to feelings of estrangement, lack of trust, feelings of inadequacy, anger, perception of lack of relevance to self in relation to either past or current experience of education and training. The book is intended for concerned professionals who are engaged in the management, provision or supervision of organised learning and training opportunities for adults. It is intended to help them to evaluate their own current provision and to develop courses and programmes which will attract, support and extend all adults who participate in organised learning and to review and modify institutional or organisational policy and regulations in order to meet the needs of disaffected learners.

The book is divided into three sections, each of which addresses a major theme. Section One of the book deals in some depth with access issues. Section Two focuses more on people's progress with their learning in relation to different kinds of provision. The third section examines the different notions of success in relation to adults' learning achievements and the implications for adult learners of new approaches to assessment and accreditation. Each Section has two objectives: to consider the major aspects of the theme of the section in relation to the needs of disaffected adult learners, and to introduce and discuss practical examples which overcome some of the problems raised by disaffection.

Section One: Courses which were designed to support and encourage disaffected learners to get access to other forms of education and training such as 'Return to Learning', 'Second Chance', and other such courses have been with us now for many years. 'Access' courses are a relatively new phenomenon. In chapter one, Roger Harrison debates the issues surrounding the introduction and use of these courses and raises some challenging questions about the primary aim of Access courses. He argues that it is because of sectional interests that such courses are focusing more on 'single exit' courses which prepare adult learners for access to traditional further and higher education rather than on what are called 'multiple exit' courses which develop the potential of individuals as learners and which aim at a much wider range of options for further study or training.

The growing national importance of adults in higher education and the problems for adults of fitting into a system designed for school leavers is discussed in chapter two. Malcolm Tight reviews the available evidence on the numbers and characteristics of adult students in higher education and describes the variety of special arrangements which currently exist for enabling adults access to higher education. The theme raised in this chapter and in other chapters in the book concerns the extent to which adult learners are expected to adapt to existing provision. In chapter three Stina Lyons points out the double-edged nature of special access arrangements to further and higher education. She draws attention to the fact that the use of special entry arrangements can result in negative effects for black minority students. Ironically, success in achieving access to further and higher education can, if not followed up with sensitive support, lead to later disaffection because black and ethnic minority students can feel labelled as 'second class'.

By no means all Access courses lead on to further and higher education. The first section concludes with a case study of a local Access project. In a candid account of a far-sighted and innovative experimental scheme set up by Oxfordshire LEA, Brenda Walters draws attention to the reality of the impact of Access opportunities on people's lives. In particular she highlights how, because of the planning and implementation problems actually faced by agencies attempting to introduce change into an existing framework of provision, there can be a real danger that the hopes of participants in such schemes about future education and training opportunities may not be met.

Section Two: The issue of the range of barriers which adults must overcome if they are to take advantage of any of the diverse forms of provision now available is taken up by Colin Titmus in his overview chapter. He points out the trend towards self-reproduction among the types of courses developed so far, and argues that alternative solutions are needed if the UK is to break out of the existing framework of provision and start moving towards Scandinavian levels of participation in adult education and training. This theme is continued by Eric Midwinter in relation to the particular needs of older adults. The University of the Third Age (U3A), which has been so successful in France, has been rapidly gaining popularity in the UK. In chapter six the success of this particular scheme in reaching out to a group who are not motivated by vocational needs, and who are particularly susceptible to lack of confidence about their learning ability is analysed in some detail. As Dr Midwinter points out, this particular form of provision uses very much a face-to-face community-based approach.

Other alternatives to the traditional institution-based mode are Open Learning and Distance Education. However the distinction between these two modes appears to be diminishing rapidly; as indeed does the distinction between the face-to-face institution-based provision and Open Learning. In chapter seven, Robert Leach and Roger Webb describe a number of models of Open Learning which range from institution-based face-to-face provision supplemented by materials-based independent study to what is, in effect, distance education. The advantages of the group support offered by such models as the employment-based open learning provision is, however, unavailable to such groups as the housebound, the unemployed and the retired. In chapter eight, Alan Woodley discusses the appropriateness of the distance education mode for disaffected learners and concludes that although distance education has much to offer them, there is evidence that modifications can be introduced which more effectively meet the needs of disaffected adults. Woodley also discusses how well disaffected learners cope with Open University degree courses. One of the points he makes is that success should not be measured only in terms of whether or not the final qualification, i.e. a degree, was achieved.

Section Three: The need to take a wider view of adult learning and success is a theme which is developed in my own chapter which opens Section Three. Changes in the aims of education and training, in their funding and in the flexibility of new forms of provision mean that perceptions of success and measures of success are becoming both more complex and sophisticated. However, although measures such as Performance Indicators have a role to play for institutions, they do have considerable limitations. For example, what is perceived as success by a learner at one point in time may not be seen in the same light in the longer term once all the costs have been counted. Similarly what is perceived as success by a learner may not be seen in the same light by the provider or sponsor.

Great changes are also occurring in the design and structure of vocational qualifications at the present time. Recommendations in the government's White Paper on higher and further education accelerated those changes. For example, there were radical proposals to replace older style vocational qualifications by a comprehensive framework of National Vocational Qualifications (NVQs) by 1992. Peter Raggatt discusses some of the issues related to the introduction of NVQs in chapter ten. At the same time, the growth of schemes such as the Assessment of Prior Learning (APL) through which earlier learning in non-formal settings, and even knowledge and skills acquired through experience, can be formally recognised and accredited should be given a considerable boost. Linda Butler Miles explains the development and the potential of this exciting new strategy for recognising competencies, however gained. For adult learners and particularly for disaffected learners, such developments could make an immense difference to the achievement of their vocational aims, to their perceptions of themselves as learners, and to the likelihood that, once drawn into a formal system which is geared to their needs, the cycle of disaffection might be broken.

An issue which the agencies involved in adult education and training share is the problem of the amount of time which education and training can take. Just as employers find it difficult to plan their detailed training requirements with any accuracy very far ahead, so adults can find it difficult to commit themselves for long periods of time to one particular institution for their education and training.

The geographical mobility of adults, and the various crises and life events which occur with little if any warning, has meant in the past that long courses were often left part way through and uncompleted. However, institutions are increasingly taking into account and recognising learning which has been undertaken in other places and at other institutions. The development and growth of credit accumulation and transfer schemes, described and discussed by Geoff Layer in chapter twelve, should prove an important step in meeting the needs of learners, employers and indeed the institutions themselves. The growth of credit transfer schemes is encouraging the modularisation of many courses which in turn is enabling providers to be much more flexible about part-time and intermittent patterns of study which are much better suited to the needs of adult learners.

It is perhaps a fitting conclusion to the book that the final chapter, from Marian Lever analyses the strategies used by a highly successful local initiative to get disadvantaged and disaffected adult learners to participate in organised learning. The community-based project which she reports has been operating for ten years, using both intensive local group work and highly developed independent learning materials. This chapter brings together and addresses many of the issues raised in earlier chapters and in a sense, emphasises the spiral nature of adult education. That is, that an important set of outcomes for disaffected learners from involvement in organised education is that access to further provision becomes possible, psychologically, socially and academically. The experience of the project workers is that, for such learners, some form of external recognition of their learning is very important.

The outlook for the provision of education and training for adults is mixed. The potential of many of the ideas which have already been tried out is clearly enormous. Adult educators and trainers have an exciting range of approaches which appear to have the capability of reaching out to and supporting even disaffected adult learners. At the same time, however, there is clearly a tension between the needs of individual learners and the immediate and short-term needs of employers. It is clear that only if employers and the government begin to look to the long term and to educate for flexibility and change rather than for narrow or specific skills will the needs of all the parties involved in adult education and training become congruent.

Acknowledgments

It is always a pleasure to have the opportunity of thanking those who have helped in so many different ways to bring an idea to reality.

To Neville Jones, whose original idea it all was and to Christine Cox, Falmer Press, and Ros Morpeth, NEC for their support and ideas during the early discussions and to Malcolm Clarkson of Falmer Press for his guidance during the end stages; to Nick Farnes and Mary Thorpe of the Open University for reviewing some of the early drafts of the manuscript; to the secretarial staff, Anne Wood, Wendy Morgan and Margaret Harkin who typed much of the manuscript.

I would also like to thank the contributors, who were a pleasure to work with; and, not least, my family, for their encouragement and support even when the going got really rough.

Part 1

Access Issues

1 Disaffection and Access

Roger Harrison

Introduction

Access is a word which has achieved a high profile among administrators and academics over the last ten years. A very wide constituency of educationalists, from those in the most elite institutions of higher education, to those involved in community-based outreach work, are prepared to vouch for access as a 'good thing'. It has drawn together those who are concerned with equal opportunities, those who are concerned with skill shortages in the labour force and those who are concerned that a decline in the number of 16–19 year olds in the population will threaten the power base of the major institutions of further and higher education. It is not surprising that this unholy alliance has led to the term 'access' being constituted into a number of different meanings, and its implications for practitioners interpreted in a number of different ways.

In this chapter I want to suggest that the 'access debate' in education has been hi-jacked by sectional interests in a way which has diverted attention from the real issues of inequality, disaffection and non-participation; that the real meaning and significance of access is at variance with the manifestations of access work which currently predominate in post-compulsory education. I want to locate the attitudinal factors implied by the term disaffection at the centre of the access debate, and to suggest it is here that educational programmes must start if they are to reach non-participating groups. Finally, I want to identify some of the broad approaches which seem to be effective.

Policy Aims

The aims of access are clear and uncontroversial. They appear as a sort of 'dream ticket' for educationalists; a fortuitous coalition of moral and pragmatic imperatives. On the one hand social justice; a concern that everyone should have equal rights to educational opportunities which can enable them to fulfil their individual human potential. On the other, a concern with changing demographic patterns, the need for a flexible workforce, and a requirement to recruit adults into retraining and skills updating courses.

Describing developments in access to higher education Philip Jones, Secretary to the Access Courses Recognition Group, identified these two main driving forces:

One is the perceived need for social equity, and the ensuing commitment to include in higher education increased numbers of students from parts of the community which are traditionally under-represented, such as the working class, women and black people. The other is the country's increasing need for well-trained personnel, which, combined with a fall in the birth-rate, could create a considerable shortfall of highly-educated people in the 1990s.

In the Treasury White Paper for 1988 one of the government's five aims for education was given as: 'to widen access to further and higher education and to make them more responsive to the needs of the economy'. Robert Jackson, then Minister for Higher Education, stated: 'Unequal access is not just uneconomic, but it is unfair and unjust as well' (April, 1980).

Few would argue with the importance of these aims but then, few people would disagree with the proposition that people should have clean air to breathe. What is required in addition to the statement of normative policy aims is some analysis of how they might be achieved in practice. Over the last decade educationalists and politicians have been strong on policy statements which indicate their view of access as a 'good thing'. At the level of institutional practice a great deal of effort and ingenuity has gone into developing methods and devices for attracting adults into education. But there has been an absence of analysis, of the development of theory, and the translation of this into an overall strategy which is capable of addressing the central issues of access: this is the simple but unavoidable fact that the majority of adults choose not to participate in any form of education or training, and those who do participate are predominantly from groups which are socially, economically and educationally advantaged. Any analysis of access must start from here, and must build theories or models as to how adults become engaged in learning opportunities which can benefit them, their communities, and society in general.

I would argue that professional educators have been willing to skip this analysis and theory building as they hurry towards quick fix access solutions which are opportunistic and self-serving. To support and explain this I want to look at how the term access has been constituted and interpreted over recent years.

Definitions

A feature of the access debate of the last few years has been the diversity of interpretation of the term itself. One way of describing this diversity is as a spectrum between two extremes. At one end of the spectrum would come those courses which have the single minded aim of enabling students to gain entry into institutions of higher education. The Further Education Unit (1987) had this type of provision in mind when it stated: 'Access courses are designed to facilitate entry into higher education for non-traditional students.' Non-traditional students are defined as: 'all those who do not follow the traditional route to university through the acquisition, in a sixth form, of the required number of 'A' levels at the age of 18.'

The government White Paper 'Higher Education: meeting the challenge' (1987) saw Access courses as providing a 'recognised route into higher education — for those, mainly mature entrants, who hold neither traditional sixth form nor vocational qualifications'.

Access is characterised as a process of helping less confident and able students by building up their skills, knowledge, and confidence to the point where they feel able to tackle a professionally produced programme of study in higher education. Courses which advertise these aims are referred to as big 'A' access, or 'single exit', courses. The assumptions they operate under are that learners are motivated to study the courses on offer, but there are factors which prevent them from doing this. These obstacles, or barriers, are interpreted as partly to do with circumstances — for instance the difficulty of arranging child care, or work commitments — but largely in terms of skills and knowledge deficits. So some Access courses do have crêche facilities and do allow flexibility in time and place of study, in an effort to overcome these barriers. But the emphasis is on study skills, and shortfalls in required skill and knowledge bases. Because the objectives are defined in terms of 'what people need to know', these courses are characterised by what Knowles has described as a 'transmission model' of teaching in which the user is seen as an 'empty vessel' into which 'acceptable knowledge' is transferred by the teacher (Knowles, 1978). To use Groombridge's terms, such courses are 'prescriptive' in that 'experts with authority decide what is to be learned and whether it has been learned satisfactorily' (Groombridge, 1983).

At the other end of the spectrum of Access courses are those which are less specific in their assumptions about learner destinations. The emphasis here is on 'negotiated' content and 'learner-centred' processes, with the aims of raising awareness of the possibilities in education and training and developing the confidence to pursue them. Courses of this type are sometimes referred to as little 'a', or 'multi-exit' courses.

The UDACE disscussion paper, 'Developing Access', (1988) had this broader definition in mind when it expressed a concern with access to:

> education and training opportunities provided by the public, voluntary and private sectors (including employers). This includes formal, informal, open and individual modes of learning at all levels from basic to higher education. These opportunities may be designed to meet either vocational or general needs, and some may lead to formal qualifications while others will not.

The discussion paper identifies the role of access initiatives as being: 'to help education and training agencies to respond to the learning needs of adults'. This broader definition of access gives equal weight to the value of all forms of learning. It places the emphasis on the learning needs of adults, rather than the requirements of entry into higher education. It acknowledges the variety of learning projects in which adults are involved as they interact with complex and changing circumstances, as they extend their knowledge and understanding in the contexts of work, leisure, family, community, through the media of books, friends, television, open learning, work or college-based courses.

Figure 1.1: *Approaches to Access*

'Provider Model'	'User Model'
Curriculum is fixed and determined by professionals (educators)	Curriculum is negotiated between users and tutors
Users take it or leave it — choice is limited to the range of options on offer	Range of options is infinite (subject to resources)
Education is concerned with passing on a fixed body of knowledge by an active tutor to relatively passive students	Education is a joint learning experience where the values and knowledge of all participants are recognised. The tutor creates situations in which people learn rather than acting as a font of knowledge
There is a limited opportunity for negotiation within a group to meet the needs of individual learners	Learners can determine the content and method of the learning. Learners can even be involved in tutor appointments
Courses tend to be located in educational establishments (our territory)	Courses/groups are located in community settings including people's own homes, community centres, libraries, halls, etc. (their territory)
Learning goals are predetermined	Learning goals may change, or grow through experience
Access is solely concerned with the routes people take to reach a fixed position. (For example enrolment procedures, publicity, pre-entry Access courses).	Access is concerned with changing the nature of the provision to meet user's requirements (for example, content, place, teaching methods)

(*Source*: REPLAN (1989), *Access in Action*)

This spectrum of approaches to access work has been summarised in a REPLAN document 'Access in Action' (1989). The ends of the spectrum have been characterised in terms of a 'Provider model' and a 'User model'. These should not be seen as either/or alternatives, but as two ends of a continuum, with most access initiatives falling somewhere in between.

Interpretation

What has happened over the last few years is that the access debate has become increasingly framed by an interpretation of access which tends towards the provider end of the spectrum. Access is taken to mean access to further and higher education, rather than access to adult learning opportunities. McGivney (1990) has noted that in the later 1980s most of the access rhetoric 'centred on opening up the advanced sector of post-compulsory education and it is in higher education that measures to widen access have been concentrated'. If we look at the phenomenon of access in terms of its impact on the world of post-compulsory education, and ask the question 'what has actually changed?' the answer is revealing.

The most noticeable effect has been the exponential growth of Access courses. In 1985 there were about 130 programmes of study defined as Access courses. By 1987 there were about 400 courses catering for some 5,000 students. A 1989 survey indicated at least 570 Access courses with places for about 11,000 students. (Access to Higher Education: Courses directory. ECCTIS, 1989). These are 'single exit' Access courses which provide a route into existing, pre-determined, higher education courses, and would locate towards the 'provider' end of the continuum. A whole industry has grown up around the requirement to develop, define, validate and generally control these courses, culminating in the development of a national framework of quality assurance for Access courses.

Malcolm Tight (1988) has noted the tendency in many quarters to equate 'access' with 'Access courses', and identifies the inherent conservatism of this approach. He says of Access courses:

> They tend, explicitly or implicitly, to accept higher education for what it is, and concentrate on providing an alternative means of entry to this unchanged commodity for a limited number of people.

The way in which the meaning of 'access' has been framed in the discourse of professional educators, tells us a lot about their concerns and preoccupations. The major stakeholders in this debate are the professionals involved in the government-funded apparatus of further and higher education. The concerns here are to do with a sufficient supply of students to justify current levels of public expenditure. A fall-off in student numbers threatens not only jobs, but the status and power bases of the main actors as well. The self-interest inherent in this concern with student take-up is nothing new; its influence on professional and institutional thinking was pointedly identified a decade ago by Sean Courtney (1981):

> Because participation in adult education is, in the main, voluntary then all those with an investment in the area are anxious about increasing it.

He concludes:

> Recruitment is a political rather than a theoretical issue for most adult education administrators, even academics.

The momentum behind the current Access bandwagon is undeniable. What is questionable is how far it is piloted by political and interest group concerns, and how far it is guided by a real interest in the issue of adult participation in learning opportunities. Are 'non-traditional learners' being seen simply as an alternative source of students by the major stakeholders in the education system; a pool of potential clients which can be drawn off to solve pressing short term problems. Or is this a genuine attempt to examine why it is that the majority of adults choose not to participate in education and training opportunities, and to take positive action.

It has to be said the signs are not good. A feature of the debate on access has been its tendency towards an atheoretical, even a knee-jerk response to the facts of non-participation. An indication of this can be seen in the way in which learners are treated in the professional discourse. They are categorised — women, minority ethnic groups, older people, and so on — and we are given to understand that they must be 'drawn-in', or 'persuaded' to attend classes. It is noted that there are 'barriers' which impede their progress, and which educators must help them to surmount. But it is largely an instrumental view of the learner, designed to facilitate the educator in dealing with less pliable raw material, yet producing the same quality of end product. There is little attempt to enter the domain of the learner, take on board their perspective, experience, attitudes and expectations. By contrast, there is a great deal of activity in the professional domain — defining policy, laying down guidelines, establishing frameworks, setting standards, drawing up curricula. One major national initiative has been the setting up of a framework for ensuring quality control and comparability between Access courses. The initiative is being handled by CNAA and CVCP and it has given the aims of the framework as being to:

> Support and extend opportunities for student admission to higher education whilst safeguarding against the risk of erosion of standards.

This statement neatly summarises the extent of the aims, and the nature of the anxieties of the educational establishment.

The message reads: There is nothing wrong with the learning opportunities currently on offer, the challenge is to persuade and educate a disaffected audience to join in, whilst ensuring that standards are maintained. The operation becomes one akin to marketing, and Access courses fit in neatly as part of the softening-up of customers. They provide a less threatening entry point for non-traditional learners, and a gentle ramp up to the standards of skill and knowledge required by existing courses. The prevailing interpretation of access allows no questioning of the traditional notion of human learning as synonymous with curriculum teaching. Knowledge, in this framework, can still be defined in terms of subjects which are easily assembled into purveyable chunks which are carefully graded, standardised, consumed and certified (Richardson, 1974). What Freire (1970) described as the digestive theory of learning is retained, with the effects on adult learners being 'to domesticate rather than educate'.

'Access' as a dynamic and potentially radical issue in education has been emasculated and domesticated. It has led not to a reassessment of what, as educators, we are actually offering people, but to the growth of a new service industry for the institutions of further and higher education. The fact that Access courses are being promoted as our best shot at changing patterns of participation is, as we have seen, convenient and pragmatic for the institutional providers. It is convenient administratively, since Access courses can simply be bolted on to the front of existing provision, with a minimum of disruption to the curriculum or to institutional practices. It is also convenient morally and philosophically because it allows the responsibility for representative take-up to be located with the Access course providers, or better still, with the individual learner.

Since little fault can be found with the existing structure of opportunities, the fault must lie with the individual who is unable to perceive what a good thing education really is. Low take-up is not problematised in terms of the nature of the education being offered, its relevance to the individual, the assumptions behind it. Neither is it problematised in terms of the way in which teaching and learning is expected to take place.

Non-participation is represented as stubborn, if not deviant, behaviour. For instance, in a discussion of how to reach 'hard-to-reach' adults Darkenwald and Larsen (1980) write '. . . we must *persuade* adults to participate in our programmes' (my italics). McGivney (1990) talks about the difficulty of getting through to 'hard core non-participants'. Non-participation begins to carry connotations of disaffection, of being marginal, or outside the consensus, where the consensus is that existing structures and patterns of provision adequately define the boundaries of adult learning. There has always been a deep thread of paternalism in education. It is prepared to offer a helping hand to those who want to sample its riches, but the treasure itself is well guarded and strictly non-negotiable. To put it another way, the pill can be sweetened, it can be packaged, and marketed, but it remains the same pill. For access to be designated a role as that 'little bit of sugar, helps the medicine go down' belittles the potential of access ideas to challenge the basic inequalities in the distribution of educational opportunity.

Participation and Non-participation

As we have seen, the policy aims of access are to broaden the constituency of adults currently taking part in post-compulsory education. We can't begin to design strategies for how this might be achieved until we know more about the adults who currently participate, and those who don't. A recent survey of take-up of adult learning opportunities in Britain found that 15 per cent of adults were currently engaged in some form of education or training (Londoners Learning, 1990). A further 15 per cent had been involved in some kind of study during the previous three years. This is a total of 30 per cent of the adult population who are 'currently' involved in educational courses in the sense of being involved in them now or having been involved in them within the past three years. These figures are slightly higher than the ACACE 1982 survey findings which recorded 12 per cent and 10 per cent respectively, giving a total of 22 per cent 'currently' involved.

As we have noted earlier, this group of participants is by no means a cross-section of the adult population. The recent NIACE survey found that 44 per cent of adults in social classes A and B were studying now or have studied recently, but the figure drops to 30 per cent for C2s (skilled manual workers) and 18 per cent for the D and Es. In short, the middle and upper classes stay at school longer, and then go on and use adult learning opportunities at a higher rate. The group of participants is also unrepresentative in terms of age and ethnic background. Only 9 per cent of people over the age of 65 were studying or had studied recently. Evidence of participation by black people is not included in the Interim Report, but many recent studies have shown that black and others from ethnic and linguistic minority groups are under-represented in education and training provision.

There is little here to encourage us to think very much has changed since the ACACE report of 1982 which noted:

All the indications show that those with the largest initial education, those who are in higher social classes, the young, men, and those seeking vocational education are consistently better able to take advantage of existing opportunities for continuing education.

Reviewing the evidence from a comprehensive survey of participation in post compulsory education Woodley *et al.* (1987) were able to state:

> ... the empirical evidence from our own study and from many others consistently shows that adult education of all kinds recruits disproportionately from certain parts of the adult population: those of working age rather than the retired; those in non-manual rather than manual occupations; and those with more than minimal previous educational success.

and they concluded:

> ... mature students clearly do not represent a cross-section of the population.

McGivney (1990) has drawn together a clutch of local and national surveys on the take-up of learning opportunities in continuing education to confirm this finding, and to point out that it appears to be consistent across national boundaries. This is hardly news to many who currently work in adult education, and it is interesting to reflect on why there is a perceived need to keep repeating surveys which tell us that little has changed in thirty years.

In 1961 Cyril Houle summed up a review of the factors which influence participation as follows:

> But the most universally important factor is schooling. The higher the formal education of the adult the more likely it is that he will take part in continuing education. The amount of schooling is in fact so significant that it underlies or reinforces many of the other determinants. . . .

So we know the facts of adult participation. If we are serious about changing the unequal distribution of adult learning opportunities across the population, what kind of action is likely to be effective? Before putting forward any propositions, we need to know more about *why* certain groups currently don't participate.

A bewildering array of possible theories and explanations are available to answer Cyril Houle's outline of the basic problem:

> No other subject is more widely pondered and discussed by people interested in the education of adults than the motives which lead men and women to introduce systematic learning into the pattern of their lives. (OECD, 1979)

Houle himself identified three categories of adult learner: those who are goal orientated, seeking to fulfil conscious objectives; those who are learning orientated, seeking knowledge for its own sake; and those who are activity orientated, taking part for reasons of companionship or to fill time. Subsequent categorizations of motives for learning have come up with a more detailed set of motives. These can be summarised as:

- A desire for knowledge
- To meet personal development goals
- To meet occupational goals
- To meet social and community goals
- To comply with external expectations
- To find activity or diversion
- To meet economic needs
- To fulfil religious needs
- To fulfil family responsibilities
- To develop, or to move on.

Woodley *et al.* (1987), in attempting to define a conceptual model of adult participation in education, looked at three distinct approaches. First, those theories which are to do with motivation. These are largely derived from psychology, and are similar to those developed from Houle's work. They seek to explain participation in terms of a desire to satisfy needs or achieve goals. Goals or needs may change over time, and there may be several different ones working together at any given time.

Second there are those theories which draw on sociology and explain non-participation as an outcome of social and class position. School performs the functions of selection and rejection, effectively placing individuals in the existing social stratification, and post-school education perpetuates the ethos and the values embedded in the school system (Hopper and Osborn, 1975). Both consciously and unconsciously barriers are placed in the path of non-traditional students, and the formal and informal practices of teachers tend to perpetuate patterns of disadvantage and inequality of opportunity (Thompson, 1983). Those who emerge from the school system as failures are not only ill disposed to return to the scene of that failure, but they also understand themselves to be part of a culture or class that has no truck with education (O'Shea and Corrigan, 1979). Non-participation is explained in terms of a lack of congruence between the social and cultural patterns of the individual, and those which are taken as norms within the education system (Boshier, 1971). People are made acutely aware of these disparities, not only by tutors and other students, but also by their own friends and family. For instance, a basic education student on the south coast of England, when asked whether she had thought of moving into an adult education class replied: 'Oh, I wouldn't go into the adult education class down there because they've all got their yachts and I haven't' (Harrison, 1988). Family and friends can feel threatened by the possibility of changes in established roles brought on by a commitment to learning.

> There are spouses who fear their mate's educational endeavours will affect the relationship and family members who are concerned that household responsibilities will be traded off against school obligations. (Lewis, 1988)

Third there are the 'supply side' models which focus on the way education is organised and presented, and on the effect this has on take-up by different sections of society. An important factor here is the tendency towards 'academic drift' among institutions of adult, further and higher education. Tyrrell Burgess (1977) has defined this as 'the tendency of institutions established in the service tradition to seek autonomy'. Thus colleges which were founded to be accessible and provide widely available adult education opportunities have tended to evolve into higher status institutions, with all that this entails in terms of structure, curriculum, entry requirements and student audience. Adult education in its wider sense has always been powerful ideologically, but has been marginalised in terms of the resources available to it. This marginalisation has in turn influenced the demand for education, and the expectations adults have of post-compulsory opportunities.

Research which has focused on the question of why adults *don't* participate in education has given us the 'deterrent concept', which suggests that there are a number of barriers which stand between the potential learner and his or her participation in a learning opportunity. (Scanlon and Darkenwald, 1984; Cross, 1981.) The deterrents to participation have been categorised in a number of ways. Perhaps the best known is that used by Cross (1981), when she summarised them as situational, institutional and dispositional.

Situational barriers arise from an individual's life situation; the fact that work or home responsibilities may leave little time for study, that courses may cost too much money, that child care arrangements may not be available, or that transport may be a constraint.

Institutional barriers include the rules and regulations which define the time, place and entry requirements of courses of study, or simply the non-availability of a course of study required by the individuals.

Dispositional barriers relate to the learner's own attitudes and self-perceptions. Common among these are that learning is too difficult or threatening, that learning is something that children do at school, not something which adults should be involved with or that learning is useless and irrelevant (K.P. Cross, 1981).

Non-participation by any individual is likely to be caused by a complex combination of factors, rather than one or two easily identifiable barriers. 'All too often, analysis focuses on only one reason for non-participation, resulting in simplistic and ineffective attempts at solutions' (Darkenwald and Larsen, 1980). Several researchers have suggested that it is the dispositional factors — attitudes, perceptions, expectations — which form the most powerful deterrents, and tend to be underestimated by the survey results.

The ACACE report of 'Continuing Education from policies to practice' asserted that: 'The major unstated barrier to access is probably the attitude which assumes that education is only for the young as a preparation for adult life.' It notes that this antipathy towards post-compulsory education is cemented by the fact that 'the education system has systematically and effectively labelled some people as successful learners and others as failures'.

McGivney (1990), drawing on the NIACE survey of 1987–9, confirms the importance of attitudinal factors:

> . . . the most powerful barrier to access is attitudes and expectations.
> Education is simply not part of the value system and behaviour pattern
> of a disturbing number of people.

She points out that in the survey conducted as part of the NIACE research over 60 per cent of non-participants claimed to have no interest in adult education, and many expressed strong hostility to education in general. She suggests that survey work will tend to underplay the importance of attitudes as against more tangible and 'acceptable' reasons for non-participation offered by institutional or situational barriers. This is a phenomenon which has been characterised as respondents putting on their 'best face' or reproducing what they see as a 'culturally normative pattern' (Laslett and Rapoport, 1975). Since education is widely perceived as a desirable commodity in our society it would not be surprising to find interviewees preferring to give the reason that they are 'too busy at present' or that 'the college is too far away' in preference to saying that they do not value what is being offered.

The Learner's Perspective

Whilst the analysis of participation we have been looking at is in some ways helpful, and gives some clues as to why participation is generally low and restricted to particular sections of the population, it provides only a partial answer to the question with which we began this section. What is lacking in this analysis is any real feeling for the experience of adults as they engage in learning projects. What are the satisfactions and frustrations, what processes and feelings lead to them engaging and continuing with learning? This is where the type of large-scale survey research we have been drawing becomes less useful.

The problems of using social survey research techniques as a way of gaining a better understanding of why people do things has been pointed out by, among others, Usher and Bryant (1989). By using pre-arranged categories as a way of organizing and comparing responses, limitations are imposed on the range of experience which can be recorded. Because surveys can deal in large numbers, they give the impression of being 'comprehensive', and because they yield figures which can then be subjected to statistical treatment, they are often seen as 'scientific'. What is questionable is whether they are capable of giving researchers real insight into what McGivney (1990) has described as: 'the mesh of inter-related attitudes, perceptions and misconceptions which prevent many people from considering education as an option'. Other researchers have expressed a dissatisfaction with the direction taken by this body of research on participation.

Courtney (1981) identified the need to escape from 'participation scales, constructed along psychometric lines and channelled through the sieve of factor analysis', towards a more interpretative approach which would go beyond the mere 'count' value of participation variables as they so often appear in surveys, and which concentrated instead on the 'internal logic' which individuals express in their description of their conscious reasons for entry. Torbert has criticised survey-based research in education as an attempt to gain unilateral control by the institutional providers of education. Researchers start off with a knowledge of what is significant, design a research programme which will focus on this, and then proceed to 'implement the pre-defined design as efficiently as possible' (Torbert, 1981). The research tends to be both self-regulatory, since researchers are investigating their own institutional practices, and to a large degree self-confirming since it is rarely suggested that teaching practices require examination and change (Usher and Bryant, 1989). So, for instance, an 'academic way of looking at things' might be identified as a problem only when the problem is located with the student who is having difficulty coming to terms with it, rather than as a problem of relevance or communication which requires consideration by the teacher.

Not only has the predominant work on participation been shaped by professional and institutional perspectives, it has failed to explore the subjective experience of non-traditional learners as they contemplate and engage in educational opportunities. Research which has given us an insight into this subjective experience has followed a qualitative approach, using unstructured, in-depth interviews. Rather than imposing pre-arranged categories of response to questions about attitudes to learning, or patterns of study, this approach allows interviewees to develop their own theories and interpretations of themselves as learners. Weil's (1986) research on non-traditional learners in higher education uses a qualitative design and grounded theory procedures suggested by Glaser and Strauss (1967) to ask how adults make sense of their experiences of higher education; and how they relate this to their sense of themselves as learners.

> A deeper understanding of adult learners' experience of higher education, as interpreted in the context of lifelong learning, can help to illuminate the issues, challenges and changes we must come to grips with if greater access is to become a prominent — and successful feature of our higher education system. This is especially important if such provision is to meet the needs, interests, and concerns of the diversity of adult learners in today's learning society — *including* those whose needs, by virtue of their gender, race and social class, may not have been catered for equally by the formal system.

In looking at some of the barriers to learning in higher education which have been identified by mature students Weil develops two related constructs. The first is of a 'learning context' which, '. . . incorporates formal and informal structures operating in a learning environment, institutional or departmental ethos and culture, and the ways in which non-traditional learners relate with and to peers and "teachers"'. The second construct is that of 'learner identity' which refers to the emerging sense of the individual as a learner — 'the process of "coming to know" oneself as a learner through interactions within and across different learning contexts over time'. The construct suggests the acquisition of values and beliefs about 'learning', 'schooling' and 'knowledge'.

Weil notes that the discovery of learning and the emergence of 'learner identity' is rooted in experience which lie outside any formal education. For many this has been through involvement with non-formal courses, often made available through community education, self-help groups, consciousness raising groups, political groups, or non-traditional training courses. Through these experiences adults had discovered themselves as learners, and had developed the self-confidence and self-esteem which had helped to propel them towards higher education. Wendy Moss (1988) also draws attention to the importance of non-formal education in developing an adult's sense of herself as a competent learner. A student from one of the Fresh Start courses at the Polytechnic of North London, reflected on what she had gained in these terms:

> I learned that I was capable of doing whatever I decided I wanted to do, not like a brain surgeon, I do know my limitations, but I realised that my

limitations were far fewer then than I at first thought. . . . I feel confident about going into full-time study now . . . they just brought my interest back into wanting to learn.

Two quotes taken from in-depth interviews with working class adults in inner city Glasgow illustrate the same point. For both of these adults their involvement in studying Open University Community Education courses through the Strathclyde Open Learning Experiment (SOLE) has been their first experience of education since leaving school.

I'll try things now, I'll take a challenge now. . . . It gave me confidence to go ahead when I was approached about the Youth Leadership course. . . . It gave me confidence and willingness and motivation to learn.

It made me feel I was not disoriented about education. It made me feel more alert, it opened my ideas about further education, that my life could still go on learning more and more and not stopping because I was a wife or mother. (Farnes, 1990)

In her review of the use of Open University Community Education material by more than half a million adults, Ballard (1987) notes:

One of the main features to emerge from our several studies is how often the material acts as a catalyst, boosting people's confidence to go on to other things. . . .

This emerging sense of self as a competent learner is a crucial factor in empowering adults to move on to further and more challenging learning experiences. But for many the move into higher education is experienced as an assault on the identity which had begun to emerge through learning in other contexts. Weil suggests that this is partly because the non-formal, learner-centred courses they have experienced serve to heighten awareness of the 'hidden agendas' operating in the formal system. 'Examples of the personal impact of the hidden curriculum and how it operates — against diversity generally, and, in particular, against those who are non-traditional in more than one dimension — are disturbingly frequent'. Weil quotes from one of her own interviews to illustrate this point.

The first year you realise that the boundaries are clearly defined by the institution. You're ignorant. You don't know what to expect. There was a useful comment one lecturer made. 'Undergraduates have no opinion'. You are made to feel that way, to say, 'I am the clay, you are the potter, shape me, mould me'. (Black working class man)

Wendy Moss quotes from one of her interviews with women who moved from a Fresh Start course to a college of further education.

Everybody I met was white, male upper class, and under 30. I felt they wouldn't know anything about me and I wouldn't know anything about them. It wasn't an environment in which I would thrive at all. I could feel myself wilting. . . . (Working class woman)

These learners are experiencing a disjunction between what they have come to know about learning, based on experiences in contexts other than formal education, and what they are presented with in an institution of higher education. Moss describes the difference between these two approaches to learning and to the individual learner. She says of the Fresh Start courses:

These courses had an approach that is traditionally not found in FE or HE: they had negotiated curricula; they were informal, supportive and participative: women were strictly encouraged to explore their personal experiences and to learn from and develop these.

This contrasts with her description of HE and FE courses as experienced by her interviewees:

At least part of the problem seemed to be that the women faced the unspoken assumptions, values and expectations of an academic (and dominant) culture, where a shared background knowledge was taken for granted and in no need of explanation.

Weil's study identifies a number of important disjunctions experienced by adult and non-traditional learners. First, between learners' expectations and their actual experiences of higher education. Many arrived inspired by high ideals but expressed shock at the contradictions between professed values — fairness, objectivity, the development of critical thinking — and actual practices. Second, a disjunction between values and beliefs about the nature of knowledge, its constitution, transmission and assessment, held by adult learners and their teachers. Third, a disjunction between the perspectives of teachers who have been socialised within the formal education system, and adult learners whose learning has been experiential and non-formal, and whose understandings are rooted in their experience of age, gender, class and race.

Conclusions

This analysis of the way in which adults introduce learning into their lives, and of their subjective experience in doing so, suggests some pointers to policymakers and practitioners who are seeking a more accessible and equitable system. It suggests that Access courses are not a sufficient response to the clear inequalities in the distribution of educational resources to adults. There is a place for courses which teach study skills and provide knowledge top-ups for entrance to existing courses, but it is not at the leading edge of a national access initiative.

More importantly, it suggests the need for a shift away from a 'provider model' of adult education towards a 'user model'. Higher education practices have much to learn from community education approaches which have been successful in presenting learning opportunities which are more congruent with the situation of non-traditional learners. The opportunities that would appear to be most effective in overcoming attitudinal barriers and developing a more secure sense of 'learner identity' are characterised by a tone which is relatively informal, an approach which is learner centred, a choice of subject matter which is perceived as relevant and useful by the learner, a setting which is community based, and an assumption on the part of the teacher that participants are not blank slates or empty vessels, but competent adults whose experience and opinions have relevance and validity.

Two examples which would illustrate these general points are a course of study for parents on being a parent and raising children, and a course for volunteers on the management of voluntary organisations. A course or programme of study built around either of these audiences would be dealing with subject matter which has a clear relevance to the individuals concerned, introducing elements of new knowledge, developing abilities in analysis, reflection, problem solving, communication, and critical thinking. Each of these elements in the learning process would seem to lie at the heart of the whole enterprise of education. As an introduction to what education is really about, and therefore as an access initiative, they would seem to have far more to offer than more formal Access courses.

> The major emphasis in official measures to widen access has been facilitating access to higher education. However, most people in non-participant categories perceive higher education as completely beyond their reach. Getting people to the point where they will cross the threshold from non-participation to participation requires attention to the first stages of access: reaching people and mounting informal learning activities in the community. (McGivney, 1990)

A further conclusion must be that the linkages between an individual's own learning career, and the continuation of that career into higher education, need to be clarified. We have seen how adult learners bring with them a wealth of experience and knowledge to any new learning project. Any form of education which fails to take account of that experience is pedagogically authoritarian, seeking to mould a specific final product rather than to encourage independent enquiry, analysis and critical thinking. Failure to take account of the diversity of adult experience would firmly anchor the enterprise of education in the domain of the professional educator, with all that this implies in terms of cultural bias. It would confirm the existence of 'fundamental social-structural barriers that lurk beneath the more ostensible pedagogic hurdles' (Neave, 1976).

Higher education institutions need to be clear about where they stand in relation to this analysis, and honest about their real aims. If the purposes of higher education really are about the stimulus of critical thinking and analysis, the encouragement of creative and independent thinking, the promotion of personal development, then there is a requirement to recognise that it is possible for this development to take place in contexts which lie outside the domain of higher education institutes.

> If the purposes of higher education are to put people through examinations, to churn out qualifications, and to manufacture people who may be ill-equipped to deal with a changing society, let us have the courage to make those purposes explicit. If, however, there is a genuine commit-

ment to continuing access within a lifetime of tertiary education, I would argue, even at this early stage in my research, that crucial questions are being raised by non-traditional learners about the ability of the system to provide them with an education that is relevant to the learning agendas they bring with them on their return to the formal system. (Weil, 1986)

If 'learning' is offered on the terms, and according to the definition, only of the professional educators it can never achieve equality of access. It will always be less attractive to those outside the current audience of habitual participants. Disaffection with education is more intractable than a simple itemising of 'barriers' would suggest. Easier admission procedures, more flexible study patterns, crèche facilities, Access courses, all have a part to play in creating a more accessible system, but unless we are prepared to take account of the prior experience of adults, not just at the point of entry into formal education, but as an integral part of any learning project, the wider policy aims of access will always be subverted.

References

ACACE (1982) *Continuing Education: from policies to practice.*

ACACE (1987) *Adults: their educational experience and needs.*

BALLARD, A. (1987) 'Meeting Community Needs — Community Education at the Open University' in THORPE, M. and GRUDGEON, D. (Eds) *Open Learning for Adults*, Longman.

BOSHIER, R. (1981) 'Motivated orientations of adult education participants: a factor analytical exploration of Houle's typology', Adult Education (US), 21.2.

BURGESS, T. (1977) *Education after School*, Penguin Books.

COURTNEY, S. (1981) 'The factors affecting participation in adult education: An analysis of some literature', *Studies in Adult Education*, 13.2.

CROSS, K.P. (1981) *Adults as Learners*, Jossey Bass.

CVCP/CNAA (1989) *Access courses to higher education. A framework of national arrangements for recognition.*

DARKENWALD, G.G. and LARSEN, G.A. (1980) *Reaching hard-to-reach adults*, Jossey Bass.

DARKENWALD, G.G. and VALENTINE, T. (1985) 'Factor structure of deterrents to public participation in adult education', *Adult Education Quarterly*, 35,4.

DES (1987) *Access to further and higher education. A discussion document*, London, HMSO.

ECCTIS (1989) *Access to Higher Education: Courses directory.*

FARNES, N.C. (1990) 'The place and influence of community education in people's lives', Ph.D., Cranfield Institute of Technology.

GROOMBRIDGE, B. (1983) *Adult Education and the Education of Adults*, Milton Keynes, Open University Press.

HARRISON, R.M. (1988) *Learning Later. A handbook for developing educational opportunities with older people*, UDACE/Open University.

HMSO (1987) *Higher Education: meeting the challenge,* April.

HOOPER, E. and OSBORNE, M. (1975) *Adult Students: Education, selection and control*, London, Francis Pinter.

HOULE, C. (1961) *The Inquiring Mind*, University of Wisconsin.

HOULE, C. OECD (1979) Quoted in Woodley *et al.* (1987) *Choosing to Learn: adults in education,* The Society for Research into Higher Education, Open University Press.

JONES, P. (1990) 'Access courses into the 1990s', *Adults Learning*, Vol. 1. No. 5. Jan.

KNOWLES, M. (1978) *The Adult Learner: a neglected species*, Houston, Gulf.

LASLETT, B. and RAPPOPORT, R. (1975) 'Collaborative interviewing and interactive research', *Journal of Marriage and the Family*, 37.

LEWIS, L. (1988) 'An Issue of Support', *International Journal of Lifelong Education*, 4.2. 1988.

MCGIVNEY, V. (1990) *Education is for other people: access to education for non-participant adults: a research report,* NIACE.

MOSS, W. (1988) *Breaking the barriers. Eight case studies of women returning to learning in north London,* ALPHA.

NEAVE, G. (1976) *Patterns of inequality,* Windsor, NFER.

NIACE/ILEA (1990) 'Londoners Learning'. An interim report of the ILEA/NIACE survey of adult learners in inner London.

O'SHEA, J. and CORRIGAN, P.L. 'Surviving adult education', Adult Education, 52.4.

RICHARDSON, K. (1974) 'The institutional mythology', in HOUGHTON, V. and RICHARDSON, K. (Eds) *Recurrent Education,* Ward Lock.

HM TREASURY, *The Government's Expenditure Plans 1988–89 to 1990–91,* London, HMSO.

THOMPSON, J. (1983) 'Learning Liberation: women's response to men's education', Beckenham, Croom Helm.

TIGHT, M. (1988) 'Access — not access courses', *Journal of Access Studies*, Vol. 3, No. 2, Autumn 1988.

TORBERT, W.R. (1981) 'Why educational research has been so uneducational', in REASON, P. and ROWAN, J. (Eds) *Human Inquiry: A source book of the new paradigm Research,* London, Wiley.

USHER, R. and BRYANT, I. (1989) *Adult Education as Theory, Practice and Research. The captive triangle,* Routledge.

WEIL, S.W. (1986) 'Non-Traditional Learners within Traditional Higher Education Institutions: discovery and disappointment', *Studies in Higher Education*, Vol. II, No. 3, 1986.

WOODLEY et al. (1987) *Choosing to Learn: adults in education,* The Society for Research into Higher Education, The Open University Press.

2   Adult Access to Higher Education

Malcolm Tight

Introduction

Adults are now firmly on the higher education agenda in the United Kingdom for the first time since the immediate post-war period. Our higher education system's love affair with the well qualified school-leaver began to pale in the late-1970s, when the likely effects of the downturn in the birthrate became apparent (Department of Education and Science, 1978). The increased recruitment of mature students was seen as one obvious way of maintaining student, and thus staff, numbers. The resulting expansion in the opportunities for adults to enter higher education has been reflected in a range of guides directed at them and their advisers (e.g. Bell, Hamilton and Roderick, 1986; Pates and Good, 1989; Rosier and Earnshaw, 1989).

The growing interest in mature students has been strengthened by the general rhetoric of expansion now favoured by the government. Thus, the current public expenditure White Paper states the following as one of the five aims for education as a whole:

> to widen access to further and higher education and to make them responsive to the needs of the economy. (HM Treasury, 1990, p. 4)

Of course, many of those involved in higher education suspect the motivations behind these developments, note the inevitable economic caveat and doubt whether adequate resources will be made available to support expansion on the scale envisaged. But we are, for the moment at least, giving these policies our broad support.

There are, however, considerable practical problems to be overcome if we are to significantly increase adult access to higher education. Our higher education system is not designed with the needs, aspirations and expectations of adult clients in mind. At present, most mature students who enter higher education have to fit themselves into a system designed for relatively compliant and predictable 18 year olds. More adult students can only be satisfactorily accommodated if we are prepared to change the existing patterns of provision and practice better to suit their different and varied needs.

The remainder of this chapter is in four main sections:

Table 2.1:   Higher Education Students by Sex, Age and Mode of Study, United Kingdom 1987/88

Mode	Sex	Total ('000)	By Age Group			
			18	19–20	21–24	25+
	Men	346	52	128	107	59
Full-time	Women	281	48	110	78	45
	Total	627	100	238	185	104
	Men	224	9	29	47	139
Part-time	Women	143	3	10	24	106
	Total	367	12	39	71	245
All Students		994	112	277	256	349

Source: Central Statistical Office, 1990, tables 3.19 and 3.20.

1   The available evidence on the numbers and characteristics of the mature students currently in higher education will be reviewed.
2   The arrangements which have developed to enable adult entry to higher education will be described from the point of view of the provider.
3   The barriers which adults have to overcome to enter, and then satisfactorily complete, higher education courses will be considered.
4   A range of existing examples of good practice, which seek to overcome these barriers and encourage adult access, will then be examined.

Mature Students in Higher Education

National Statistics

In 1987/88, the latest year for which comprehensive national statistics are available, a total of 994,000 higher education students were recorded in the United Kingdom (Central Statistical Office, 1990, tables 3.19 and 3.20). Of this total, some 35 per cent were aged 25 years or more, with a further 26 per cent aged between 21 and 24. It makes sense to use the lower limit as a definition of maturity for undergraduate entrants and the upper limit for postgraduates. On this basis, the number of mature students increased by more than one-third in the six year period from 1981/82 to 1987/88 (*ibid.*, p. 61).

Table 2.1, which disaggregates these figures by sex, age and mode of study, illustrates a number of further points. Most mature students (70 per cent of those aged 25 years or more, 52 per cent of those aged 21 years or more) are studying on a part-time basis; whereas younger students are predominantly full-time (87 per cent of those aged less than 21 years). Men and women are represented amongst the young and mature student bodies in equal proportions: 57 per cent of those aged over 25 years were men, the same proportion as for the total student population. Female students are in general under-represented on part-time courses, but are on average older than the men involved. The statistical reports produced separately for the different sectors of the higher education system (the universities and the polytechnics and colleges) show further disparities.

Universities

In 1987/88, there were 76,689 new home entrants to full-time university undergraduate courses (out of a total enrolment of 264,803). Only 6 per cent of them were aged 25 years or more, with another 6 per cent aged between 21 and 24 (Universities Statistical Record 1988, table 1). By comparison, 8 per cent of those who applied to enter but were rejected were over 25 years old, and 15 per cent were over 21. This does not necessarily indicate a bias in admissions procedures towards younger candidates, since the mature students tended to have poorer entry qualifications. Mature entrants were concentrated in arts, education, humanities and social sciences; and were relatively uncommon in science, engineering and medicine (Universities Central Council on Admissions (UCCA), 1989, tables B1, B2, B5; see also Woodley, 1981).

The 22,811 new home entrants to full-time postgraduate university courses naturally tended to be older than the undergraduates. But, while almost all of them were over 21, 60 per cent were under 25 years old (Universities Statistical Record 1988, table 1).

The British university which has by far the most impressive record for encouraging mature students does not teach full-time or face-to-face: it is, of course, the Open University. In 1988, 83,598 undergraduate and associate students were registered by the Open University. Virtually all were over 21 and 95 per cent were over 25 years old. The majority, 58 per cent, were over 35 and a substantial minority, 21 per cent (or 17,714 students), were over 45 (Open University, 1990, table 4).

Polytechnics and Colleges

There are many more mature students studying in the polytechnics and colleges than there are in the universities. Of the total of 453,608 students enrolled on higher level courses at polytechnics or colleges in England in 1987/88, 35 per cent were over 25 years of age, with a further 29 per cent aged between 21 and 24. Yet only 19,052 students were over 45 years old, not many more than those studying through the Open University (Department of Education and Science, 1988a, table F3).

Mature applicants to polytechnics and colleges tend to be more successful in gaining admission than those in the university sector. In 1987/88, only 16 per cent of home applicants for full-time first degree or diploma courses who applied through the Polytechnics Central Admissions System (PCAS) were aged 21 years or more. Of those admitted, 24 per cent were aged 21 years or older. For those aged 25 years or more, the proportions were 7 per cent and 12 per cent respectively. The subject distribution of mature students in the polytechnics and colleges is similar to that in the universities. Above average numbers are to be found in arts, humanities and social sciences, with relatively few studying science, languages, business and, surprisingly, education. Substantial numbers are, however, enrolled on engineering courses (Hollinshead and Griffith, 1990, pp. 5 and 7).

Survey Data

A number of recent surveys provide more detailed information about the characteristics, experience and attitudes of mature students.

Alan Woodley and his colleagues carried out a comprehensive survey of adults participating in organised education throughout England and Wales in the early 1980s (Woodley *et al.*, 1987). The great majority of those taking higher education or other qualifying courses were middle class. They tended to have had a better school education, and to have gained more qualifications, than the general population. Most were involved in education for instrumental reasons related to personal career development, and they were generally positive about the courses they were taking. This group was, however, far from homogeneous:

> Among our group of adult students we can find large numbers of highly successful school-leavers who were in no way 'rejected' by the school system, but nevertheless 'failed' to carry on and acquire degrees after their A levels. At the other extreme are those who left school early, and here the evidence suggests that the majority either chose to do so or were forced to do so by home circumstances, rather than being literally 'rejected'. (*ibid.*, p. 68)

Tom Bourner and his colleagues carried out a survey of students on part-time degree courses accredited by the Council for National Academic Awards (CNAA) in the mid-1980s (Bourner *et al.*, 1988). Their average age was 32 years, and most were in full-time employment. Most had left school aged 17 or less, but had continued studying, and were well-qualified when they started their degree course. Their aims were primarily vocational:

> The findings of this study are consistent with a picture in which taking a CNAA part-time degree course is part of a process of upward social and economic mobility. There is also a suggestion in the findings that a significant proportion of the part-time students are in families in which continuing education is perceived as a route to enhanced economic life chances and that the students were continuing a process of upward socio-economic mobility started by their parents. (*ibid.*, p. 7)

Studies of the Joint Matriculation Board scheme for mature entry — operated by Birmingham, Leeds, Liverpool, Manchester and Sheffield universities — show that their recruitment tends to be from a less well-qualified group (Roderick *et al.*, 1981, 1982). Yet, when carefully selected, these students proved to be highly successful:

> Unqualified adults admitted through the mature entry scheme were found, on average, to do rather better than other university students in terms of the qualification achieved. (Smithers and Griffin, 1986, p. 147)

Summary

Mature students are a substantial and growing force in higher education. They form a much more heterogeneous group than the traditional school-leaver intake. Most are studying part-time, either face-to-face in a polytechnic or college, or at-a-distance with the Open University. Most mature students are, however, comparatively young: in their twenties or thirties. Many are relatively well-qualified on entry to higher education: they are taking a 'second bite' rather than seeking a 'second chance'. Most are middle class and are studying mainly for vocational reasons, seeking further career advancement and upward social mobility.

In other words, the adults currently engaged in higher education are not representative of the general adult population. Most adults have not seriously considered — and are thus effectively excluded from — participation in higher education (Advisory Council for Adult and Continuing Education, 1982a; Tight, 1982).

Entry Arrangements

Those adults who are aware of, and who wish to gain access to, higher education have to satisfy the entrance requirements set by institutions and validating bodies, and variously interpreted by departments and admissions tutors. So far as undergraduate study is concerned, five main types of entry arrangements may be recognised: standard entry, entry with equivalent qualifications, special entry, open entry, and entry via an Access course (Tight, 1987a). Curiously enough, mature students with the requisite experience can find it easier to enter higher education at postgraduate level, where a more flexible attitude towards prior qualifications is sometimes taken.

Standard Entry

Possession of the standard entry qualifications — i.e. a minimum of two subjects at Advanced level, plus at least three others at GCSE level — remains the normal method by which mature students gain entry to higher education. The grades asked of adult entrants, particularly for part-time courses will, however, typically be lower than those demanded from school-leavers.

Equivalent Qualifications

Most institutions of higher education will now accept an extensive range of professional, foreign and other qualifications as equivalent in standing to A levels, having built up a list of precedents over the years. Indeed, some courses in some subjects — such as education, management and nursing — are expressly designed for experienced mature students with qualifications of this nature. In other cases, much may depend on the individual student's circumstances and performance in interview, and on the appropriateness of their qualifications to the subject in question. Entry may be made conditional on satisfactory performance during a probationary period of study.

Special Entry

This covers cases where prospective students do not have the normal entry qualifications or their equivalent, and tends to be much more time-consuming and contentious. Most institutions now allow, at least in principle, for the possibility of special entry, but a strong case has to be made regarding the ability and potential of each individual concerned. The numbers of students admitted through special entry arrangements has increased in recent years, but they remain a small minority. A survey of mature students on full-time CNAA undergraduate courses carried out in 1989 found that only 17 per cent said they had been admitted through a special concession (Hollinshead and Griffith, 1990, p. 17; cf. Evans, 1984).

Open Entry

Open entry is essentially confined to just one institution of higher education: the Open University. This arrangement reduces the question of entry to one of resources; i.e. first come, first served. It also necessitates high levels of support and preparatory provision if recruitment is from the general adult population. This is an issue which the Open University has only just begun to get to grips with, now that its initial wave of teacher-students has largely passed through the system.

Access Courses

These are structured periods of preparatory study, planning and confidence building designed for adults seeking entry to further or higher education. They typically require two years of part-time attendance. About 600 courses, with about 12,000 students enrolled, are now operating in the United Kingdom; many of them offered through 'open colleges' or regional networks (Educational Counselling and Credit Transfer Information Service, 1989; Millins and Jones, 1990). A framework of national arrangements for recognition has been set up by the CNAA. Most Access courses have only been established for a few years, however, so it is too early to assess their impact on higher education.

All adults who wish to enter higher education have to take one of the routes just described. Those who do not wish to study with the Open University, and who lack the standard entry qualifications or their equivalent, are confined to seeking special entry or taking an Access course. Both of the latter routes impose considerable demands, and neither entry nor eventual success is guaranteed. Indeed, in some cases the students concerned might well be better advised to take one or two A levels instead. The conventional route can be quicker and cheaper.

Barriers to Access

There are many other barriers, in addition to entry requirements, which limit adult access to higher education. Table 2.2 offers a simple categorisation of them.

Adult Access to Higher Education

Table 2.2: Types of Barriers Affecting Mature Student Access to Higher Education

Barriers	Potential Student Groups Affected				
	Manual Workers	Married Women	Ethnic Minorities	Disabled People	Elderly People
Dispositional					
Attitudinal	x	x	x		x
Informational	x		x	x	
Institutional					
Geographical		x		x	x
Financial	x	x			x
Structural	x			x	
Situational					
Child care		x			
Work release	x				
Educational					
Qualifications	x		x		x
Preparation	x	x	x		x

Source: adapted from ACACE 1982b, p. 65.

Four main groups of barriers (dispositional, institutional, situational and educational) have been recognised. Their possible impact on different kinds of mature students — manual workers, married women, ethnic, minorities, disabled people, elderly people — is indicated in the body of the table (ACACE, 1982b; Carp, Peterson and Roelfs, 1974; Cross, 1981).

Dispositional Barriers

The attitudes held by adults are themselves major barrier to their participation. Most people in the United Kingdom still assume that higher education is only for well-qualified school-leavers, and that it involves leaving home to study 'full-time' for three years at a university or college. Most adults are unaware that it is possible to pursue higher education on a part-time basis through face-to-face study, combining learning with work or domestic responsibilities (Tight, 1987b). Little wonder, then, if they conclude that higher education is not for them.

To date, most institutions of higher education have made only limited efforts to dispel these views, and to inform potential mature students of the benefits of engaging in study. It can be very difficult, even for a highly motivated adult, to get accurate information on the study opportunities available. Institutional prospectuses and admissions staff, as well as both of the national admissions systems (UCCA and PCAS), remain geared to the needs of the sixth-former seeking a full-time course.

Institutional Barriers

The physical inaccessibility of higher education creates further barriers. The availability of higher education, both full-time and part-time, varies considerably between different parts of the country. In England, for example, many 'rural' counties — including Buckinghamshire, Cumbria, Lincolnshire, Northumberland, Shropshire, Somerset and Wiltshire — are poorly provided for (Tight, 1987c). Where institutions are geographically accessible, they may not offer an adult environment for study, or may physically exclude certain groups, such as the disabled.

Financial barriers present obvious problems. Although adults accepted for full-time higher education courses are normally entitled to receive grant aid, they are likely, unless they have been unemployed, to suffer a substantial drop in income. Even with supplementary support, considerable financial strains will be placed on those with families. This helps to explain the attraction of part-time study, since it can be undertaken without giving up employment, even though most part-time students receive no grant aid. By offering alternative modes of study, higher education institutions can begin to break down some of the structural barriers to adult participation.

Other structural barriers relate to the level and content of courses, and to the teaching and learning methods used. Courses designed to meet the perceived needs of school-leavers are unlikely to be as successful with, or as acceptable to, adult students. Mixing adult and young students together may, therefore, present problems, though the potential benefits to be gained from using the adults' diverse experience as a learning resource are considerable.

Situational Barriers

These have to do with the context of adult life: work, domestic, leisure and social responsibilities and activities. Those with young children cannot undertake serious study unless arrangements can be made to look after their children while they are studying. Those in employment may need, and would almost certainly benefit from, some paid release from work to pursue their studies.

Educational Barriers

Finally, there are the various educational barriers to expanding adult access to higher education, including lack of formal qualifications and lack of adequate preparation, which were highlighted in the previous section.

All of these barriers may affect mature students not just at the time they are seeking entry into higher education, but throughout the period of their studies. Much the same set of barriers have been identified in studies of mature student dropout or non-completion: e.g. problems with the course or the institution, changing domestic or employment circumstances, altered expectations and difficulties with motivation (Woodley *et al.*, 1987, chapter 9).

For the school-leaver seeking a full-time course, getting into higher education is the main problem, given the competition for places. Once in, it is relatively easy to survive three years of grant-aided residential study and come out with some kind of qualification. For the mature student, the problems do not end with entry, but are likely to be there — sometimes in the foreground, sometimes in the background — throughout the duration of the course.

Susan Weil has characterised the experience of adults in higher education as a continuing cycle of discovery and disappointment:

> Adults contrasted the largely negative feelings associated with initial schooling with the excitement, enthusiasm and potential they discovered through learning as an adult . . . certain experiences of higher education can easily reactivate previous anxieties, memories and feelings of inadequacy. These seem to occur in spite of positive recollections of learning and the self which have been experienced in non-traditional learning contexts . . . once self-esteem is re-established in the formal system, personal interpretations of being a learner — based on traditional and non-traditional experiences — can more easily be generated. (Weil, 1986, p. 224)

Indeed, problems may linger on even after the course is over. Some adults experience difficulties in reconciling what they have experienced through higher education with their previous social and employment background. Mature age study can be an important factor in family break-ups, and may disrupt established friendships. And those who take degrees as mature students can find difficulty in gaining suitable employment, given the prejudice of many employers towards young graduate entrants (Graham, 1989).

Examples of Good Practice

All of the barriers to increased adult participation in higher education that I have described can be overcome, and many are currently being overcome in particular institutions. If higher education is to be made more accessible to mature students, further action is required on the part of institutions, educational authorities, employers, national bodies and government departments, as well as by adults themselves (National Institute of Adult Continuing Education, 1989). Many examples of existing good practice could be given here to illustrate the possibilities. In the space available, it is only possible to discuss briefly some selected examples. The discussion will again follow the categorisation presented in Table 2.2.

Overcoming Dispositional Barriers

This chiefly requires action by institutions and local education authorities (Duke, 1989). Some of the former have already reviewed their admissions practices, and have supplemented their standard prospectuses with specific guides for mature students (Fulton and Ellwood, 1989). Some, more positively, are completely rewriting their prospectuses so that they are generally useful for both young and mature applicants. Open days are being organised for potential adult students, and former adult students are being used as unofficial ambassadors in their local communities, spreading information and helping to change attitudes by word-of-mouth.

Some local education authorities have adapted their careers advisory services so that they are of use to adults as well as to young people. Some support the work of independent local educational guidance services for adults. These typically operate from shop fronts or other accessible locations, and can be very

Table 2.3: *Increasing the Diversity of Institutional Provision*

Part-time only <-----------> Mixed Mode <---------->	Full-time only
Evening provision <------> Day and Evening <-------->	Daytime provision
Distance provision <-------> Mixed provision <------->	Face-to-face provision
Single site <-----------> Multi-site teaching <-------->	Credit Transfer
Modular study <--------> Intermediate awards <-------->	Degree only
Open entry <------------> Special entry <---------->	Standard Entry
Independent study <-------> Curricular options <-------->	Fixed curriculum

Source: adapted from Tight, 1990, p. 3.

helpful in assisting adults to explore the various options available to them (Unit for the Development of Adult Continuing Education, 1986).

Overcoming Institutional Barriers

Some of the possible responses here are illustrated diagrammatically in Table 2.3. The provision of higher education can be organised on a full-time or part-time basis. Or it can be arranged so as to enable students to mix periods of full-time and part-time study to suit their varying needs and the changing demands upon their time (Hubert, 1989).

Part-time provision can be organised during the day, with crèches available for those with young children (Michaels, 1979). It can be provided during the day and evening for those who can get release from their employment. Or it can be offered wholly in the evening for those who cannot get work release. It may be provided primarily through face-to-face contact, or primarily by distance means, as at the Open University. Or it can mix elements of both distance and face-to-face provision in order to reach students who cannot attend an institution regularly, but who do not wish to study wholly by distance means: this is the model now being developed by the Open Polytechnic.

Instead of teaching courses solely on one site, they can be made available — where the demand is sufficient — at a number of locations. The Mundella programme in Sheffield, for example, enables students to take the first part of their degree at their local college, moving on later to the university if they wish. Credit transfer schemes extend these benefits more widely. The CNAA's national credit accumulation and transfer scheme is enabling an increasing number of students to transfer credit — gained from studying a course, or part of a course, at one institution — to help them to complete a related course at another institution (CNAA, 1989).

In a related development, many institutions, including Newcastle and Oxford Polytechnics, have broken their courses down into units or modules of study. Students are able to put together their own study packages from the modules available. They can leave with intermediate awards as well as full degrees, or they can opt to study one module at a time (Watson *et al.*, 1989). These developments are particularly relevant for mature students, who tend to be both busy and occupationally mobile.

Course contents and teaching methods can be adapted to suit adults' differing expectations and needs, and to make use of their considerable and varied experience.

Courses may be based in part on experiential learning methods (Weil and McGill, 1989); with, for example, students leading sessions on subjects in which they have expertise, or basing project work on their employment or spare-time interests. In some institutions, notably East London Polytechnic and Lancaster University, complete independent study courses have been developed. These give individual students the responsibility for devising their own curricula, methods of study and assessment criteria (Percy, Ramsden and Lewin, 1980; Stephenson, 1980).

A much greater degree of equity in the state support given to different kinds of students is required to break down the financial barriers to access. It seems neither just nor sensible for the state to pay the fees of, and give grants to, home students taking full-time higher education courses, while offering no support as of right to those taking equivalent part-time courses.

The new system of student funding, by which grants will be steadily supplemented by top-up loans, is similarly unjust in focusing entirely on full-time study (Department of Education and Science, 1988b). And those mature students who do study full-time, given their heavier dependence on benefits (now largely withdrawn), are likely to suffer more from these changes than are school-leavers (Bryant, 1990; Wagner, 1990).

Overcoming Situational Barriers

Employers also have a role to play here in breaking down financial and situational barriers. They should encourage and support their employees to undertake study, typically on a part-time basis, since they stand to benefit from the increased motivation, understanding and skills of those involved. This support may take the form of a contribution towards the direct costs of study, or it might involve granting limited release from work during the period of study. Examples of such schemes include Sheffield City Council's paid educational leave scheme for its staff (Twentyman, 1990), and the educational allowances which Ford have now made available to all of their employees.

Overcoming Educational Barriers

Educational barriers to adult participation can best be alleviated — at least in the short term — by ensuring that those who lack the conventional qualifications expected for entry to higher education, and who do not have recent experience of formal study, are given adequate preparation and support before undertaking their courses. This will probably involve attending some kind of access course, although other forms of preparation should also be available (Tight, 1988). Adults who have developed appropriate knowledge, understanding or skills outside formal education could have this prior experiential learning assessed and accredited. The assessment might take the form of an interview or examination, or might involve the presentation of a portfolio (Evans, 1988).

None of these examples are unproblematic. They are not applicable in all cases, and it may prove very difficult to accommodate the varying needs of a heterogeneous group of adults (in addition to those of younger students) within one course. Many of the suggestions made may be awkward or time-consuming to implement. They may encounter misunderstanding and resistance from established staff. They also have resource implications for all of those involved in higher education: students, institutions and employers, as well as local and central government.

However, if we are serious about significantly increasing and broadening adult participation in higher education, then we need to adopt and adapt, in as flexible a way as possible, these kinds of measures. The benefits to be gained from doing so are likely to extend beyond greater adult participation: by increasing the value of the higher education experience for all of those involved, including younger students and staff.

Conclusions

Three main conclusions may be drawn from this discussion. First, it is both possible and desirable to increase significantly adult participation in higher education in the United Kingdom. Second, it would be unwise to attempt to do this without changing the nature of the higher education experience to which adult students were gaining access (Fulton, 1989; Parry and Wake, 1990). Such changes would focus on enhancing the flexibility and relevance of the provision made for all concerned. They should not, as is often feared, affect the standards used in the established higher education examinations, though they might well add to these (Ball, 1990). They ought, however, to improve the quality of teaching and learning throughout higher education.

And, third, it is probably misleading to talk about adult disaffection from higher education as such. Those adults who enter, or seek to enter, higher education usually benefit from the process in some way, even if they do not complete their courses. Those who do not seek to enter have usually never seriously considered participation in higher education, mainly because of their childhood disaffection from education as a whole. To overcome that disaffection we may attempt to reach out to adults directly, but — and particularly in the longer term — we should also endeavour to tackle the problem at source in schools, homes and society in general.

References

ADVISORY COUNCIL FOR ADULT AND CONTINUING EDUCATION (1982a) *Adults: their educational experience and needs*, Leicester: ACACE.
—— (1982b) *Continuing Education: from policies to practice*, Leicester: ACACE.
BALL, C. (1990) *More Means Different: widening access to higher education*, London: Royal Society of Arts.
BELL, J., HAMILTON, S. and RODERICK, G. (1986) *Mature Students; entry to higher education. A guide for students and advisers*, Harlow: Longman.
BOURNER, T., HAMED, M., BARNETT, R. and REYNOLDS, A. (1988) *Students on CNAA's Part-time First Degree Courses*, London: CNAA.
BRYANT, R. (1990) 'Loans and Adult Students', *Adults Learning*, **2**, 2, pp. 40–1.
CARP, A., PETERSON, R. and ROELFS, P. (1974) 'Adult Learning Interests and Experiences', in CROSS, K., VALLEY, J. *et al.*, *Planning Non-traditional Programs*, San Francisco: Jossey-Bass, pp. 11–52.

CENTRAL STATISTICAL OFFICE (1990) *Social Trends 20*, London: HMSO.
COUNCIL FOR NATIONAL ACADEMIC AWARDS (1989) *Credit Accumulation and Transfer Scheme: regulations*, London: CNAA.
CROSS, K. (1981) *Adults as Learners*, San Francisco: Jossey-Bass.
DEPARTMENT OF EDUCATION AND SCIENCE (1978) *Higher Education into the 1990s*, London: HMSO.
—— (1988a) *Statistics of Education, Further Education November 1987*, Darlington: DES.
—— (1988b) *Top-up Loans for Students*, London: HMSO, Cm 520.
DUKE, C. (1989) 'Creating the Accessible Institution', in FULTON, O. (Ed.) *Access and Institutional Change*, Milton Keynes: Open University Press, pp. 163–77.
EDUCATIONAL COUNSELLING AND CREDIT TRANSFER INFORMATION SERVICE (1989) *Access to Higher Education: courses directory*, Milton Keynes: ECCTIS.
EVANS, N. (1984) *Access to Higher Education: non-standard entry to CNAA first degree and DipHE courses*, London: CNAA.
—— (1988) *The Assessment of Prior Experiential Learning*, London: CNAA.
FULTON, O. (Ed.) (1989) *Access and Institutional Change*, Milton Keynes: Open University Press.
FULTON, O. and ELLWOOD, S. (1989) *Admissions to Higher Education: policy and practice*, Sheffield: Training Agency.
GRAHAM, B. (1989) *Older Graduates and Employment*, London: Career Services Trust.
HOLLINSHEAD, B. and GRIFFITH, J. (1990) *Mature Students: marketing and admissions policy. Strategies for Polytechnics and Colleges*, London: CNAA.
HUBERT, G. (1989) 'Mixed Mode Study: has it got a future?' *Studies in Higher Education*, **14**, 2, pp. 219–29.
MICHAELS, R. (1979) 'A Custom Built Degree for Mature Students', *Studies in Higher Education*, **4**, 1, pp. 103–11.
MILLINS, K. and JONES, P. (1990) *A Survey of Access Courses to Higher Education: analysis and prospects*, London: CNAA.
NATIONAL INSTITUTE OF ADULT CONTINUING EDUCATION (1989) *Adults in Higher Education: a policy discussion paper*, Leicester: NIACE.
OPEN UNIVERSITY (1990) *Open University Statistics 1988: students, staff and finance*, Milton Keynes: Open University.
PARRY, G. and WAKE, C. (Eds) (1990) *Access and Alternative Futures for Higher Education*, London: Hodder and Stoughton.
PATES, A. and GOOD, M. (1989) *Second Chances: a national guide to adult education and training opportunities*, Sheffield: Department of Employment.
PERCY, K., RAMSDEN, P. and LEWIN, J. (1980) *Independent Study: two examples from English higher education*, Guildford: Society for Research into Higher Education.
RODERICK, G., BELL, J., DICKINSON, R., TURNER, R. and WELLINGS, A. (1981) *Mature Students: a study in Sheffield*, Sheffield: University of Sheffield.
RODERICK, G., BELL, J. and HAMILTON, S. (1982) 'Unqualified Mature Students in British Universities', *Studies in Adult Education*, **14**, pp. 59–68.
ROSIER, I. and EARNSHAW, L. (1989) *Mature Students' Handbook: a survey of courses and career opportunities*, Richmond: Trotman.
SMITHERS, A. and GRIFFIN, A. (1986) *The Progress of Mature Students*, Manchester: Joint Matriculation Board.
STEPHENSON, J. (1980) 'Higher Education: School for Independent Study', in BURGESS, T. and ADAMS, E. (Eds) *Outcomes of Education*, London: Macmillan, pp. 132–49.
TIGHT, M. (1982) *Part-time Degree Level Study in the United Kingdom*, Leicester: Advisory Council for Adult and Continuing Education.
—— (1987a) 'Access and Part-time Undergraduate Study', *Journal of Access Studies*, **2**, 1, pp. 12–24.
—— (1987b) 'The Value of Higher Education: full-time or part-time?' *Studies in Higher Education*, **12**, 2, pp. 169–85.

—— (1987c) 'The Location of Higher Education', *Higher Education Quarterly*, **41**, 2, pp. 162–83.

—— (1988) 'Access — not Access Courses', *Journal of Access Studies*, **3**, 2, pp. 6–13.

—— (1990) *Higher Education: a part-time perspective*, Buckingham: Open University Press.

TREASURY, HM (1990) *The Government's Expenditure Plans 1990–91 to 1992–93. Chapter 11: Department of Education and Science*, London: HMSO, Cm 1011.

TWENTYMAN, T. (1990) 'Take Ten: the Sheffield scheme for paid educational leave', *Adults Learning*, **1**, 8, pp. 218–20.

UNIT FOR THE DEVELOPMENT OF ADULT CONTINUING EDUCATION (1986) *The Challenge of Change: developing educational guidance for adults*, Leicester: UDACE.

UNIVERSITIES CENTRAL COUNCIL ON ADMISSIONS (1989) *Statistical Supplement to the Twenty-sixth Report 1987–88*, Cheltenham: UCCA.

UNIVERSITIES STATISTICAL RECORD (1988) *University Statistics 1987–1988. Volume 1: students and staff*, Cheltenham: USR.

WAGNER, L. (1990) 'Adults in Higher Education: the next five years', *Adults Learning*, **2**, 4, pp. 94–6.

WATSON, D., BROOKS, J., COGHILL, C., LINDSAY, R. and SCURRY, D. (1989) *Managing the Modular Course: perspectives from Oxford Polytechnic*, Milton Keynes: Open University Press.

WEIL, S. (1986) 'Non-traditional Learners Within Traditional Higher Education Institutions: discovery and disappointment', *Studies in Higher Education*, **11**, 3, pp. 219–35.

WEIL, S. and MCGILL, I. (1989) *Making Sense of Experiential Learning: diversity in theory and practice*, Milton Keynes: Open University Press.

WOODLEY, A. (1981) 'Age Bias', in PIPER, D. (Ed.) *Is Higher Education Fair?* Guildford: Society for Research into Higher Education, pp. 80–103.

WOODLEY, A., WAGNER, A., SLOWEY, M., HAMILTON, M. and FULTON, O. (1987) *Choosing to Learn: adults in education*, Milton Keynes: Open University Press.

3   The Experience of Black Minority Students

Eva Stina Lyon

Introduction

Over the last decades a great deal has been written about race, ethnicity and schooling. Within the educational establishment, the debate has on the whole focused on issues of 'underachievement' and its many causes, and on a meritocratic notion of equality of opportunity based on some undefined norm of equality of performance. From more critical educational and political quarters have come the arguments that such an approach, centred as it is on the perceived educational 'problems' of the minority groups themselves, fails to take on board the more important issue of racism, both individual and institutional, as the prime obstacle to the educational advancement of black minority pupils. This debate continues to generate much research and analysis, though considerably less action to alleviate proven disadvantage and injustice than the situation should demand.

In comparison, the situation facing adult black minority group members intent on continuing into further and higher education, whether straight from school or later in life, has had much less attention directed to it, either as regards the role of further and higher education in consolidating the consequences of earlier 'underachievement' through meritocratic recruitment procedures, or as regards the extent of racist practices within their own confines. The aim of this chapter is to attempt to redress this imbalance by discussing a few of the many hurdles and obstacles that impinge on the progress of black minority students from secondary and tertiary education through to higher education and into the graduate labour market. The focus of the chapter will be on higher education, entry to which many minority students seek as adults later in life, for reasons often related to their earlier rejection by schools and in the labour market. The role of further educational establishments in creating opportunities to prepare students for entry will also be looked at, as will issues in the systematic monitoring of the progress through the education system of Britain's black minorities.

Taken in isolation the hurdles to be discussed are not uniquely faced by black minority students. They are those of class in a selective and elitist system of education with credentials reflecting social position more than ability. They are also those of age and gender in a system that puts a primacy on the educational and vocational success of young people and men. They are those of race, racism and discrimination in a society that largely ignores the many rejections faced by its black members. Taken together and in complex interaction with each other, these hurdles make formidable obstacles indeed for many black minority group members wishing to continue their educational careers, and to use the fruits of their educational labours in employment. The path to higher education and into the professional end of the labour market is one which 'only the fittest of the fittest will survive' (McKellar, 1989).

There are many conceptual difficulties inherent in the discussion of race and ethnicity in education. As issues of racist discrimination and exclusion, and the consequences thereof, constitute the focus of this chapter, I have chosen to use the term 'black minority students' to refer both to students of Asian origin, i.e. mainly either Indian, Pakistani or Bangladeshi, and to those of African and Afro-Caribbean origin. Referring to such groups by the characterisation of ethnicity alone, obscures the fact that cultural difference is only one aspect of their marginal position and used by itself fails to account for the colour dimension of prejudice and discrimination. It is the dimension of colour, and with it that of prejudice and racism, which puts the problems facing black students in higher education firmly in the lap of the white educational establishment. When other studies cited below employ a different terminology, I will make this clear as far as possible in the text. I will also, when relevant, make distinctions between these groups, each one characterised by different social and educational histories.

The discussion will be based on a variety of sources of evidence, both direct and indirect, collected in some recent research projects on the position of black students and graduates. I do not aim to add to the literature cataloguing relative achievement, but will instead focus on the barriers to educational success highlighted by black higher education students themselves in various retrospective comments about their educational careers. The qualitative evidence presented below derives from interviews done with black minority students for a CNAA/CRE funded project on graduates in the labour market, and from investigations by black students themselves doing project and dissertation work in my own institution. Though the process of entering higher education, and the experiences and perceptions of its students will constitute the main focus of this chapter, the perceptions presented here relate as much to stages lower down the educational ladder as to higher education. Comments on institutional practices and procedures are partially based on my own experiences as teacher, researcher and course administrator in higher education.

Accounting for Race and Ethnicity: Out of Sight, Out of Mind

The first issue to take on board in the discussion of the position of black minority students in and *en route* to higher education is that of official statistical 'invisibility'. Whereas the processes and consequences of discrimination and racism in schools are by now quite well documented, there is a marked paucity of information about the consequences and continuation of such practices into further and higher education. A decade ago, Little and Robbins, in the first article on race bias in British higher education, observed that the position of black minorities in higher education was 'easier to observe than to prove' (Little and Robbins, 1981). In the same year, the Rampton Report recommended that the DES should arrange for the collection of information from all higher education establishments about the ethnicity of their students. Except for a few urban polytechnics and colleges of further education, the situation for adult black students has continued to be easier to observe than to prove. It was only in 1990 that the DES finally started to monitor systematically the ethnic background of applicants processed through the central admission bodies of both universities and polytechnics. It will be a while before detailed analysis of this evidence will be available. For schools, decisions about monitoring have, until now, been in the hands of local authorities, though this may be about to change, on instigation by the DES. For colleges of further education, monitoring decisions have been taken by local authorities or individual institutions themselves, or, as with programmes sponsored under the Training, Education and Enterprise Directorate of the Employment Department (previously the Manpower Services Commission and the Training Agency), on an individual course basis in relationship to employers' perceptions of the issue of equal opportunity.

It follows, that information at present at our disposal about the progress of black minority students into higher education is scant and patchy, and based largely on individual sample surveys. Studies all point to an under-representation in higher education relative to white students of Afro-Caribbean students and students of Pakistani and Bangladeshi origin. Asian students of East African and Indian background show participation rates similar to that of white students, but they, like other black minority students, are less likely to go to universities than to the former polytechnics and more likely to be concentrated in a limited range of courses. Black minority students are also more likely to enter higher education from further education establishments than sixth form colleges and to be older at the point of entry than their white counter parts. (For a summary of some of this evidence, see Lyon, 1988; Tomlinson, 1989; Brennan and McGeevor, 1990). That differences in educational attainment and progression to higher education cannot be interpreted as resulting from lack of motivation, is evidenced by research showing that both Asian and Afro-Caribbean students are more likely than white students to pursue further study, both full-time and part-time, after leaving school (Eggleston, *et al.*, 1986). Further, the difference between black minorities and the white population with respect to educational credentials increases sharply with age for both men and women, due to patterns of immigration over the last forty years. To this should also be added the fact that for older members of Asian minorities, especially women, educational disadvantages are compounded by lack of fluency in English (Brown, 1984).

As a result of the decision to monitor the ethnicity of all applicants to higher education, alongside the educational background characteristics, it will in the future be with some greater confidence that differences in the patterns of educational progression can be scrutinised and the disadvantaged position of black minorities brought more clearly into the open. There are many reasons to welcome this monitoring and to hope that it will gain support from both students and institutions. First, there is today a stronger consensus by community groups in favour of monitoring for purposes of official accountability for the consequences of discrimination, than there was a decade ago. This is illustrated by the public support for the inclusion of an ethnicity question in the census (Bhrolchain, 1990). With ethnic monitoring increasingly becoming standard practice for schools, often in response to demands from parents, there will be a growing pressure on educational establishments for adults to follow suit and become more public and accountable about recruitment patterns.

A further reason in support of systematic monitoring by all higher education establishments is the small size of the population of black minority students on many courses and in many institutions, and the different racial and ethnic composition of the local communities in which institutions are placed. These factors make national aggregated figures estimated from sample surveys difficult to interpret. A metropolitan inner-city education establishment can learn little about its own performance on recruitment, except perhaps complacency, by comparing itself to national estimates and surveys done elsewhere (Lyon, 1988). The concentration of the black minority population in particular locations is considerable. It is estimated that, in all, three-quarters of the British black population live in a set of enumeration districts in which are found only a tenth of the white population (Brown, 1984). This is an urban concentration, and while 31 per cent of the white population are resident in metropolitan areas, the corresponding figures for the British population of West Indian, Bangladeshi, and Indian and Pakistani origin are 81 per cent, 79 per cent and 66 per cent respectively. It has been estimated that a third of all Asian peoples in Britain, and half of the West Indian people, as opposed to only 11 per cent of whites, live in London (Brown, 1984). ILEA monitoring led to the estimate that close to a quarter of all London secondary school pupils are from black minority groups (ILEA, 1984). With national competition for places in higher education, institutions can largely ignore the needs of their local communities, if more 'desirable' qualified candidates are available from elsewhere. The system of monitoring now set in train by the DES will enable a better-informed debate about differences between the characteristics of students applying to courses, and those that are being recruited. This will isolate subject areas and institutions where discrimination in the recruitment process is prevalent.

The way racial and ethnic monitoring is done is often in itself a contentious matter. It is an inherently political process with concepts and methods used open to continued scrutiny and reformulation in the light of changing political realities (Bulmer, 1986). Twenty years ago, the concept of 'immigrant' was used in most educational research on black minority participation in schools to refer to what was generally seen as a large and amorphous group of 'outsiders' to the system. A decade later, much educational research used a simple dichotomy of 'West Indian' and 'Asian' to refer to black minority students, with an emphasis on ethnic background. The growing amount of research into the differential educational achievement patterns of various ethnic groupings covered by such general concepts has meant that much recent educational research uses more complex 'lists' of ethnic categorisations. Such detailed emphasis on ethnicity has been criticised for putting too much emphasis on aspects of culture and the characteristics of the minority groups themselves, thereby obscuring issues of colour prejudice and racism in white educational establishments.

It must finally be emphasised that ethnic monitoring, however visible it may make inequalities and areas of neglect and discrimination, is not in itself an answer to the issues faced by British black minority students seeking and passing through higher education. It is only an indication of processes at work. As monitoring of adults in higher education has to depend on the goodwill of those filling in forms, the political acceptability of such 'lists' becomes important, as does a sense of trust in the purposes of such monitoring; trust that it will 'make a difference' and be part of a more general commitment to the alleviation of disadvantage (Booth,

1985). With financial difficulties facing many higher educational establishments, and a political climate on the whole hostile to anti-racist and equal opportunities initiatives in education, there is little ground for optimism that such trust will develop between potential black students and the further and higher education establishments they wish to attend, unless the political rhetoric of numbers becomes converted into the rhetoric of action and change. The seeds of distrust in the willingness of educational establishments to support their aspirations are already sown much lower down the education system for black students. Unless clear signals of supportive change are forthcoming in response to the monitoring information expected in the next few years, black minority students will continue to remain largely outside the system.

The Motivation to Succeed and its Obstacles: Class, Race and Gender

The motivation to seek further educational opportunities in adult life is the result of a long process of educational decision-making determined by a variety of factors, beginning with the family, its socio-economic location and the possibilities and expectations generated by this. It is beyond the confines of this chapter to discuss the many reasons why the British working class has been under-represented in post-school education. But given this situation, it is evident that the marginal economic position of Britain's black minorities and their main location in poor areas of large cities, make factors of class chief contributors to their absence in any sizeable numbers from higher education. The class distribution of black minorities in Britain is markedly lower than that of whites. According to a recent major PSI survey into the economic position of Britain's black minorities, whereas 42 per cent of white men were found to be in non-manual work, this was true of only 26 per cent of Asian men and 15 per cent of West Indian men. Similar, though less marked, differences were shown to exist for women. There are also differences between these groups with respect to women's participation in the labour market, with a higher proportion of West Indian women in full-time occupation than either white or Asian women (Brown, 1984). The different participation rates previously referred to between various black minorities correlate directly with the above. The supposed 'success' of Asians in higher education is not universal, but is tied to black minorities' overall unusually low position. Recent Labour Force Surveys have shown the extent of the economic differences between blacks and whites in Britain, with unemployment overall for whites at 10.2 per cent compared to 16.4 per cent for ethnic minorities. Much the highest unemployment rate amongst the minorities discussed here is that of Pakistani and Bangladeshi groups (29 per cent) followed by West Indian (17 per cent) and Indian groups (13 per cent). Though unemployment is less for those with higher educational qualifications, differences remain, with the unemployment rate for black minorities over three times as high as that for whites (Brennan and McGeevor, 1990).

The evidence that is available on the socio-economic origin of black students in higher education not surprisingly shows that they are considerably more likely than their white counterparts to have fathers employed in manual or intermediate occupations (Lyon, 1988; Lyon and Gatley, 1988; Brennan and McGeevor, 1990). This evidence on class also relates to the fact that minority students are often older

37

and enter as mature students from work, or through further education establishments, a traditional alternative route into higher education for working-class
adults. For many black minority adults as for mature working-class aspirants to
higher education, cheap and easy access to further and continuing education will
remain the only possible pathway into degree studies. For black school leavers
and their parents set on 'getting on', special circumstances may be required. The
women in Tomlinson's study of a small group of black women students at
university, felt that their educational success had been enhanced by moving to a
middle-class area with few blacks in the schools (Tomlinson, 1983). In her study
of a group of African and Caribbean women who had gone through higher
education, Tueje observed that black women who had been in a small minority
in their schools felt they had received more encouragement (Tueje, 1989). Such
educational 'advantages' are gained at some emotional cost, however. As one
Afro-Caribbean male, who had gone to grammar school, expressed it in the survey of minority graduates:

> There were 90 of us in the first year's intake and only four of us were
> black. So . . . I did get some kind of prejudice. I remember the headmas-
> ter, he used to do the racist stereotype things a bit. There were four of
> us and he used to call me by someone else's name. I'm pretty sure he
> knew I wasn't that person . . . it was another black guy. He used delib-
> erately to do it to try and wind you up a bit. It was only the headmaster
> . . . most of the teachers were great. (Brennan and McGeevor, 1990)

The obstacles of class become compounded by those of both race and gender,
when pupils and students are faced by barriers, erected by the school and its
various professional advisers and gate keepers, in whose power it is to open and
close doors to future educational and occupational aspirations. It is beyond the
confines of this chapter to discuss the position of women in higher education, an
issue of importance as regards subject choice and types of professional training,
but also when it comes to the marginal position in higher education of mature
women with family responsibilities, (Acker and Warren Piper, 1984). The university women in Tomlinson's study saw themselves 'lucky' to have received university education because of both their race and gender. The progression of black
pupils as well as girls and women through the education system, has been shown
to be marred by the low and stereo-typical academic and vocational expectations
held of them by both teachers and careers advisers. Regular school processes of
decision-making with and on behalf of pupils may not be intentionally designed
to exclude and discriminate, but may in practice have that effect. One of the
reasons comparative scores of achievement between different racial and ethnic
groups tell us so very little about the potential *ability to benefit* from higher education is that such scores are based on the results of only those pupils that have
been given the *opportunity* to prepare for and sit particular secondary school
examinations. The comment of one girl in a study of black school girls, summed
up her feelings about her careers advisor thus, 'It seems she wants you to end up
in TESCO's, packing beans' (Riley, 1982).

This sentiment is echoed by many black students interviewed about their
school experiences. The negative role of careers officers and teachers in 'blocking'
or 'defusing' aspirations rather than supporting and encouraging them is evidenced

by studies of both black school leavers and graduates (Tomlinson, 1987; Wrench, 1990; Brennan and McGeevor, 1990). Here are two quotes, one from an Afro-Caribbean woman graduate, the other from a male Indian graduate.

> I was told if I wanted to be a nurse what I had to do. That is all they went on about, nursing or working in a bank as a clerk. They didn't go on to the professions, not lawyers or doctors or accountants or anything like that. Things like that were sort of unheard of in the school we went to.

> Some teachers underestimate the sort of students they have got, so when you go for a reference or something like that they don't say 'alright then, let's hope you get that place', they say 'come off it', phrases like 'I don't think you can get those sorts of grades' rather than 'put some effort into it'. (Brennan and McGeevor, 1990)

Tueje's graduate women interviewees expressed a sense of being 'man-oeuvred' out of pre-higher educational qualifications and pointed, like many other black graduates surveyed, towards teacher *encouragement* as an important factor in supporting them to continue up the educational ladder. But teacher encourage-ment was on the whole perceived as absent by the black women graduates in her study, and teachers' lower expectations of them in comparison with those of white pupils was seen as yet another form of racial discrimination. All her in-terviewees felt that the advice received in school was negative, biased and based on teachers' low academic expectations of pupils. A permanent need to 'prove' themselves had been felt. The general feeling expressed by these women was that of being treated as 'not bright enough' to enter for exams (Tueje, 1989).

The motivation to proceed with education despite discouragements and a sense of rejection seems to relate to several factors. The findings from all the studies of black graduates point to the significance of both teacher and parent support and expectations. Sometimes this is fuelled by religious values and faith in the work ethic, as well as refusal to accept the lack of encouragement shown by schools. Further, education is seen as a way to achieve economic independence, and as the only means of upward mobility available, (Riley, 1982; M. Fuller, 1980). For some of the women in Tueje's study, helping their own children's educational careers was also seen as important. As one women expressed it, education helps women, 'to be more articulate, especially when dealing with the children's schools, or talking to white people in positions of power' (Tueje, 1989).

For mature students, vocational aspirations and the desire to 'move on' be-come important motivational forces, strengthened by the knowledge that in order to do 'well', black employees in the labour market have to do better than their white collegues. As expressed by two black students in Caine's study, one a student of law, the other of social science:

> You feel you have to achieve more, whereas with a white student it is not such a big thing for them, they'll always gain a job.

> Even to apply for a job in a bank, where a white person may get the job on their A level grades a black person will be required to have higher qualifications in order to be considered. (Caine, 1990)

Motivation and support in the effort to succeed educationally are important steps on the way towards further and higher education, but the process by which a student becomes accepted for a place on a degree course is a different thing altogether. It is to the processes of selection for entry into higher education that I will now turn; a process of exclusion and redirection far more 'hidden' than those known to operate in schools.

Admissions to Higher Education: A Hidden Gate to a Secret Garden

Access to higher education is expanding, and there is a great deal of discussion about Britain entering a new era of 'mass' education. But the system has a long way to go before it can be described as 'open'. The selection process into both further and higher education is complex and guided by principles largely invisible to the outside world, and hence open to the same opportunities for discrimination and abuse as careers advice in schools and recruitment processes in the labour market (Jenkins, 1986; Wrench, 1990). The educational and vocational aspirations of students are both guided and circumscribed by the various entry standards, both formal and informal, laid down by institutions, course teams, employers and various regulatory professional bodies (Fulton, 1988). What makes the system or recruitment 'elitist' and a hidden arena for 'racist' decision-making, especially in higher education, is its dependence on a very narrow, specialised and academic system of secondary school qualifications. The attainment of these have repeatedly and over a long time been shown to relate to class, gender, race and ethnicity. Much research and major governmental inquiries have established beyond doubt that most black minority group pupils leave school less formally qualified than white ones (DES, 1981; DES, 1985). This means, first, that some minority groups are becoming channelled into the lower end of the higher education structure, into lower status institutions and subjects with fewer career opportunities, by virtue of a combination of low economic status, and discriminatory practices lower down the system. Secondly, the 'hidden nature' of the admissions system makes it open to all the charges of institutional and hidden racism that has been directed against recruitment systems in the labour market. An important distinction is drawn by Jenkins, as a result of his research into racism in employment recruitment practices, between what are seen as 'suitable' candidates, i.e. sufficiently formally qualified, and 'acceptable' ones, i.e. for more nebulous reasons 'desirable' candidates in the context at hand.

Given the element of preference and choice exercised by students in the process of entry to higher education and academic and professional disciplines, courses in great demand amongst highly-qualified candidates (such as medicine and law), can command higher and more complex 'packages' of entry qualifications, than those where students are either in short supply (such as at present teaching and engineering), or where the demand is high only from less-qualified candidates (such as a variety of areas in the social sciences). Courses and disciplines, as well as institutions in higher education vary considerably in the number and quality of O and A levels asked for as a formal pre-requisite for entry. Students who for various reasons were guided or opted out of doing maths and science at O levels (presently GCSE), or who completed school with a weak A level profile are automatically excluded from a large number of courses, and as a result also from a whole range of occupations and professions. What makes this of special importance is the strength of the evidence available that many black students, especially those of Afro-Caribbean, Pakistani and Bangladeshi origin, have in the past been 'steered' away from subjects and examination levels acting as entry tickets to educational options higher up the academic ladder (Tomlinson, 1987). From the evidence available on discrimination in the Youth Training Scheme, there are reasons to believe that similar processes are at work in the role played by further education establishments in narrowing the educational and training options open to black minority students (Wrench, 1990). That the nature, quality and numbers of secondary school credentials influence recruitment both into courses, and later into the labour market, in ways which are not supportive of black minority students is known from studies such as that undertaken by the CRE into accountancy education (CRE, 1987).

With the overall demand for many courses high, some form of further 'selection' takes place amongst candidates with equal educational background qualifications. This means that a selection is made on the basis of interviews, additional tests or straightforward 'paper' rejection or acceptance by admissions tutors, letting experience and 'a hunch' or even an informal 'quota' system guide their choice. An important study into racial and sexual discrimination in the selection of students for medical schools in London, showed such processes at work and the resulting exclusion of some categories of students with equal entry qualifications (Collier and Burke, 1986). The system of admissions is thus not only diversified, but also hierarchical both between subjects and courses, as well as between different types of institutions and students. The proposed system of ethnic monitoring of applicants, as well as of candidates finally accepted to courses and institutions, will enable some better-informed discussions about instances where intended, or unintended, discriminatory practices rather than the nature of qualifications have determined the profile of the student entry. Vocational courses where standards are set by occupational organisations, can use entry standards as systems for controlling entry to particular vocations and professions. When the demand for places on courses in a particular area is high, entry standards will remain high, unless some system of 'targets' or informal 'quotas' are operated to accommodate the particular kinds of students it is desired to recruit for social, political or moral reasons. This is one of the ways in which even courses in high demand can accommodate mature students without the 'normal' standard qualifications. Many former polytechnics have succeeded in improving their recruitment of black minority students by supporting the development of 'alternative entry' preparatory courses in further education establishments, and accepting students from those courses either in open competition, or through the use of some form of recruitment 'targets'. It is to a discussion of such courses that I will now turn.

The Access Route to Higher Education: A 'Back Way In'?

The DES Access course initiative, launched in 1978, was aimed at increasing the participation in higher education of educationally disadvantaged groups in selected local authorities. Since then the range of activities designed to assist mature students without standard qualifications has grown. Such activities range from short 'Return to Study' courses to more extensive Access courses acting as 'tailor-made' preparatory courses for particular types of degree schemes. One target group for such courses since their inception has been mature students from black minority groups. This was because of the recognised need to redress labour market inequalities and to train black professionals for entry to a range of professions such as teaching, social work and nursing (Millins, 1984). The emphasis of such courses is aimed less towards particular subject specialisms than is the case with traditional A level syllabuses, and more towards general study skills, new forms of 'portfolio' evaluations and the development of intellectual and personal confidences. The aim is to reduce the perceived barriers between having left school early, voluntarily or involuntarily, and entering some form of higher education. Through the establishment of systems of discretionary grant awards, individual local authorities have up to now been able to foster a shorter, educationally broader and more focused entry route to higher education. These awards are designed to increase the participation rate of students who for various reasons have been disadvantaged earlier in their educational careers. The location of Access initiatives at colleges of further education, traditionally institutions with greater contacts with the local community, has contributed to their greater accessibility in comparison with higher education establishments. Because of the direct involvement of CNAA and individual course teams from higher education in the design, assessment procedures and accreditation of such courses, they have provided some assurance about the standards and quality of the preparatory education offered.

It is estimated that there are now in the region of 600 Access courses in operation, and a national scheme for the recognition of the academic quality of such courses has been established through the auspices of the CNAA (Ball, 1989). With official blessing from the centre, such courses have and will continue to provide an important alternative to A levels for some black students (Brennan and McGeevor, 1990). Access course students are seldom entirely without educational qualifications of some kind, and higher education establishments have always been able to take mature students without A level qualifications. However, the nature and quality of these qualifications may not by themselves offer enough background for direct entry as a mature student, nor may they be sufficient to provide enough confidence to take the 'plunge' into a degree course or a course of professional training for someone who has been out of education for some time. As the successful completion of an Access course may offer a guarantee of a place on a particular degree course, this gives 'local' mature students the opportunity to be kept out of 'open' national competition on courses in high demand from more highly-qualified candidates.

There can be no doubt that such courses have acted as a 'launch pad' into higher education for many black minority students wishing to enter higher education, a second chance for students who would not otherwise see themselves as educationally prepared for degree studies. As policies on extending Access have focused on mature students in local communities, and given the urban location of many former polytechnics involved in such schemes, this has meant that black ethnic minority students have been making good use of such schemes. Various studies show the contribution of Access courses to the enrolment into higher education institutions, especially for Afro-Caribbean students (Millins, 1984; Lyon, 1988; Brennan and McGeevor, 1990). Access courses located in communities with a high proportion of minority school leavers could be said to be the closest the

British higher education system has come to implementing what in the US are referred to as 'affirmative action programmes'. Such programmes are designed to remedy the present consequences of past discrimination by offering opportunities designed to *promote* the recruitment of minority groups.

Given the failures of the school system in the past to provide equal opportunities for groups of students, and given that positive discrimination and quota recruitment is against the law in Britain, Access courses in local and accessible further education colleges have come to be significant because of their power to *attract* black minority students with the promise of support, encouragement and tangible outcomes in admission and degree results. They have also enabled higher education establishments to go some way towards the implementation of equal opportunities policies and to work towards 'recruitment targets' of non-standard entrants, knowing that a proportion of such students will come from black ethnic minorities.

However, such courses also present a dilemma. Despite the advantages noted above, some students express concern about the perceived low status of Access courses and how this can undermine their reputation both as students inside higher education itself, and subsequently as graduates in the labour market. There is a real danger of stereotypes of low-achieving black students being reinforced with the implication that alternative entry routes do not teach 'proper' skills. In the small study done by Caine of her fellow African and Afro-Caribbean students on degree courses in law and social sciences in a polytechnic, such fears were clearly and strongly articulated:

> There is a certain snobbery towards A level students because I think Access is viewed as a back entrance into higher education.

> Access courses are good for black students, but there is a stigma attached to them because they are geared too much to black people, which tends to price it down, it is not seen in such a good light. (Caine, 1990)

Students expressed concern that staff downgraded Access students, and that there was an assumption that all Afro-Caribbean students came through the Access route, which is by no means the case (Lyon, 1988). There is also the dilemma posed by students on the one hand not wishing to be singled out as special students with special needs, but on the other needing tutorial support and encouragement to keep pace with recent A level school leavers. In my own experience as a tutor of Access students, there is a strong feeling amongst such students that once in higher education, they are there on an equal footing with everyone else, a situation which at times creates unreasonable pressures on the declining staff resources.

Employer perceptions about qualifications were also seen to present a problem. There was concern expressed by students in Caine's study about putting Access course qualifications on job applications. Such concerns must also be seen in the context of Access students studying for degrees from the old polytechnics rather than from the traditional universities, in itself a perceived drawback in the labour market for minority students. As I will show later, there is firm evidence that such concerns are both realistic and warranted. Employers do indeed look for a wider range of indicators than the degree qualification itself when recruiting, and one such set of indicators is secondary school qualifications both in terms of their nature and quality, and in terms of the timespan over which they were gained (Royzen and Jepson, 1985). So in all, Access courses leave students in a double bind. On the one hand, in the words of one student, they give mature students who previously had a bad deal from education: 'the opportunity to achieve something previously seen as impossible', (Caine, 1990), but they do so at the cost of reinforcing old stereotypes of minority under-achievement and by creating a new kind of low status credential for students already burdened in the labour market by other low status characteristics. As with all policies for affirmative action and equal opportunities, special Access course programmes must be seen as temporary measures until such time that either *all* mature entrants to higher education have to qualify by passing through such programmes, or the school system itself improves the quality of education it is able to offer minority pupils. As this is not very likely to happen in the near future, Access courses will remain important as a route into higher education for previously disadvantaged students for some time to come and employers need to be educated about their educational role and significance.

Student Maintenance for Minority Students: Who Will Foot the Bill?

The development of alternative entry routes to higher education is not only, however, about creating a variety of educational options for groups previously disadvantaged and discriminated against. They are also about making them accessible. Such opportunities mean very little if financial resources are not provided to enable those entitled to take them up. Given the social and economic position of the main sections of Britain's black minorities, economic obstacles may well prove more insurmountable than those of credential meritocracy and varieties of institutional discriminatory practices within higher education itself. The economic restructuring of Britain over the last decades towards greater market orientation and a reduction of public sector funding, both local and national, has disproportionately affected the poorer sections of British society, and hence large proportions of Britain's black minorities, both as workers and as recipients of various public sector services such as housing, health care and education.

For higher education, the recent educational reforms leave a confused message. There is, as has been noted above, strong governmental support for increased participation rates in higher education, which in view of declining cohorts of 18 year olds, can only be achieved through the recruitment of students from sections of society traditionally under-represented in higher education, mature students, working-class students and ethnic minority students (Ball, 1989; Pearson and Pike, 1989). But the planned expansion of higher education will only benefit students from less-favoured backgrounds, mature students and students with family responsibilities if financial resources are made available. This, however, will not be the case. The expansion is expected to take place largely within existing resources, both as regards student maintenance and institutional funding available from the public purse. The growth in costs is expected to be paid partly through an increased direct involvement of industry in the funding of courses and research, and partly by students themselves through loans and supplementary course fees (Williams, 1989). There seems little doubt that changes in the system of student maintenance, which include the necessity for loans, restrictive social security measures and an obligation to pay, albeit reduced, poll tax, mean that finance will become even more of a major hurdle than it already is for many students. This will be especially so for black minority adults, given their economic position in British society, and given that, as we have seen, many of them enter as mature students with family responsibilities. But it will also be difficult for those minority school leavers who come from financially insecure backgrounds, and for whom loans will be perceived as yet another insurmountable obstacle to fulfilling aspirations.

Local authorities with concern for equal opportunities have in the past been able to contribute to the educational aspirations of late 'returners' through further education provision and systems of discretionary grants. With the introduction of the poll tax, their opportunities to finance such programmes will in the future be increasingly limited and the cost for further and continuing education is likely to be passed on to students. The withdrawal of local authority involvement in the old polytechnics in London had an immediate and detrimental effect on access for non-standard entrants with the abolition of the ILEA discretionary grant for full-time Access course students. Given the immediate and urgent needs of statutory universal educational obligations towards primary and secondary schools, a grant system for students wishing to prepare themselves for higher education is not likely to be on top of local authority agendas.

The message which recent reforms give to black minority students is not one of encouragement or support. A polytechnic student in Caine's study expressed well the fears felt by many in higher education, both students and staff:

> I believe the proposals are specifically aimed at reducing the proportions
> of black entrants like myself to go back into education. Because you have
> to make quite a lot of sacrifices financially and emotionally, and to actually
> depend now on a loan is an added burden and you'll have to think twice
> whether you'll manage. (Caine, 1990)

Unless some greater financial resource input is made into student maintenance, and extra support provided for mature students wishing to return to study, there is little hope that there will be a widening of opportunities for access to higher education for large numbers of black minority students.

Choice of Institution and Subject: First Choice, Second Best?

For those working in higher education, it has for many years been 'easy to observe' that polytechnics, especially those located in metropolitan areas, are more multiracial institutions than both universities, and polytechnics outside the larger urban conurbations. A few recent sample surveys have begun to present some evidence for this, showing that black minority students are considerably more likely to gain their higher education from polytechnics than from universities. This is not true for white students in higher education, of whom the majority go to universities (Craft and Craft, 1983; Brennan and McGeevor, 1990). Even with the rapid moves towards unitary system of higher education the two formerly seperate sectors of higher education are not equal, either with respect to facilities and resources, or to the kind of learning opportunities they offer. Despite moves to make the old polytechnics independent self-validating bodies like the traditional universities, the divide remains.

There is some considerable evidence to show that employers are not as attracted to the products of polytechnics as they are to graduates from universities (Roizen and Jepson, 1986; Boys and Kirkland, 1988). Evidence collected in the CNAA/CRE survey on ethnic minority graduates in the labour market shows that black minority graduates are aware of this and resent it. In the words of two of their interviewees:

> There is more discrimination between place of education than colour of skin. I'm sure an Indian who studied at a polytechnic and got a first would not get a job which an Indian with a first from a university went for. There is more discrimination between polytechnic and university. (Indian male)

> It really annoys me because the place I'm working there are lots of graduates, a few women, and their degree is no better than mine — in some cases it is, in some cases it is not — but because they are typical graduates and have been to university rather than a poly they have risen above me and I get really frustrated (Afro-Caribbean female). (Brennan and McGeevor, 1990)

We are here again faced with a dilemma for minority group students. They must either seek academic excellence in an 'alien' community, or remain with the 'second best' without a sense of isolation. The sense of loneliness and isolation experienced by black students in universities comes out strongly in several studies. One of the university women interviewed by Tueje expressed the view that: 'perhaps, I would have been much happier had I studied for a first degree at a Polytechnic' (Tueje, 1989).

It is not only in their distribution across the old binary divide, that black minority students differ from white students, but also with respect to the subjects they choose. The CNAA/CRE survey throws some light on this, albeit in a sketchy way given the limitations of the survey. Black minority students in engineering and sciences were more likely to be Asian and to be concentrated in computer science, chemistry and engineering, whereas black students in the area of social studies were more likely to be Afro-Caribbean and female. Subjects such as economics, geography and town planning, as well as business studies and humanities were characterised by only small proportions of minority students. This confirms the subject and gender distributions found in research done in my own institution in London (Lyon, 1988). Such differences relate to the degree of flexible admissions policies and the proportion of non-standard entrants accepted on particular courses. These differences illustrate the significance of 'hierarchies' of knowledge in higher education, with low status subjects such as engineering and social studies being the ones recruiting more black students, subjects not high on the list of preferences for white middle-class A level school leavers.

Several of the black social sciences students interviewed by Caines, had chosen law as their preference, but had not reached the required competitive standards, and had had to settle for 'second best', i.e. social sciences (Caine, 1990). The women students interviewed by Tueje expressed worries about their choice of social sciences, a discipline area which, they felt had not got them very far in the labour market. In the words of one graduate:

> I would not have done a social science degree if I had been given good advice. Though it was my decision to go on to the course, it was a decision based on advice given. A lot of black people are advised to get into courses and careers white people are getting out of. If black people are not careful, they will always be one step behind white people. A social science degree does not lead anywhere. (Tueje, 1989)

I will later look at the consequences of subject choice for the experience of black minority graduates in the labour market.

The Experience of Higher Education: Shining Through the Odds

In discussing her own educational career, B. McKellar notes that the educational system is in practice making additional requirements of black pupils (McKellar, 1989). The Afro-Caribbean students in the small survey undertaken in my own institution, expressed serious fears about two aspects of the learning process, both of which allowed the subtleties of racism to operate: the system of assessment and the white ethnocentric bias of the information presented. First, the 'hidden' nature of the evaluation process in many subjects allows undefined 'taken for granted' aspects of cultural skills to be evaluated, such as discursive styles, linguistic background, the confidence to be critical. As such skills, related to 'cultural capital' as they are, depend on social class and previous school experience, this is an area where dimensions of disadvantage go together and low staff expectations about potential ability to perform, is seen to have an effect.

> Black students really have to shine through all the odds for teachers and lecturers to realise their ability and potential. (Tueje, 1989)

> Black students go into the library night and day, working hard to get information, but find out when they produce their essays it is not what the lecturers want. On the one hand you have white students using three books to write their essays and get top marks. On the other hand, black students load themselves up with books and get nowhere. (Tueje, 1989)

The sense of cultural isolation in white organisations leads to a quest for an 'alternative' view and a concern about white staff ignorance about the social locations and histories of Britain's black population. This is an as yet difficult area to write meaningfully about in view of the absence of critical research on ethnocentricity in the higher education curriculum. Again, inner-city polytechnics with larger black minority student intakes and well-monitored equal opportunities policies have begun to monitor the *quality* of their courses with respect to their relevance to Britain's black minorities. The situation elsewhere is very different, and little pressure for change can be discerned except in institutions with centres specialising in minority group issues.

The sense of cultural and social isolation can only be enhanced by the absence of black staff in all institutions of higher education, a situation again more easily 'observed' than 'proved'. The meritocratic nature of academic credentials and appointments is often seen as incompatible with the implementation of equal opportunities employment policies. There is as yet no system for monitoring the ethnic composition of staff in higher education. With resource constraints, a low turnover of staff, and few opportunities for the recruitment of new staff in higher education, little change can be expected in the near future, even if institutions became more pro-active in equal opportunities recruitment. Like other professions in Britain, the academic establishment has been slow to respond to the changing nature of British society and it is perhaps time it became subject to the same kind of scrutiny as, for example, teaching, accountancy and law.

The sense of having to work harder than others and to shine through the odds, also relates to the pessimistic labour market expectations black students bring with them to higher education. Three of the black law students interviewed by Caine put it thus:

> I think being black and on any course in higher education you have to work twice as hard as any white individual. People are going to see you as black first regardless of what qualifications you have.

> You feel you have to achieve more, whereas with white students, it's not such a big thing for them, they'll always gain a job.

> It is important to do well because I'm disadvantaged in a lot of ways. Firstly language, where I am competing with white students from middle-class backgrounds, and secondly being black. (Caine, 1990)

There is evidence to show that such concerns are realistic and do reflect the situation in which black minorities find themselves in the labour market.

Degrees into Careers: A Major Leap Forward, Several Steps Behind

There is a growing body of evidence on graduate labour market recruitment that points to the 'realism' of the above perceptions. The benefits gained by black minority students who make it into higher education in comparison with the many other black minority members that do not, are considerable. It has improved their qualifications, made them more experienced and confident and, as we have seen above, the process of going through the system is likely to have fostered strength in coping with obstacles and set-backs. But they are still, in comparison with their white fellow graduates, as far behind as they were before they began the process of seeking higher education credentials (Brennan and McGeevor, 1990). Despite their elite status, and despite their entering a part of the labour market that is supposed to be characterised by more meritocratic recruitment procedures, black minority graduates experience more difficulties in the transition to work than their equivalently qualified white counterparts. They are less likely to find themselves in the job they initially would have preferred, and more likely to feel overqualified for the job they have. In the difficulties they encounter, they make more job applications, get fewer job offers and experience more rejections. Once in a job, their promotion prospects, both real and perceived, are poorer than for white graduates.

The interviews conducted for the CNAA/CRE study showed that for the graduates themselves, their 'ethnic origin' is seen to be the most important hindrance in their path to a desired job. As summed up by Brennan and McGeevor, they felt this was the factor that most often influenced the conduct and outcome of job interviews. Few could give direct evidence of their suspicions of discrimination, because of the 'hidden' nature of the recruitment processes within which it took place. But the outcomes of these processes for the position of black minority graduates relative to equally-qualified white graduates in similar subjects make it, as Brennan and McGeevor argue, difficult to conclude anything but that there is racial discrimination in the graduate labour market. As with the admissions process to higher education, the balance of power in the labour market recruitment process lies deeply embedded in institutional contexts of bureaucracy, prejudice and the tendency of white organisations, consciously or unconsciously, to 'bias' the rules in favour of white majority applications (Jenkins, 1986). What the evidence continues to show is that entry into the elite labour market does not depend on qualifications alone, and that the likelihood of recruitment of a member of one of Britain's black minorities is less than equal. The improved position of black minority graduates relative to other black minority workers, who are more than twice as likely to be unemployed, will continue to act as a strongly motivating force in seeking and gaining higher qualifications. But with increasing social and political pressures towards 'credentialism' for everyone, black minority adult students will continue to have to work that much harder in their educational endeavours to remain one step behind.

Towards the Future: The Changing Role of Higher Education

Looking towards the future, there are reasons to believe that post-school education in general and higher education in particular are going to have to become more actively involved in the educational progression of British minority students. During the last decade, both social and economic demands for an expansion of further and higher education has grown. Such pressures derive both from adults themselves placed in a labour market where skilled labour is in great demand, and from higher education institutions faced with declining cohorts of 18 year olds and a system of funding dependent on student recruitment. They also derive from a political concern about the low participation rate in further and higher education of the British population in comparison with those of competing industrial nations in Europe and North America. There is both in industry and the government a growing quest for better vocationally trained and educated workers, often, as Wright argues, in the simplistic belief that this on its own will resolve Britain's economic crisis (Wright, 1989). The 'demographic timebomb' of declining numbers of 18 years olds, will mean that any expansion in higher education is going to have to come from mature students, especially those previously under-represented in higher education: women, minority and working-class adults. This will be especially so in areas of labour market shortages such as technology, science and finance, but also in management services professions more generally, as well as in those public sector professions no longer able to recruit young entrants straight from school and college. The pressure is on higher education institutions to change their approach to both recruitment, admissions and the curriculum to make themselves both more attractive and more accessible to students other than those from the traditional white middle-class elite.

What are the issues that emerge as important for an improved participation rate in higher education for Britain's black minorities? Perhaps the first and most important one is the acknowledgement that there indeed is an issue, an issue that will not be solved by secondary school reforms alone. Institutions need to look towards adult students who, for various reasons to do with the history of their presence in Britain, and with racism, discrimination and neglect lower down the educational hierarchy, were unable to seek or were denied the opportunity to gain 'standard entry qualifications'. Higher education sets the goal posts, and if these are set too narrowly in line with those of a typical middle-class pupil applying straight from school, there will be little change.

First, this means that attention has to be paid to introducing monitoring procedures to establish the extent to which recruitment patterns include or exclude minority students, and to developing initiatives of various kinds to attract such students where they are absent. If used effectively, systematic monitoring will enable not only an overview of national participation rates, but also comparisons between different institutions in similar locations and between different courses and subjects. If used effectively, such information can become an instrument to force a public debate long overdue, and enable a more meaningful establishment of 'targets' to be aimed for.

Secondly, institutions need to develop closer links with other educational establishments in the community, especially in further and continuing education. They need to do so both to assist and support the development of preparatory entry courses, and to foster good relations with the minority community in order to establish trust amongst individuals who so far in their lives may have had little reason to put their faith in 'white elite' institutions. Given the hostile social, economic, political and educational environment in which Britain's black minorities find themselves, there is not much confidence amongst potential students in the commitment of higher education to accommodate them, let alone treat them fairly. Nor is such confidence likely to develop until a more thorough and public scrutiny has been made of the higher education establishment itself in terms of both curricular content, staff recruitment and behaviour, and the profile of its students. British schools have come some way towards trying to eliminate racism and its consequences in the class-room. The further and higher education establishments have hardly begun to ask the questions. It is high time they did.

References

ACKER, S. and WARREN PIPER, D. (1984) *Is Higher Education Fair to Women?*, Guildford, SRHE/NFER-Nelson.

BALL, C. (1989) *Aim Higher: Widening Access to Higher Education*, Interim Report for the Education/Industry Forum Education Steering Group, RSA.

BAKER, C.A. and THOMAS, K.C. (1985) 'The participation of ethnic minority students in a college of further education', *Journal of Further and Higher Education*, Vol. 9, No. 1.

BALLARD, R. and HOLDEN, R. (1975) 'The employment of coloured graduates in Britain', *New Community*, Vol. 4, No. 3.

BARBER, A. (1985) 'Ethnic origins and economic status', *Employment Gazette*, December.

BHROLCHAIN, M.N. (1990) 'The ethnicity question for the 1991 Census: Background and issues', Paper presented to the British Sociological Association's Annual Conference, 1990.

BOOTH, H. (1985) 'Which "ethnic question"?: The development of questions identifying ethnic origin in official statistics', *Sociological Review*, Vol. 33, No. 2.

BRENNAN, J. and McGEEVOR, P. (1990) *Ethnic Minorities and the Graduate Labour Market*, London, Commission for Racial Equality.

BROWN, C. (1984) *Black and White Britain: The third PSI survey*, London, Heinemann Educational Books.

BULMER, M. (1986) 'A controversial census topic: race and ethnicity in the British Census', *Journal of Official Statistics*, **2**, pp. 471–80.

CAINE, C. (1988) 'Black Students in Higher Education', unpublished B.Sc. Project, London, South Bank Polytechnic.

COLLIER, J. and BURKE, A. (1986) 'Racial and sexual discrimination in the selection of students for London medical schools', *Medical Education*, Vol. 20.

CRAFT, M. and CRAFT, A. (1983) 'The participation of ethnic minorities in further and higher education', *Educational Research*, Vol. 21, No. 1.

CRE (1987) *Chartered Accountancy Training Contracts: A Report of a formal investigation into ethnic minority recruitment*, London, Commission for Racial Equality.

DES (1981) *West Indian Children in Our Schools* (The Rampton Report), London, HMSO.

—— (1985) *Education for All* (The Swann Report), London, HMSO.

EGGLESTON, J. et al., (1986) *Education for Some: The Educational and Vocational Experiences of 15–18 Year Old Members of Minority Ethnic Groups*, Stoke, Trentham Books.

EMPLOYMENT GAZETTE (1988) 'Ethnic origins and the labour market', March and December.

FULLER, M. (1980) 'Black girls in a London comprehensive school', in DEEM, R. (Ed.), *Schooling for Women's Work*, London, Routledge and Kegan Paul.

FULTON, O. (1988) 'Elite survivals? Entry "standards" and procedures for higher education admissions', *Studies in Higher Education*, Vol. 19, No. 3.

HARDY, J. and VIELER-PORTER, C. (1989) 'Race, schooling and the 1988 Education Reform Act', in FLUDE, M. and HAMMER, M. (Eds) *The Education Reform Act, 1988: Its origins and implications*, London, The Falmer Press.

ILEA (1984) Research and Statistics: Statistical Information Bulletin (RS 961/84), London, ILEA.

JENKINS, R. (1986) *Racism and Recruitment: Managers, organisations and equal opportunity in the labour market*, Cambridge, Cambridge University Press.

JOHNSON, M.R.D. et al., (1989) 'Paying for change?: Section 11 and local authority social services', *New Community*, **15** (3), pp. 371–90.

LITTLE, A. and ROBBINS, D. (1981) 'Race Bias', in WARREN PIPER, D. (Ed.) *Is Higher Education Fair?*, Guildford, Society for Research into Higher Education.

LYON, E.S. (1988) 'Unequal Opportunities: Black minorities and access to higher education', *Journal of Further and Higher Education*, Vol. 12, No. 3.

LYON, E.S. and GATLEY, D. (1991) 'Black graduates and labour market recruitment', in BRENNAN, J. and JARRY, D. (Eds), *Degrees of Inequality*, London, Jessica Kingsley, (forthcoming).

McKELLAR, B. (1989) ' "Only the fittest of the fittest will survive": Black women and education', in ACKER, S. (Ed.), *Teachers, Gender and Careers*, London, The Falmer Press.

MILLINS, P.K.C. (1984) *Access Studies to Higher Education: A Report*, London, Roehampton Institute.

PEARSON, R. and PIKE, G. (1989) *The Graduate Labour Market in the 1990s*, IMS Report No. 167, Brighton, Institute of Manpower Studies.

RILEY, K. (1982) 'Black girls speak for themselves', *Multi-racial Education*, Vol. 10, No. 3.

ROBERTS, H. (1984) 'A feminist perspective on affirmative action', in ACKER, S. and WARREN PIPER, D. (Eds), *Is Higher Education Fair to Women?*, Guildford, SRHE/NFER-NELSON.

ROIZEN, J. and JEPSON, M. (1985) *Degrees for Jobs: Employer expectations of higher education*, Guildford, SRHE/NFER Nelson.

TOMLINSON, S. (1983) 'Black women in higher education: Case studies of university women in Britain', in BARTON, L. and WALKER, S. (Eds), *Race, Class and Education*, London, Croom Helm.

—— (1987) 'Curriculum option choices in multi-ethnic schools', in TROYNA, B. (Ed.), *Racial Inequality in Education*, London, Tavistock Publications.

TOMLINSON, S. and SMITH, D. (1989) *The School Effect: A study of multi-racial comprehensives*, London, PSI.

TUEJE, T. (1989) *Black Women in Higher Education*, Unpublished M.Sc. Thesis, London, South Bank Polytechnic.

WILLIAMS, G. (1989) 'Higher education', in FLUDE, M. and HAMMER, M. (Eds), *The Education Reform Act 1988*, London, Falmer Press.

WRENCH, J. (1987) 'The unfinished bridge: YTS and black youth', in TROYNA, B. (Ed.) *Racial Inequality in Education*, London, Tavistock Publications.

—— (1990) 'New vocationalism, old racism and the careers service', *New Community*, **16**(3) pp. 425–40.

WRIGHT, P. (1989) 'Access or exclusion? Some comments on the history and future prospects of continuing education in England', *Studies in Higher Education*, Vol. 14, No. 1.

4   Local Provision: An Oxfordshire Case Study

Brenda Walters

Introduction

This chapter is based on the findings from a research initiative funded by the Oxfordshire Local Education Authority between January 1989 and May 1990. A research project was set up to evaluate the impact that special funding was having on the range and numbers of non-traditional adult students taking part in Access projects and courses. The new styles of learning the students were being offered were also to be monitored. Projects were divided into four levels:

- a foundation level for skills necessary in everyday life, e.g. reading, writing, speaking, numeracy and practical and coping skills
- a return to learning (introductory) level which builds on existing skills or introduces a range of new foundation skills and subjects, e.g. learning to learn, language and mathematics, and community and group skills
- a return to learning (advanced) level which enables participants to acquire or develop basic concepts and principles of enquiry in chosen areas of study and which also enables them to achieve functional competence in languages, maths, etc.
- a fourth level which enables participants to develop the capacity for sustained study using critical and evaluative skills and understanding and which can prepare participants for entry to higher education.

The Oxfordshire access initiative involved the collaboration of a range of adult providers: Community and Adult Education Centres, Colleges of Further Education, Oxford Polytechnic, Oxford University Department for External Studies, and the Workers' Educational Association.

Oxfordshire: Provision Prior to the Initiative

Access provision in Oxfordshire had to be grafted onto the existing adult, further and higher education provision. Because the pattern of provision had just grown rather than been established according to intelligible criteria, the range of opportunities was haphazard, inconsistent and uncoordinated and it wasted both human and material resources. Access courses do *attract* people who normally would consider that their 'education' is finished, but when people are on the educational ladder, it is not always clear to them how one course relates to another or what particular providers expect of students before they begin a course.

The County was late in joining the national movement which the Department of Education and Science encouraged in 1978 in order, particularly, to train ethnic-minority teachers. By the time the idea was explored in Oxfordshire, there were three different views about the existing system. These can be very crudely outlined as follows:

- The present system is basically sound, but needs minor adjustment to allow access to the existing system for small groups of people currently excluded
- The present system discriminates systematically (though not necessarily intentionally) against some categories of people, and needs significant reworking
- The present system discriminates against large groups, perhaps a majority of adults, and needs radical change.

Whichever analysis is preferred there is no doubt that social, political and economic contexts did and still do play a major part in issues of access. The educational experience of different groups in society is very different, and attitudes and expectations vary greatly. Oxfordshire's provision, prior to the initiative, was largely taken up by white middle-class people, mainly women. The County wanted to redress the balance. (The much discussed demographic changes were also a consideration, but stressed more by officers and officials than by providers.)

Oxfordshire Local Education Authority made its first major step in 1987 and voted money for the provision of a variety of Access courses. The aim of the strategy was:

the development of a comprehensive, integrated system of educational opportunities for adults, operating at a number of different levels, directed towards traditional non-participants. The main aim is to open new pathways to continued learning in a range of possible directions from informal voluntary activity to a professional qualification, or from Basic Education to Higher Education. The objective at all stages is to equip participants with skills, knowledge and confidence to take their learning forward and to effect changes in organisational practice, curriculum and methods, to enable this to happen.

During an early pilot study all existing providers were interviewed, using a structured questionnaire, as were some of their students, with the aim of establishing whether or not the aims of the County's strategy were being met. Thereafter, detailed case studies were carried out on two Community Education projects as this area seemed at the time to be the most problematic. The findings from these studies indicated that there was some way to go before the County would have a coherent, comprehensive structure.

The Initiative as Planned

It was acknowledged that Access courses are not cheap, as they require counselling and student support systems above those normally offered to other students.

Time must also be allocated for team meetings of staff. It was envisaged that confidence-building for students would be built in through the development of literacy, numeracy and study skills. Courses should be modular, not linear or 'year long' and starting dates should not be dependent on the start of the academic year. Continuous assessment should be made and it was envisaged at this time that 'credits' should be recorded, as in an Open College Network. (This had not happened by the end of the research project but was still being worked towards.) Since the client groups being dealt with would be sensitive to the slightest hint of racism or sexism, the need for a staff development programme was recognised.

Range and Type of Courses

As mentioned in the introduction, the Oxfordshire Access initiative has involved a very wide range of adult providers from Community and Adult Education Centres to Oxford Polytechnic. In the first round of funding (1987/8) it was decided to allocate funding to as many different individual projects as possible as a pump-priming exercise. These included a full-time 'Access to Higher Education' course; a 'Second Change to Learn' course outside Oxford City; and a number of Community Education courses and outreach provision for specific groups.

Initially, a working party of practitioners was set up to oversee the development of the strategy. Very unfortunately, the working party ran into difficulties in 1988 when it was asked to consider the allocation of the next round of funding. By this time, there were more requests than could be met. People on the working party were actually competing with each other for funding, and sometimes felt unable to support new initiatives since their own particular projects might then have lost financial support. (The working party was eventually replaced by a group of three County Councillors).

No money was made available for general management, co-ordination, research or evaluation. In retrospect, this proved to be a misguided policy. This meant that the providers were unsupported and the total strategy was uncoordinated.[1] Some projects either began late or did not begin at all and others were unable to achieve their original objectives. The access initiative was not working and steps had to be taken to pull the work together into a more coherent form. The need for some additional professional support was acknowledged and the research project was set up in January 1989, both to evaluate the provision and help with the development of the strategy.

Objectives of the Access Initiative

The main objectives of the initiative were to:

- strengthen the application of the County's Equal Opportunities Policy by providing a focus on certain specific groups
- encourage and develop coherence and progression for adults across all the relevant sectors
- encourage curriculum development by financial pump-priming for a limited period.

In order to reach the target groups, careful thought was given to the barriers to participation which potential students faced. These were seen to be: pressure of time; lack of confidence; demands for entry qualifications; the nature of any assessment; possible lack of support from families and friends; lack of flexibility in relation to the curriculum; lack of information and knowledge, even of the existence of the course; the timing and location of courses and enrolment procedures.

Lack of confidence can be and is provided for through guidance and counselling. It can also, along with all the problems mentioned above, be overcome with support and understanding from both staff and other students. Time pressure and lack of family support are perhaps the most difficult problems to tackle, but again additional personal support can help. It is also important to remember that many adults have low expectations about their capacity to learn and are still conditioned in their thinking by the negative verdicts on their capabilities expressed when they were at school. This has implications for the design of learning opportunities and makes it unlikely that educationally-disadvantaged adults will respond to conventional appeals to participate in education. 'Education' means something unpleasant. Access strategies seek to change this by creating opportunities which emphasise confidence-building, and the development of learning skills; by helping students to study alone or to work effectively in groups; and by developing different approaches to teaching methodology.

Funding

The Education Committee had voted £110,000 for the Access Initiative in 1987/88 and a further £200,000 in 1988/89. By January 1989 the County had been funding Access projects for two years, and fifty-two projects were being supported to varying degrees. The intention was that research and evaluation should begin immediately; however, this was not possible. It was not that anyone working on the projects was reluctant to be evaluated or to evaluate their own work, but they felt, in general, that they had not reached the stage where they could step back and look objectively at what they were doing. There were, however, criticisms of the way that money had been distributed and confusion as to what kind of evaluation was expected; in particular, what criteria would be applied, and whom the evaluation was from. One of the early tasks of the researcher was to try to disseminate information about evaluation to the project managers.

Monitoring and Evaluation Strategy

A familiarisation exercise was carried out to ascertain existing practice in the county. The researcher met most of the project leaders and administered a questionnaire with the aim of learning about the nature of the project. Information was collected about the type and number of students involved; what special provision was made for transport and child care; the length of the courses and their venues. A summary of these findings was presented to the County Council Members' Working Party in February 1989. The findings reinforced the strong feeling that Access had to mean something distinct and that the projects should provide a 'different' sort of adult education than had been available before. The distinctiveness of Access should lie in the people it wished to attract back into learning, the new forms of learning offered and pathways to be opened up to enable people to progress more easily in the educational system. Provision at all four levels should be available in the five divisions (loosely based on District Council areas) in the County.[2] Neither of these aspirations was being met in the spring of 1989, although individually some good work was being done.

Project Guidelines

At a day-long workshop the following guidelines for project proposals were drawn up:

- *Client groups*: Careful monitoring of gender and the social, educational and ethnic background of participants will have to take place.
- *Project organisers* should show that they have taken into account the needs of students beyond their particular programme and consult other interested groups in the same area.
- *Curriculum design* and *methodology* should give attention to providing students with the skills (including effective approaches to study) required to progress in their learning. There should also be evidence of student involvement in course design and evaluation, as well as of participative teaching methods.

For the various types (levels) of provision, guidelines for curriculum and methodology were further broken down:

a) Adult basic education courses funded by Access should demonstrate that they are working in new ways, e.g., integrating disabled people into mainstream classes; adapting curricula to introduce skills like basic electronics and computing; and moving people on from basic one-to-one provision to other forms of learning.

b) Courses at Return to Learning level should develop skills such as note-taking and should be designed to encourage maximum student input through discussion and project work, and they should build on the skills and knowledge that students already have.

c) Access to Higher Education courses should be skills-based rather than knowledge-based, with an emphasis on student-centred learning and also include information technology. The courses also have to pass fairly rigorous validation procedures at the Polytechnic and have 'exit counselling' built into them. Students are also encouraged to think about the skills they already have to help build up their confidence.

d) Outreach work should cover all sectors, but is perhaps most appropriate in community education. It should build up an individual's confidence, help people to enunciate and to recognise the skills they already have, and should help people to find ways of making demands (for example, for classes at more convenient times) from the education system.

- Student-centred assessment should take place at all stages. However, progression should not be seen simply as moving on to another level of access provision, but could mean training, employment or community involvement.

- Evaluation should be carefully structured into all projects. Records will be kept to aid this process, which will be thorough but not intrusive and completed with the full cooperation of the tutors and students whose views would be sought.
- Guidance and counselling of students should be built into every project. (Everyone at the workshop felt that this is an essential element which cannot be overstressed.)
- There should be emphasis on the provision of curriculum-led staff development for the need of different locations and different disciplines.

Each project was, in future, to be written with the above in mind, and would be evaluated against them and against their own stated objectives. To people who have long been involved in Access, none of this is revolutionary, but it did form a major part of the early discussions for this *local* provision and it was often stated that Oxfordshire wanted to find its own solution. Oxfordshire's style, particularly that of allowing Community Education Centres to be autonomous bodies, responsible to Management Committees, created problems for evaluation. The Access initiative should have been centrally controlled from the beginning but even when an element of control was introduced in 1989, it was still not possible to *force* providers to keep records and work towards achieving their objectives, except by the threat of discontinuing funding.

The Role of the Evaluation

Problems were also created because 'evaluation' means different things to different people. It has an elastic quality that allows people to include almost anything they want. But there is a general feeling that evaluation means being under the microscope and is therefore to be regarded with suspicion and this is what happened in Oxfordshire. Some people think that evaluation will produce the answers to all their problems, whilst others believe that it is no more than a boring ritual to be completed as painlessly, and with as little effort, as possible. Still others fear its findings. No doubt amongst the Oxfordshire Access providers all these feelings occurred. The problem was complicated because evaluation had not been built in from the beginning and the providers felt that it was being introduced as a means of checking their expenditure. To a certain extent they were correct. The money had been given in the first instance without question to an under-resourced service.[3] But now the County, both at officer and member level, wanted to know that the money was being spent as intended. Until the new proposals could be put in place, an answer was sought to the question 'What is it necessary to know?', by trying to elicit answers to the following questions:

1 The goals of the individual project
2 Who decided the goals?
3 Do they meet the aims of the County's strategy?
4 Does everyone working on the project agree about the goals?
5 Are they achieved?

6 Who uses the services/attends the course? Are they from the target group identified in the project proposal?

7 What is their motivation? What do the users gain from the service? How does it affect their lives? What problems do they encounter?

8 Is follow-up made of people who leave?

9 How might the service be improved?

These questions formed the basis of interviews with project managers — mainly face-to-face, but in a few cases on the telephone. General answers were received but to get further information in-depth analysis and long discussion with providers and students would have been necessary, particularly since it was clear that few people were keeping records. Such an analysis did take place in two of the projects and form the basis of the case studies which now follow.

What Actually Happened

The two projects to be considered here were chosen from basic community education provision. Both were novel in their approach, and raised many questions.

A Self-help Group

The first project was a womens' self-help group which developed and broadened to take on the role of forging a link with the local Community Education network. The group was based in a small village (population of about 2,000) with no shop or school, on the outskirts of Oxford. It has a reasonable bus service and a minibus for the elderly. The village is unusual for the area since it has a council estate of seventy houses. There had been an influx of young couples with families over the previous three years because the original, now elderly, tenants had moved to smaller houses outside the village. The new people were often from large, busy council estates and were used to easy access to more facilities. They tended to find the village boring and quiet and accused people of being unfriendly. Opportunities for people to meet were few and new people, especially people without children, found it difficult to get to know village people because of the lack of places to meet. The nearest evening classes are two miles away and public transport stops at 6.20 p.m; only one-third of the families on the council estate have cars. In the village there was a high proportion of women in the 25–35 age group. Most of them had young children and some worked part-time. Very few of them drive and even fewer had access to a car during the day. For these women an educational interest outside the village would require organising transport and child care at added cost. The County's Access strategy does at least begin to address this problem through 'minor awards' in needy cases.

In January 1988, a group of women in the village decided to form a self-help group in order to lose weight, without professional help. At this stage, they claimed that although their husbands felt it was all right for them to meet as a slimming group, they would not want their wives to spend an evening talking together. It was suggested by the women that their husbands would feel threatened.

They worried less about this as their confidence developed. At the weekly weigh-in the group would also discuss the types of food they should avoid in order to lose weight. As they became more knowledgeable about nutrition, they started to discuss such matters as food additives and obesity in children — topics usually inspired by an article in a newspaper. The discussions were frequently of practical value as it was often found that they shared the same problems and could compare notes on possible solutions, e.g. suggestions from a doctor. Sometimes a woman would volunteer to find out more before the next session, e.g. on pre-menstrual tension, and an experiment was carried out by some in taking Vitamin B6. The organiser said that this simple description of self-help does not adequately show the value of the discoveries that the women were making about themselves and about the world they lived in. They began to question why such matters were not more widely discussed and researched. Their conclusion was that this was because it was a woman's problem! (This does seem to be a conclusion they reached for themselves.) From health matters, discussion broadened into the subject of house-work and the socialisation of women to be housewives. They discussed the attitudes of their husbands to this. For the first time, in many cases, the women were able to share these resentments and discuss them openly. The group began to develop and to discuss issues of wider importance. One woman said that she had gained sufficient confidence from a discussion on shoddy goods to write a letter of complaint after a poor meal in a restaurant.

The prime mover of the group was a woman who grew up locally and who took it upon herself to be the leader and organiser of this local development. She was not a professional and had received no training in this type of work, but she was a member of the Management Committee of the nearby Community Education Centre. The group operated for a year on a self-help basis. In 1989, funding from the Access budget was made available for its further development, and to pay the organiser as a part-time worker. The organiser did not act as a neutral agent of change but rather acted from the beginning as a personal counsellor and later as an educational counsellor. On occasion she worked in ways which strongly influenced the other women to act in the way she herself felt most appropriate.

Eight out of the ten regulars of the group were in some kind of paid employment, but only one had a full-time paid job. All were low paid, but no travel was involved and they could virtually choose which days to work on and fit in with the children. Two women, although well-qualified, were not able to work because of the commitment to very young children. All the women had had full-time paid work before having their children. All said that the break from work had left them feeling devalued and lacking in confidence. Although the skills involved when managing on a tight budget — organising meals, shopping, house-work, child care, etc. — were pointed out to them, the general attitude was the 'anyone could do it'. Some wanted to retrain or get more qualifications but were afraid of night-school. School experiences were on the whole, negative, and a few had hated school. All of them were convinced that Adult Education was just school for grown-ups. They had a mental picture of sitting in classrooms, taking notes and being told what to do by a teacher. They wanted a basic introductory course of some description which would result in a completion certificate. The thought of taking GCSEs sounded far too difficult and reminded them of the failures some had had in their youth. Conversely, they felt that there were too many 'hobby' classes like floristry, and some subjects that they could not relate to at all, like fifteenth-century Dutch painting. They wanted to go back to work and to try something a bit different.

One example of the membership of the group was a women of 32 with two children aged 13 and 15, who had hated school and had left half-way through the 5th year just to get away. She started training as a hairdresser but became pregnant, and was married with a baby just before her 18th birthday. She had been completely immersed in family life, but now her family were growing up and becoming much more independent. As she was beginning to think about her future, she suffered five bereavements in one year. After years of being someone's wife, mother, daughter, sister, she did not know who she was unless it was in relation to someone else. She felt resentful at the way her life was turning out. She was afraid to look at what the future would bring, and wanted something to look forward to and to plan for.

The organiser helped her with some 'counselling', in particular getting her to list all the things she could do. Through this, the organiser tried to convince her that she was not stupid just because she did not have any certificates. The organiser also suggested to her that some of the blame for her lack of education was due to bad teaching methods and low expectations by her parents and teachers, and also to her social background. The student wanted to try something new and, after initial resistance, she was persuaded to join a community education course. The organiser told her she would get used to meeting strangers again, to being back in the classroom and to listening. She would also be committing herself to attending one evening a week; this time would be hers alone and would not benefit the other members of her family at all.

Indeed, there were other negative sides to the process. Her husband was worried by her unhappiness and blamed himself for not being able to change it. He became angry and impatient. He also felt that if she 'bettered' herself she would see his failings and leave him. The organiser again intervened 'by keeping him informed of what we had been talking about, and always asking his opinion. He was reassured and felt relieved that someone else was listening to his wife's problems and the whole family could see how much happier she was'. The wife's new-found confidence has resulted in her becoming much more involved in village projects, including youth work. This sort of progression into further study and community activity is exactly what the Access strategy seeks to achieve.

Another participant was a women of 26, who had one child. She was a very confident and outspoken woman who was not afraid to speak to new people. She was determined to go back to work once her child was old enough for school and wanted to improve her skills in the meantime. It was suggested that a shorthand course and perhaps an advanced typing course, would add to her existing typing skills. She was not even aware she could do these things part-time. Once again, a husband proved a problem since he was worried that once she was better-qualified she would end up earning more than him. He felt threatened by this and he worried that the housework and care of the child would suffer. The organiser advised her to reassure him, although she felt angry at his lack of support. She claimed she would only want to work part-time and that the extra money would be very useful. She said she felt strange at the thought of going back to school since she had hated it and had spent most of her school years playing truant. The organiser pointed out that she would be with other adults and this time she would be choosing the subjects.

Here the organiser acknowledged that her own role, or indeed that of anyone giving encouragement and helping to boost the confidence of someone, could cause complications. Later the young mother saw her old job advertised and rang for details. She was offered the job and her husband was very annoyed as she had not discussed it. But undeterred, the organiser pointed out the practical difficulties and the problems she would face if she was to take on a full-time job then. Her son would not start school for another year and the work's crèche had a waiting list of twenty; she did not have access to a car and buses through the village did not fit in with her work hours. It was also pointed out that she was going back to exactly the same job she had held before having her child, and if she did the courses she would have more of a choice when things were easier. She realised that perhaps this was the wrong time to make this move and became determined to get other qualifications for use in the future.

The organiser did have some misgivings about moving on from a self-help group to counselling individuals. The project was funded as a self-help group. In the original proposal the role of the organiser was not spelled out, although the implication was that 'organiser' meant the person who booked the hall, etc. She recognised the level of commitment needed, and that if an offer of help was made, e.g. to find out certain information, this was always done. She helped women who were nervous about making telephone calls and writing letters. She discussed the temptation to suggest particular jobs or courses of action to people and genuinely seemed to think she was a neutral advocate. She thought that nothing should be suggested that might be beyond the reach of the person concerned, and said she suggested smaller goals and how they might be achieved, saying

> then confidence is gained with each success. It is also easy to do too much for a person who is lacking confidence. This can be overcome by giving 'phone numbers, names of contacts and then encouraging people to make the calls themselves. Obviously if this is really out of the question then one should always step in, but there must be an opportunity for the individual to find out for themselves — this in itself is a way of attaining goals and of learning.

When funding was awarded, the transition from slimming club to discussion group had already taken place. Indeed, it was this fact that made the local Community Education Tutor request the funding; he felt the organiser needed a 'reward' in the form of a small payment and that the group should be able to buy materials such as the Open University 'Health Choices' course. He also felt it would give the group 'status'.

It is interesting to note that the original slimming group would *not* have been funded as it would not have been seen as educational. It was only after it developed into a discussion group that it could even be considered under the terms of the initiative. Yet a discussion group could not have been started without this basis and its (almost) spontaneous evolution. When considering provision like this it is worth bearing in mind that many of those involved think that it is only education if they attend a course to train for a specific job, and are unaware that they have been taking part in an educational experience. Indeed, that the community has been educating itself. The women were receptive and able to accept new ideas and cooperate with each other over child care arrangements and transport. Although one person had the information required it needed communication and cooperation between the women themselves for some to attend classes or start new work.

Open University material on 'Health Choices' and a pack prepared by the Oxfordshire County Council Training Officer were used by five of the women. They found them interesting and in parts 'educational'. They also felt self-conscious at first about doing some of the written exercises, and some of the methods recommended in the Training Officer's pack for recording past experiences were quite new to them, e.g. spider diagrams and spirals of influence. It was also difficult for some to write at length as they were out of practice — writing was confined to the odd letter and shopping lists. It is interesting to note that some of the women felt that the language of the pack was difficult to understand; one woman commented: 'You have to be educated to understand the education pack'. Although it was stressed that this pack was just an interesting experiment, all the women felt they were learning or being taught something. The group leader found the pages on aims for the group and for herself were most useful. She found the whole pack interesting but in need of more simplified language and less abstract methods of recording thoughts and feelings.

Originally the group filled a social gap. It also quickly highlighted the very real need for such groups in small rural communities. The group, created simply for weight-watching developed into a forum where women could share and, in many cases, come to grips with their own family problems. In this sense, the original group did have an educational function, since it helped women to understand more about their own lives and the social pressures which shape their lives. The group also became a means through which the women could learn how to broaden their experiences and skills.

This project was already reaching one of the groups which were targeted by the Access Initiative before funding was offered. In that sense it was not a new initiative, but the funding allowed it to be adopted by the Community Education Service. The money did allow the group to move from discussing newspaper articles and television programmes to using more structured materials. That is, it allowed them to move on to a different style of educational experience. It will be interesting to see what will develop next.

An Adult Learning Project

This project was based on the work of two unemployment Outreach Workers who felt that the unemployed people they were meeting would benefit from more education and training and would then be better able to re-enter the job market. Provision was made for an afternoon course and an evening one. Each course lasted for ten weeks. In addition, one joint four-hour session was held on a Saturday early in the course; also a joint two-day residential weekend was held at the end of the course. In view of the high drop-out rate there may be something to be said for having a residential weekend nearer the beginning of a course in order to help build commitment and group cohesion.

There were seventeen women and eight men, whose ages varied from 21 to 76, with five over 60 years of age. Child care expenses were paid to students who needed them. This was taken up by three students, one of whom would have preferred a crèche on the premises. Only four students of the twenty-five students were from ethnic minority groups. Three of the four had dropped out by the sixth session. Course tutors suggested that the course may not have been sufficiently geared to meet their needs. However, similar problems have been met in attempts elsewhere in the City to start a 'College' specifically for Asians and Afro-Caribbeans. In terms of the Access criteria, the course succeeded in attracting women, the unemployed and those wishing to improve their educational qualifications. It was not successful in retaining a racial mix or in catering for the disabled.

Both courses met in a church hall in the centre of Oxford. This venue had the advantage of a central location accessible by public transport from a wide surrounding area. As only seven students had access to a car this was important. However, the City Centre is not a pleasant place at night and the area around the church is particularly bleak and dismal even in the summer. One student did drop out for this reason. The room in the church which was used for the afternoon class was not ideal, with stairs and little signposting. The room used for the evening group was cramped. This meant that disabled students could not be included on the course. However, at the time the course was set up, no more suitable place was available. Ideally, a light, airy room with chairs and tables which could easily be moved into different positions would have been preferable. Similarly, it would be better to have had a more easily accessible room with clear signposting — although, of course, the tutors could have prepared signs and/or waited for possible participants at the front door on the first evening. The timing of the courses was chosen by the students and the resulting day/evening split should have offered plenty of opportunity for people to attend. However, the afternoon group suffered a high drop-out rate. The course was designed to have a break in the middle. This resulted in some of the students not returning immediately afterwards, although most of them did reappear later. Reasons people gave for leaving both courses were various, such as disliking another student, being unhappy about walking through the City at night, and not being happy with the tutor. The tutors who run these courses are warm and friendly and it could, as mentioned above, have been the siting of the courses that caused some of the problems. Five of those who dropped out and those who completed all or most of the course all stayed in touch with the tutors afterwards and sought help and advice about future opportunities for educational and vocational courses.

The content of the courses was based on study skills, using a variety of materials relevant to students' interests. The study skills included: note-taking, statistics, critical thinking, reading, writing, and finding out information (including about further educational opportunities). The subjects and the way they were taught was decided by the tutors with the course organiser. The teaching and learning methods included small group work, discussion and project work. Some of the students found having to do work at home difficult, but on the whole they derived great satisfaction from their project work.

In general, expectations of the course seem to have been high. From the analysis of a detailed questionnaire completed by the students at the beginning and end of the course, from a brief period of non-participant observation, and from interviews with the students, it seems that most gained enormously from the course experience, particularly from each other and from the tutors. They also benefited from the commitment and individual attention given by the course organiser. It may be that people attend a course of this type expecting it to solve all their personal, social and educational needs. This is clearly unrealistic, but such courses can give confidence and knowledge and information, which can, in themselves, prove very satisfying. A high level of support is vital to Access students and should be a feature of all Access courses and such groups should ideally consist of about twelve people: small enough for individual attention, but large enough for people to get confidence in group work.

Conclusions

It is difficult to give the full flavour of the local provision, but the two case studies, one rural and one based in the City, show some of the problems that arose. Initially, provision across the County was patchy with most money going into the City, which is the largest centre of population and which has the largest number of economically deprived people. But Oxfordshire is a rural county and this poses its own problems. Also, there is a tendency to equate economic deprivation with educational deprivation, and this is not always the case. Many of the people with low educational achievement are not necessarily short of money, but they may be unwilling to spend it on attending courses.

What can be Learned from Oxfordshire's Early Experience?

The main problem was that a well-intentioned addition to the educational provision got off to a bad start because the decision was taken to put 'once off' money directly into course provision. Two problems followed from this: firstly, many providers felt strongly that the short-term nature of the funding would raise expectations among students and potential students which might not be met. It was frequently said, 'You cannot change the world overnight.' Time is needed to consolidate strategy and establish courses to meet the needs of those who have traditionally been non-participants in continuing education. Secondly, the lack of administrative support led to confusion and a certain wariness on the part of providers.

What was Learned?

By the end of the project it was generally felt that providers need the security of long-term funding to enable planning, coordination and effective outreach to take place. They would be helped by more information on how funds are distributed, on the current Access situation in the area, and on options available to students in order to give guidance and counselling. Many staff are part-time and feel that this means that their work is not valued. They also feel there is no recognition of the importance of outreach work and the fact that it is time-consuming and may appear to show few results. All providers need administrative support and opportunities to collaborate with colleagues in other areas of work and to develop networks. Training and staff development are necessary for Access tutors on student-centred learning, negotiation and guidance.

Students need to receive information on available courses through well-organised and widely distributed publicity material; through counselling, both prior to and during courses, and access to independent information and advice at all times (not just during traditional hours). To assist in their development, they need an acknowledgement of their prior experiential learning in work and life together with forms of assessment such as profiling which are relevant to their situation. This would also give learners opportunities to explore and express their own needs. More people would be enabled to attend if grants were available to part-time students, if more free provision and free crèches and other child care facilities were also provided. They should have appropriate teaching methods which recognise their adult status and experience and a range of opportunities catering for different needs (different times, locations, lengths of courses) and flexible enrolment procedures with some roll on/roll off provision. There should be local opportunities which respond to local needs. Perhaps above all they need to be offered the opportunity to develop understanding and reasoning and not just skills.

To help all this to happen, the County needs to acknowledge the importance of all levels and types of Access work and to support programmes which will lead to increased knowledge and improved practice in specific areas. Clear policy decisions have to be made on how funding is distributed so that providers have a clear idea of what is eligible. The main task might be said to be the recognition of the long-term nature of Access work when assessing success. All in all, Access provision needs to become more flexible and participant-centred, but with clear guidelines to follow. In order for all this to happen, institutions need to change and to incorporate the ideas which are being developed.

When the project ended, these things were beginning to happen and a more coordinated approach to Access provision was being made. It could be that the most transferable lesson to be learned is, having taken the decision to move in the direction of funding Access provision, a clear policy needs to be agreed. Action before thought can lead to short-term provision. This can lead to the hopes of potential students, who very probably got little out of school, being raised and to their becoming once again alienated.

Notes

1 Because of this, and the way in which providers put money towards something other than was funded, it is impossible to say how many projects ran in that first year, but it was about thirty.
2 Oxfordshire County Council Education Committee Minute 5/89 Resolution (e).
3 Oxfordshire's allocation of money for adult and community education ranks thirty-third out of thirty-six counties.

Part 2

Provision and Progress with Learning

5 The Scope and Characteristics of Educational Provision for Adults

Colin Titmus

This will, I hope, turn out to be an overview of adult education provision, of such a kind that it may suggest to the reader ways in which the disaffected adult may be drawn to participate in it, either by changing the provision, or the adult, or by modifying the world in which the former exists and the latter lives. There may be other ways of achieving this desirable aim, but for the moment I cannot think of any. This seemingly simple task is a problem that has occupied the minds and sometimes the actions of educators — with only limited success — since the beginning of adult education.

In fact, leaving its fulfilment on one side, the task is less easy even to envisage adequately than most writers on the subject have appeared to think. There is not a clear division between affection and disaffection, but rather a continuum running from high enthusiasm to undertake systematic study in adult life, through indifference, to violent detestation of any such activity. Nor is the scope of this attitude precisely defined. In the case of any given individual does it cover all systematic study, or only certain kinds? Is it the content, the nature of the learning situation, or the outcome that inspires or repels? Does one's attitude spring from experiences, not necessarily overtly educational at all? Is it really disaffection that people feel, in the sense of indifference or alienation, or do they feel it is attractive, but other activities competing for their time are perceived as being more pleasurable or more worthwhile? Is their position on the continuum fixed, or is it liable to change — and if it is, what kinds of influences are likely to change it?

Since the answers to these questions are likely to change with the individual of whom they are asked, there is almost certainly no single prototype of the disaffected adult and therefore no single way of drawing such adults into participation. Indeed, it seems a daunting task, perhaps even unrealistic, to address so many and such diverse cases. Against this, however, one may set the vast array of provisions of content, mode and outcome now to be found in adult education. So much is there that one is tempted to wonder whether the task is less one of finding new provisions than of matching examples of what already exists to the target individual. If that proves not to be the case, then the solution to the conundrum of the disaffected adult may not lie in provision itself, however one may define it, but elsewhere.

Range of Educational Experiences on Offer

Continuation of Initial Education

Today, as for many centuries past, much full-time education, begun in childhood, continues into adult life. In most countries those who are fortunate enough to undergo higher education do not complete their studies until they are in their middle or late-twenties. In the Federal Republic of Germany, for example, where students who enter university straight from school do so at the age of 19, but where many do military service first or spend a period of other activity outside education until a place in the desired course is available, the average length of higher study before graduation is 6.5 years (Teichler and Sanyal, 1982). Increasingly in advanced countries the minimum age for leaving school is 16 and the majority of young people, as in the USA, stay on at least until they are 18. Then many follow a course of general post-secondary education in institutions such as a Folk High School or a Community College, or of initial preparation for an occupation requiring several years of study after leaving school.

Nevertheless, even today education is an activity essentially associated, even in the mind of educators, with childhood. In spite of the volume of intentional learning, structured and organised, undergone after childhood by people throughout the world, when one speaks of education, one is normally referring to initial education. It is therefore not surprising that education after childhood is perceived and practised in terms of its relationship to childhood education and is determined by this perception to a degree that is perhaps too little realised. One not only talks but thinks of processes and organisation of systematic study for persons beyond school age as post-initial, post-secondary, tertiary or further education, all terms expressing a perceived position relative to childhood schooling.

In advanced countries it is impossible to ignore this. The school system is there, by statute. Any subsequent educational provision derives its basic assumptions about its clients from its perceptions of what the system has done or failed to do. One may see post-initial education as a continuation in varying degrees of school, or, conversely, as a necessity created to a greater or lesser extent by the inadequacies of the schooling children receive. The latter was the case of *éducation populaire* in France after World War II and had as its result a movement that set out as a matter of principle to adopt characteristics — local control by users, democratic organisation, informality, learner-centred learning, emphasis on learning processes, particularly active ones — which were the direct opposite of what it saw as those of French schools (Titmus, 1967). But by behaving in that way it modelled itself according to those schools just as much as if it had set out to continue their work.

Compensatory Education

In Third World countries few, if any, can offer to all children that minimum of between nine and eleven years of continuous full-time childhood education, which is the norm in economically advanced societies. All countries do, however, aspire to this. In those that have not achieved this goal, education after childhood is largely conceived as compensation for the lack of such provision. In particular its purpose is to combat illiteracy and to inculcate basic life skills. In those societies that have quasi-universal long-term schooling, adult basic education is similarly available for those people, and there are always likely to be a few, who slipped out of the educational net during childhood. In advanced societies, as the normal length of initial education has increased, so has the perceived compensatory role of education after childhood. In some form or other all levels of initial education are covered, although not to all people. Sweden is only one of many states offering to adults opportunities to complete secondary education (Titmus, 1981:76 ff). The growing provision of places in European higher education for mature students without formal entry qualifications is, like the British Open University, in part motivated by a desire to provide a second or compensatory chance to those who, for whatever reason, did not enter higher education straight after leaving school (Titmus, 1985:90 ff).

Supplementary Education

In addition to being compensatory, education after childhood is seen as being supplementary to initial schooling. In current thinking, some post-childhood education is necessary, because it is not possible to cram all the systematic learning one will need throughout life into full-time initial study, however long that experience may be. There are indeed pertinent reasons for not extending the latter any further than the age of 18–19, usual in advanced countries. The primary one is cost-effectiveness. Most advanced countries are examining critically their expenditure on tertiary education. They are questioning, among other things, how far they can afford to continue to open conventional higher education, that is, full-time undergraduate study undertaken straight from school, more widely to a mass public. Some are considering also whether there would not be educational, as well as economical advantages, if young people, instead of remaining in full-time study until their mid-twenties, went out from school in their late-teens to gain experience of paid employment or other activities, to return later to higher or other tertiary education, perhaps on a part-time basis, as and when they felt the desire.

There is a need for some educational opportunities in adult life because, even if there were enough time to learn in childhood and adolescence all that one would need through life, one could not at that time foresee all one's later learning needs. In the past one might have relied entirely on one's general education and initial vocational training, if any, on staying in the same occupation, the same society and district all one's life, one's social roles predictable and not much different from those of one's forefathers. There is a chance that life will still be like that for some rural inhabitants of Third World countries, who will have to get by without any formal education at all. It is highly unlikely that such a career will be open to anyone else. It is now most widely argued that one has to expect at some time either to need to refresh some of the knowledge one has acquired in youth, revise it, advance it to a higher level, or acquire quite new learning. It is one of the assumptions on which the provision of education after childhood is predicated.

Re-education and Retraining

Even in the slowly changing human society of the past centuries, voluntary or involuntary shifts of one's position within it might impose upon one the need for new knowledge, although opportunities to obtain it by systematic courses of study were few. Today, even if one could conceive the societies as unchanging in any other ways, one would have to take into account transformations brought about by an increasing awareness among their members of the different roles they may have to play, of the range of role choices open, and of the value of systematic education in preparing people for their roles. To a large extent this is due to democratization and the spread of universal education. People feel entitled to change their way of life. They are not merely forced by external circumstances to change their work. Nowadays it is not uncommon even for persons who have devoted years to achieving expertise in one profession, to choose to move of their own free will to another, requiring perhaps an equal effort of study. Such behaviour is accepted as legitimate and opportunities are created to make it possible. Recently the British government has relied, as it has done on occasions in the past, on this phenomenon to help to make up for the shortage of science and mathematics teachers in its schools. It has been trying to attract men and women with suitable subject qualifications to transfer from commerce and industry.

Knowledge Obsolescence

The heightened awareness and wider expectations of individuals and groups has, however, been stimulated, if not created, by external pressures. The world in which and for which most people received their initial education is not the one in which they live most of their adult lives and this, as far as one can see, will be the situation of succeeding generations. A very great deal of the education after childhood that people may now expect to undergo has been rendered desirable, if not necessary, by factors outside themselves, by rapid changes in knowledge and society. These are making much of initial education and training obsolete.

In the employment field, to a growing extent, occupations require some specialised knowledge. Unskilled workers find it increasingly difficult to obtain employment. Even skilled ones who stay in one occupation throughout their working life may require to adapt their skills or acquire new ones — and more than once in their career. Typists master word-processors. Some occupations disappear, as for example, almost fifty years ago, in shipbuilding, riveters were replaced by welders. Because of the development of computer-aided design, there will probably be no future demand for traditionally trained draughtsmen. The need for change may arise very suddenly. In the first few years of the 1980s Ford of Great Britain had to switch apprentices in mid-course to become machine maintenance fitters rather than toolmakers (Shepherd, 1985).

Not only trades, but whole industries have either become obsolete altogether, or the demand for them has been greatly reduced, or production has shifted from the traditional centres, frequently to other countries. New industries, using new technologies and therefore requiring new skills, have sprung up. Automation has made most productive industry less labour intensive. Fewer workers are needed, jobs are lost. In advanced countries a significant shift from productive industries to the provision of services has been occurring for a number of years, paralleled in many Third World countries by a move from primary production of raw materials to the manufacture of finished goods. For a multiplicity of reasons, therefore, one may expect to have to undergo some occupational retraining in the course of one's working life.

Education for Social Change

The effect of accelerating knowledge growth is not confined to working life. In areas where the whole economic base is changing, and they are numerous, people have not only to move away or learn new skills, but they are frequently obliged to make substantial personal, family and social adjustments. Adult education was used in the early days of the industrial revolution to help transform rural homeworkers and agricultural workers into urban factory labourers. It has continued to be used to further the process of acculturation in recent decades, for example, when the Lorraine coal and steel industries were shut down (Lesne, Collon and Oeconomo, 1970).

Many adults have to undergo vocational training to obtain a job or to keep in employment at all, but on the whole workers pursue it in the expectation of improving their lives in some way, thus continuing a process that has been going on for most employees in the advanced world ever since the World War II. People look to it to heighten workers' job satisfaction, or raise their material standards and enable them to improve the quality of their life outside working hours. They are working fewer hours, with the forty-hour week, for which so much struggle was waged in Western Europe in the 1930s, becoming one of thirty-five. Paid holidays are longer, working life shorter, as workers, willingly or not, take retirement earlier. As less time has to be spent on paid labour, so that which is free of the demands of work grows longer and assumes a relatively greater importance. An increasing number of people see the purpose of work as enabling one to enjoy to the full the time outside work (Goldthorpe *et al.*, 1968–9). Taken together, increased disposable hours, greater prosperity, technical advances in, for instance, travel and communications and a higher average level of initial education have vastly enlarged the possibilities of using free time, and made individuals both more conscious of them and more expectant that they will be able to experience that potential to the full if they wish.

Education for Self-realization

Educators commonly deplore that too little advantage is taken of these opportunities to further individual enrichment by intentional learning. Nevertheless, a very large number of adults engage in systematic study for no other apparent reason than self-satisfaction, either in the end product or enriched experience through acquired knowledge and skills, or in the process of acquiring them. They learn to paint, to make music, to write stories and poetry, to dance, to make useful or aesthetically pleasing objects, to sail boats, to fish, to play games such as chess or bridge, to develop their bodies. They study history, archaeology, philosophy, botany, geology, economics and politics for the simple pleasure of understanding.

Many of these so-called leisure or hobby studies have also a social dimension. The man or woman who learns metalwork, carpentry, decorating skills, or gardening, who studies cookery, dressmaking or flower arranging may be learning to make a contribution to the quality of family life or its material well-being. But there is need and also provision for non-vocational post-childhood study with a wider social resonance.

Education to Help Solve Social Problems

Throughout human history societies have had their problems and would have benefited if their members had understood them better. Perhaps not though, because for most of that time the ills man was prone to were seen to be the work of fate or whatever gods there were and therefore insoluble in this world. Only in an afterlife, if one was a Christian or Muslim, or by escaping from the wheel of existence altogether, if one was a Hindu or a Buddhist, could one find relief. In our contemporary world, however, a strong belief has been created that humanity can master the physical world, can understand and control its own fate. Perhaps the events of this century have reduced this optimism in recent years, but it is still the predominant principle behind public policy that the destiny of humanity lies in its own hands, not least because there appears to many people to be no alternative. Knowledge and the wise application of it can ultimately resolve any difficulty, or so it is commonly believed.

Learning Personal and Social Skills

Operation on that assumption has either made the world more complicated, or we perceive more of its complexity. The more we know, the more conscious we become of what remains to be learned. We are also aware that no single person can master it all. Nevertheless, because knowledge on so many matters is publicly available, human beings have greater expectations that some knowledge exists to help solve any problem they may have. They can either master and use any part of it that they may be required to in a specific context, or, if they cannot, they count on being able to call on a specialist who can meet their needs. It is no longer feasible to draw on the body of knowledge and skills within the family and near neighbours. Members of families are less frequently living near enough to each other to be called upon, the older generation's store of experience is too often outmoded, the range of understanding and skills existing is too great to be comprehended within so small a group. However, it does not matter, since access to them outside one's own small circle is already easy and growing easier. So we call on experts, either to do things for us, or to teach us what they know and show us how to put it to use. Much of systematic learning after childhood is of this kind. It is accepted that there is a large amount of knowledge and skills, about child rearing, but living after retirement, about driving a car, which can be structured into a coherent body, so that it may be taught and learned, and, most important, usefully applied in practice.

Role Education

In the past one was prepared for taking on traditional roles in family and society, in so far as one was trained at all, by relatives or friends, or by observing the behaviour of those already in them. Increasingly such learning is considered to be inadequate, or unreliable. Family-life workshops and courses have become a commonplace in advanced countries and a significant element of educational programmes in the Third World (Brillinger and Brundage, 1985). Pre-natal courses for pregnant women (and the fathers), offered in Britain by the National Child-birth Trust, attract a large proportion of the child-bearing group. Education is available and encouraged in many societies for other social, non-occupational roles. It may be a condition of acceptance as a candidate for election to political office that one undergoes some training. Employees are commonly legally entitled to paid leave from employment in order to train for work in trade unions (Hopkins, 1985).

Society's Pressure on the Individual

To a degree that was probably only equalled in past ages in its imposition of religious observance, society now interferes in what one has been accustomed to call the private affairs of individuals. The reason is in part paternalistic, to do the best for people, whether they like it or not, at least in so-called welfare states, but principally because there is very little in any person's life that does not have at least a potential impact on the lives of others, so that it becomes a social concern. Therefore out of self-interest society may not force, but it certainly encourages, people to learn how to behave in a multiplicity of situations. One is obliged to follow a course of instruction before driving a car or flying an aeroplane, because in unskilled hands these objects may kill other people in addition to the driver. One is encouraged to learn to bring up children, not only for their benefit, but because if badly brought up they may become social or economic misfits as they grow up, and thus a burden on society. Old people, by their very numbers, constitute a growing problem, but they may be made less so by education. Education aimed at specific categories of people, or people in specific situations, is not confined to the advanced world. In developing countries much effort has been devoted to health education, especially nutrition, hygiene and the importance and means of ensuring the purity of drinking water. Considerable importance is attached to the education of women, not only in Europe and America, but also in Africa, Latin America and other parts of the Third World, as a means of redressing the age-long imbalance between the sexes.

Citizenship and political education are widespread, at whatever level of development the society may be. The former usually signifies inculcation of responsible, informed social and political behaviour in support of the form of government in power. It is commonplace in countries such as China (Hunter and Keehn, 1985). In principle, there and in other socialist states, all citizens underwent it (Onushkin and Tonkonogaya, 1984), although, as far as Eastern Europe is concerned, it is certainly no longer so. In Liberal democracies, in so far as it exists, the goal of citizenship education is much the same, but there is less overt indoctrination. Political education may also have similar objectives, in some places it is only a different name for the same thing, but in some societies it is viewed with suspicion, since it may become, either intentionally or unintentionally, an instrument to undermine the ruling regime. The work of Paolo Freire is a case in point.

Education to Combat Social Ills

The question of women's rights may be seen as one of which societies have only recently been made aware, although it has always existed. Technological and social changes, while solving problems, have also created new ones. Some threaten the whole of humanity, such as the greenhouse effect and other ecological dangers, world population growth, the growing gap in wealth and life expectations between the advanced and the Third World, AIDS and drug addiction. Some are more limited in their effect, such as the perceived need in some ex-colonies to create a sense of national identity, or the difficulties created by large-scale immigration in others. In the past the means, if any, even the right, to take action to resolve difficulties on this scale, were concentrated in comparatively few hands. The great mass of people was not expected to understand the issues, merely to behave as it was told. Today, even in the most dictatorial regimes, it suits the rulers that citizens should be made to believe that they bear a considerable responsibility for public policy. It is easier and more effective to apply, if they understand and approve what is being done. In other polities, the responsibility is real.

In some situations only mass action guided by understanding holds any promise of working. In many countries mass educational campaigns in schools and after childhood are being conducted to reduce the birth rate (UNESCO, 1978). Education is being marshalled in the fight against drug addiction and AIDS. The number of conditions suitable for this kind of action is growing as speed of communication makes the interdependence of all humanity both more actual and more apparent. Communication technology and methods of information diffusion now exist to make such understanding possible throughout the world. It is, however, one of the contemporary world's dilemmas that with sophisticated communications the potential for knowledge diffusion has grown, but so have the possibilities for its manipulation and distortion.

The Religious Element

Whatever education may do to help humanity to cure the ills of this world, not everyone sees existence in the physical universe as the be all and end all of human destiny. Some argue that there must be dimensions beyond the empirical one of the senses, an order of which the apparent chaos of life is only a part, there must have been some prime cause, some consolation beyond death to make up for the suffering of which life largely consists. Religiously inspired education for people of all ages is still a strong force. That may be less true of advanced than Third World countries, although Christian churches are major providers of general as well as specifically religious education in The Federal Republic of Germany, in the Netherlands and Scandinavia. In developing countries they play this combined role as part of their missionary endeavours. In Latin America efforts of Protestant organisations have been attacked as an attempt at an American colonisation of the spirit, and revolutionary theology is taught by Catholic priests with a political as well as a spiritual goal (Retamal, 1982). Other religions too are active. In Asia the Sarvodaya Shramadana Movement of Sri Lanka (Ariyaratne, 1985), which undertakes integrated rural development, and Khit-Pen, the Thai philosophy and programme of adult education, are strongly inspired by Buddhist ideas (Titmus, 1989).

Education having only Marginal Links to Initial Education

It may be argued that all post-childhood education which is not to be seen as compensation for that not received as initial education, or else as a final stage of the latter, is supplementary to it. That is only true if supplementation is understood very broadly. Some post-childhood learning is progressive or hierarchical, builds directly on previous knowledge, and would not be possible without it. Most advanced scientific or technological education is of this kind and that offered in adult life is usually conducted on the assumption that the learners have already achieved a certain level in initial full-time education, if not in school itself. Teaching to adults of other subjects normally learned in schools frequently assumes prior knowledge of the subject being taught and supplements it, even in such cases as history, language, literature and social sciences, which do not advance in a clear linear progression. Education after childhood often covers academic disciplines not normally included in the school programme, such as archaeology, philosophy, politics, or languages other than the two or three usually in the school syllabus, or is not concerned with disciplines at all, but about issues and behaviours, such as abortion, or nuclear power, or women's rights. These learning experiences may only be supplementary in the sense that they are built on the assumption that the learners have a body of general knowledge and experience, which may have been acquired in school, but may derive from family and other sources outside formal education.

The essential prior knowledge, to which learning after childhood may be said to be supplementary, may frequently be confined to basic literacy and numeracy. Even they may constitute a desirable, but not an essential, pre-condition of learning in many circumstances. Third World mothers can, if need be, learn health care, develop an understanding of nationhood, acquire artistic or craft skills, improve their farming practices without being able either to read or write, or do more than the most simple arithmetic. So the necessary links with childhood education may be tenuous indeed. Where prior experience is a requirement, it may well have been picked up incidentally in the course of adult life, rather than through any prior intentional learning. Even childhood life experience may be irrelevant to the participants in a pre-natal course, to people preparing for retirement, or to learners about the social dangers of AIDS or drug abuse. By this it is not meant that children cannot usefully study many of the issues commonly only examined in post-childhood education, indeed it may be desirable that they should, but that for many adults, at least, there will have been nothing in their childhood which will help their adult understanding of the issues. Some educators would in fact go further and, if they would not exclude certain areas of knowledge from childhood education, they nevertheless consider them better studied later in life. It has been said, 'I am convinced that for the studies in question (humanities and social sciences) the years after eighteen are a better age, and those after thirty better still' (Livingstone, 1941).

The Extent of Participation

In the preceding pages I have endeavoured to bring out the great diversity of educational provision for adults. It is so large and wide-ranging that somewhere, at some time, it may seem, opportunities are being offered to meet any conceivable demand for learning. Not only that, there are apparently convincing reasons why they should be taken up. Nevertheless in any given year, even in those countries where participation rates appear to be highest, as for example, Sweden and the USA, only a minority of the adult population undertake the structured, intentional learning experiences on offer. A high proportion never do so at any time in their lives. A decade ago it was calculated that in the United Kingdom and the Federal German Republic only 10 per cent of adults participated regularly, and about 60 per cent never did (Eccleston and Schmidt, 1981). Later estimates suggest that more have taken part at some time (ACACE, 1982), but the figure does not rise above 50 per cent. Jennings reckoned that about 20 per cent of the adult population took part in some organised learning experience in any given year (Jennings, 1982).

The ACACE (Advisory Council for Adult and Continuing Education) survey confirmed the information given in other studies of the age, sex and socio-economic status of participants. Of those currently in post full-time education at the time of the survey (1979–80), younger people from the lower middle class were most strongly represented. Past participants were mostly to be found in the upper and middle middle class between the ages of 25 and 64. More women than men were currently studying, but fewer had studied in the past. 60 per cent of men and 63 per cent of women would like to study in the future. There was a substantial number in each age and socio-economic group, but the percentage declined among the more advanced ages and lower classes. Whatever the precise statistics, the rate of actual and potential non-participation remains high. If we knew the reasons for this, it is argued, we might do something about it.

Issues Affecting Provision and its Improvement

Fitting Provision to Demand

To some extent the problem may be a logistic one. The particular provision to which an adult would respond may exist somewhere, sometime, but not when, where and under the conditions necessary for him/her to do so. If this is true, then the task is to fit the provision to the market. The British national survey, undertaken for ACACE (1982), indicated that this fit could be better, also that it would not be beyond the organisational skill and resources of the country to improve it, if the political will were there. It would never be perfect, however, there are limits to the educational manpower and economic resources that can be devoted to supplying those adults who have never been reached by provision. In saying this I am not referring only to extreme cases. It might be deemed impossible in Britain, for quite valid reasons, to organise practical courses in life drawing for people who cannot get to those daytime or evening classes which are held in urban centres. (I am one such person myself.)

Provision Made to Suit Providers

Only some, indeed comparatively few, of the opportunities for adult study currently offered have as their purpose, simply or even primarily, to give individual learners what they want. The history of adult education, it is true, is scattered with mutual education groups set up by the people who took part in them, to meet their own learning needs. In principle, although increasingly marginally in practice, the

Scandinavian study circle in just such a group. Most provision, however, is made by and on the initiative of people so that others than themselves may have the opportunity to study. They do it for a variety of purposes, selfish, altruistic, economic, political, religious, social, cultural. In many cases they promote what is seen to be of benefit to themselves. Employers do, for example. Religious and political groups may not be intending to further their own interests in a crude material sense, but they are trying to sell their own values. The prime goal of the state apparatus is ostensibly the good of its citizens, whether seen as a whole or as an agglomeration of individuals, but the perceived good of the state predominates, which is not necessarily the same thing, and often, even normally, coincides with that of the ruling party. Those movements which operate in adult education to improve the lot of social groups with special needs, such as women or ethnic minorities, or to raise the standard of living of particular societies, for instance Third World countries which are seen to need population education (UNESCO, 1978), or to meet a perceived need for the whole of humanity to be educated about the dangers of smoking or other drug addiction, for example, are pre-occupied with influencing the collective, not the individual.

Coercion of Participants

No provider would exclude from his/her calculations individual participants' views of their needs or desires, however. Since adult education is not compulsory, the people at whom provision is aimed have to be offered some inducement to study. It is not always a carrot. A company may use the stick of coercion on its employees. In a similar way professional associations or other licensing bodies may make it a condition of continuing entitlement to practise that a professional undergo periodic refresher and updating courses. It happens in some countries in medicine, the law and in teaching, for instance (Apps, 1985). If the pressure is sufficiently strong and despite what is said about an unwilling learner being a bad learner, then the likes and dislikes of the adult undergoing such experiences can to a large extent be ignored, as anyone who has done compulsory military training can testify.

Limitations of Attempts to Meet Participants' Needs and Wishes

Most providers, however, have to adopt a more seductive approach. Within the limits set by their resources, by their own purposes and the principles on which they are based, and by their understanding of what most nearly ensures effective learning, they try to arrange their educational offering to meet the requirements of their target public. But these provisos may be significant. Education in the place of work may be designed to capture the interest of trainees, but only in so far as that is compatible with the prime aim, to develop in them knowledge and skills useful to the employer. The Swedish government appears to have rejected an Open University on the British model at one stage, largely on grounds of cost-effectiveness (Titmus, 1981:46). It situated second chance secondary education in schools in preference to commissioning adult education associations to do it, because schools were specialists in the curriculum to be taught, even though the associations had much more experience in educating adults (Titmus 1981:79). The potential clients do not seem to have been consulted.

Even if the purpose is to offer what adults want, educators' thinking is often unclear. They take 'want' to be a synonym of 'need', apply to both their own meaning rather than that of potential learners, and confuse the issue further by filtering their understanding of what adults do 'want' or 'need' through their (the educators') own concept of what they ought to 'want' or 'need'. In the USA (and elsewhere) widespread acceptance of the concept of andragogy, as proposed by Malcolm Knowles, had as much to do with the values of educators, their concepts of the purpose of adult education and what constitutes a mature adult, as with any evidence of how adults wished to or most effectively could organise study (Knowles, 1980).

It does, therefore, seem that a more effective attempt to discover what individuals want and a more whole-hearted attempt to offer it might improve participation.

Assessment of Adult Needs and Desires

Despite the theoretical and practical objections to their way of assessing their public, it may be argued that educators get it right for some adults, since many do undertake organised study. Of course, to a large extent it is from their observation of these participants that providers derive their ideas of what will attract adults and of how they learn. Indeed, except in those areas where more coercion could be applied, the history of adult education may be said to have been disproportionately influenced by the respondents to the first speculative offers of study opportunities in that variety of fields of which it now consists. Those mechanics who attended Birbeck's science lectures in the 1880s, the labourers who went to adult schools at the beginning of the nineteenth century, the men and women who filled university extension in the 1870s or joined the Workers' Educational Association in the 1900s, confirmed to the pioneer providers that they had got it right to the extent that there was an audience for what they were offering. It was not always the intended one, it is true, and attempts were made, as in the case of the Mechanics' Institutes, to attract a different public. By and large, however, educators have settled for what they have got and have offered more of the same. So one has the phenomenon that those who first participated conformed to the preconceptions of the first providers, thus confirming them. Because of this and because it guaranteed bottoms on benches in substantial numbers, providers offered more of the same and so on *ad infinitum*. There have been large changes over the last two hundred years, that is undeniable, as the environment has been transformed, affecting both providers and learners. There is, however, a continuous thread linking the publics (and they are plural) at which study opportunities are aimed with the groups of participants in the various pioneering efforts of the past. This thread has been thickened and made more complex by successive educational initiatives and by the influence of forces outside education. Of wider significance, general theories of adult wants or needs, of how adults learn, are derived from observation of the behaviour of successive groups of participants. They are seen to work because it is the participants who provide the evidence, from the fact that they do participate.

There are always some people who are uncomfortable with this self-perpetuation of beliefs and attempt to break out of the framework to reach the successors of the non-attenders, who far outnumbered those first adult students. They operate for the most part on the fringes. From time to time there occur major initiatives to reach a hitherto untouched public. The Adult Literacy Campaign of the 1970s in Great Britain was one. The success it achieved was due to two principal features. It offered provision to meet a real need, up to then largely ignored. It also devoted considerable effort and resources to reaching and attracting its target public. At the beginning of the campaign much was made of teaching methods and organisation specifically designed to be acceptable to clients, but subsequent experience has suggested that these were less important than was first thought. The principal difficulty was to recruit students (Jones and Charnley, 1978).

Outreach

Among the inducements offered was free tuition. This carrot has been commonly used by a number of governments to encourage participation in provision held to be of special value to society and most often aimed at a target group known to be resistant, as in Swedish Municipal Adult Education (Titmus, 1981:76–82). It is one instrument of 'outreach', that is, activity specifically undertaken to contact and recruit people who have not previously taken part in any post-initial education. In its mildest form it consists of measures to make it easy for adults to participate in education, such as arranging courses at times and in places convenient to them, at a cost they could afford — taking it to them, indeed, instead of requiring that they should come to education (Osborn, 1989). More active efforts to bring people into adult study have been widely tried, including paying them to attend (Titmus, 1981:90).

In the 1970s it was hoped that the introduction of a right to paid educational leave, that is, to take time off from work in order to study while continuing to be paid, would bring about an increase in participation (von Moltke and Schneevoigt, 1977). It did and would probably have led to further growth, had it been given wholehearted support, notably by the state and employers (CEDEFOP, 1984). The indications are, however, that even with that backing it would not have achieved as much as its supporters had hoped (Cropley, 1985).

Indeed, this seems to be true of all outreach efforts. Some progress has been made, but always out of any group at which efforts have been directed a part does not respond. In some cases the reason may have been that the intended target has been treated as a collective, rather than as individuals. It has most commonly been the working class, or some part of it, because statistics show that the largest concentration of non-participants is to be found within it. The kind of study offered has usually been what the group is thought to need. Probably the largest controlled outreach experiment yet, the FÖVUX project in Sweden (Titmus, 1981:88–95) notably did not allow those engaged to choose freely what they would study, but offered one of four subjects, Swedish, English, mathematics or social studies, which were believed by the experimenters to be most useful as well as most attractive to working people.

Is Study Inherently Pleasureable?

Much of the disappointment of educators at their failure to reach all adults, particularly the so-called disaffected ones, springs from their tendency to exaggerate the extent to which study is inherently, or can be made to be, a pleasurable process. Some people certainly find it so (Houle, 1961), but many do not. It is probably a misconception or an oversimplification, inspired by wishful thinking based on the idea that human beings are naturally inclined to learning, to believe that if they do not wish to study it is always because of environmental deterrents or unfavourable past experience. Learning is not study, which is a discipline, with all that word entails, while the extent to which intentional learning can be brought about without study is limited. If one believes that adults should be free to decide whether they should undertake it, then to wish not to submit to the discipline comes within the normal range of acceptable human behaviour, it is not necessarily a pathological condition.

In fact for only a minority of people is the pleasure of the process alone likely to be a strong enough incentive to overcome the many distractions from study. For most participants their motive to study is not the educational experience, but the beneficial consequences of it, notably vocationally related ones (ACACE, 1982). It is not the provision, which is merely the means, but the outcome. It is possible that in many cases there is an inverse relationship between the attractiveness of the educational experience and the value or the certainty of the outcome necessary to bring about participation. One would not need such a high reward to draw people to an enjoyable programme, as to a tedious one, but for many, if not most, there must be a reward outside the educational experience. Therefore programming alone, in terms of learning content, organisation and methods, can only go so far to reduce non-participation, particularly if it is caused by disaffection.

Provision and the Hard Core of Disaffection

Perhaps every person has a price. There appears, however, to be a hard core in British society, and probably in others, for whom it may be outside the realms of practical policy to offer outcomes sufficiently attractive to bring them into adult education. The ACACE survey, already quoted, found that 21 per cent of its sample had never participated and had no desire to in the future. This group had fewer and less active leisure interests and, if given more leisure hours, was more likely than other groups to say that it would spend them just passing the time (ACACE, 1982). This agrees with a finding of an earlier survey, which had reported a quite widespread opinion among participants that the most common cause of non-participation was lack of sufficient desire to change, whether because of contentment, resignation, or apathy in one's present lot, or the belief that no more attractive alternative was available, or that the attraction of change was outweighed by its uncertainty, or the bother of engaging in study (Titmus and Hely, 1976).

Conclusion

There are obviously limits to what can be done by provision, even in its widest sense, to attract disaffected adults to engage in education. This chapter may have overstressed the point. By identifying what provision does not do, in the way of accurately determining individual demand and giving priority to satisfying it, and what it has had some success in doing, by way of outreach, it may, however, have suggested to the reader some means of improvement.

It is difficult to believe that nothing can be done, while less than 50 per cent of British adults take part in post-initial education at *any* time and in Sweden about 50 per cent do so *every* year. The Swedes attribute their success in large part to the great variety of forms of education on offer (Swedish National Board of Education, 1989; Swedish Institute, 1990), others would say that much of the reason for it lies in the nature of the society that has evolved in Sweden in the last half-century. It is a culture in which participation in post-initial education has become the norm. If that were the case in Britain it would bring in some non-participants, because they would be under social pressure to conform. Social approval might be a useful incentive for our disaffected to change their stance. That inspires a further, final thought. Organising provision so that participants are induced to study more frequently and so that those non-participants who are not disaffected do take part in it, until undertaking post-initial education does become the norm, would be an indirect, but ultimately, perhaps, effective way of overcoming the resistance of the disaffected.

Bibliography

ACACE (1982) *Adults: their Educational Experience and Needs*, Advisory Council for Adult and Continuing Education, Leicester.

APPS, J.W. (1985) 'Mandatory continuing Education', in Husen, T. and Postlethwaite, T.N. (Eds) *International Encyclopedia of Education*, Pergamon, Oxford

ARIYARATNE, A.T. (1985) 'Integrated Rural Development: Sarvodaya Movement', in HUSEN, T. and POSTLETHWAITE, T.N., (Eds), *International Encyclopedia of Education*, Pergamon, Oxford.

BRILLINGER, M.E. and BRUNDAGE, D.H. (1985) 'Family-life Education for Adults', in HUSEN, T. and POSTLETHWAITE, T.N. (Eds), *International Encyclopedia of Education*, Pergamon, Oxford.

CEDEFOP (1984) *Educational Leave and the Labour Market in Europe*, CEDEFOP, Berlin.

CROPLEY, A.J. (1985) 'Motivation for Participation in Adult Education', in KNOLL, J.H., *Motivation for Adult Education*, German Commission for UNESCO, BONN, K.G. Saur, Munich.

GOLDTHORPE, J.H. *et al.* (1968) *The Affluent Worker in the Class Structure*, 3 Vols, Cambridge University Press, Cambridge.

HOPKINS, P.G.H. (1985) *Workers' Education*, Open University Press, Milton Keynes.

HUNTER, C. St.J. and KEEHN, M.M. (Ed.) (1985) *Adult Education in China*, Croom Helm, London.

HUSEN, T. and POSTLETHWAITE, T.N. (Ed.) (1985) *International Encyclopedia of Education: Research and Studies*, Pergamon, Oxford.

JENNINGS, B. (1981) *Adult Education in Europe: United Kingdom. Studies and Documents No. 9*, European Centre for Leisure and Education, Prague.

JONES, H.A. and CHARNLEY, A.H. (1978) *Adult Literacy: a Study of its Impact*, National Institute of Adult Education, Leicester.

KNOWLES, M.S. (1980) *The Modern Practice of Adult Education: from Pedagogy to Andragogy*, Association Press, New York.

LESNE, M., COLLON, C. and OECONOMO, C. (1970) *Changement socio-professionelle et formation: étude d'une situation de crise dans le Bassin de Briey*, Institut National de Formation des Adultes (INFA), Paris.

LIVINGSTONE, R. (1941) *The Future in Education*, University Press, Cambridge.

ONUSHKIN, V.G. and TONKONOGAYA, E.P. (1984) *Adult Education in Europe: Adult Education in the USSR. Studies and Documents No. 20*, European Centre for Leisure and Education, Prague.

OSBORN, M. (1985) 'Outreach in Adult Education', in HUSEN, T. and POSTLETHWAITE, T.N. (Eds) *International Encylopaedia of Education*, Pergamon, Oxford.

RETAMAL, G. (1982) *Paolo Freire, Christian Ideology and Adult Education in Latin America*, Newlands Papers No. 5, University of Hull Department of Adult Education, Hull.

SHEPHERD, R.A. (1985) 'A case in the motor industry', in TITMUS, C. (Ed.) *Widening the Field: Continuing Education in Higher Education*, SRHE and NFER-Nelson, Guildford.

SWEDISH INSTITUTE (1990) *Adult Education in Sweden: Fact Sheet on Sweden*, Stockholm.

SWEDISH NATIONAL BOARD OF EDUCATION (1989) *Adult Education*, Stockholm.

TEICHLER, U. and SANYAL, B.C. (1982) *Higher Education and the Labour Market in the Federal Republic of Germany*, International Institute for Educational Planning, UNESCO, Paris.

TITMUS, C. (1967) *Adult Education in France*, Pergamon, Oxford.

—— (1981) *Strategies for Adult Education; Practices in Western Europe*, Open University Press, Milton Keynes.

—— (Ed.) (1985) *Widening the Field: Continuing Education in Higher Education*, SRHE and NFER-Nelson, Guildford.

—— (Ed.) (1989) *Lifelong Education for Adults: an International Handbook*, Pergamon, Oxford.

TITMUS, C. and HELY, C.G. (1974) 'L'individuel et le collectif dans la formation professionnelle et générale des travailleurs en Grande-Bretagne' in DAVID, M. (Ed.) *L'individuel et le collectif dans la formation professionnelle et générale des travailleurs*, Université de Paris L' Institute des Sciences Sociales de Travail, Paris.

UNESCO (1978) *Population education: a contemporary concern*, Educational Studies and Documents No. 28. UNESCO, Paris.

VON MOLTKE, K. and SCHNEEVOIGT, N. (1977) *Educational Leave for Employees: European Experience for American Consideration*, Jossey-Bass, San Francisco.

6 Face-to-Face Provision and the Older Learner

Eric Midwinter

The Question: The Perceived Contradiction of Old Age and Education

It is curious that, with wisdom associated in the popular mind with age, and with the archetypical scholar of cheap novels or science-fiction often an extremely enlightened person, that the relation of education with older age in Britain is so limited. Indeed, another popular image intrudes. Education is the province of the young, not least because, rather more emphatically perhaps over the recent years of unemployment, it has been so intensely linked with the major aspect of preparation. It is a short step from arguing that education is to provide people with the training or re-training for work to claiming that those retired and beyond work need have no call on education. In brief, older people are not expected — further, they do not expect themselves — to be concerned with education.

The Definition: Status as the Benchmark of Older Age

Yet the counter-argument — that they might be considered as in greater need of education than anyone, even children — has validity. There is a new definition of older age extant. It relates not to the misleading index of chronological age, nor to the social indicator of physical and mental decline, whereby many equate oldness with illness. There are more 'economically active' males over 70 than there are those 'permanently ill', while three-quarters of those between 65 and 74 report themselves in good or fairly good health.

The preferred threshold is that of standing in the life-span, and the construct increasingly utilised is that of a four-age division. This embraces a First Age of childhood and socialisation; a Second Age of work and family-raising; a Third Age of active independence in the post-work, post-familial circumstances; and a Fourth Age of dependence and decline. Thus those who have finished work and/ or raising a family constitute the echelon of older age, and a conservative estimate might suggest this amounts to some 11 or 12 million adults. Naturally enough, it is the policy of social gerontologists to extend the Third Age and, thereby, curtail the Fourth Age. The final advantage of the formula is its flexibility. Older people do gravitate between the Third and Fourth Age: for example, a highly dependent person might — and there have been examples — run a tutorial in their own home, even into their own bedroom, and would be, for that hour or so, in the Third Age.

It is important for adult educators to comprehend this novel precept. It has, historically speaking, arrived with some precipitation, to inaugurate a social construction hitherto unknown. That is, for the first time ever, there is a higher proportion of the population which has discharged its filial and vocational duties, and is still faced with a lengthy phase of life, in many cases for as long, even longer, than the Second Age itself. This arises because in the past, many people worked for a longer period and, frequently with larger families, sustained parenting into later life. In counterpoise, there is also greater survival now (not really, as is often rather misleadingly supposed, longer life. Many more people are not dying prematurely but are persevering to live the length of life hitherto always enjoyed by a minority). Like the controls of a concertina, the phenomena of earlier release from adult chores and greater survival draw out an expanding Third Age.

It follows that the only safe generalisation about older age is that its exponents are, technically, at leisure, in that they are, by the previous standards of humankind, 'post-adult'. What might be called the 'gold clock' and the 'empty nest' syndromes combine so to determine. Of course, there are strong moral and civic arguments for educational provision in older age. This is the generation which, having fought its way through two world wars and a couple of depressions, paid generously in rates and taxes for the biggest-ever bonanza in British educational spending during the 1960s and 1970s. Moreover, those who believe in the recurrent motif for educational activity, holding persuasively to the notion that educational service should be available throughout all the ups and downs of life, would, with equal fervour, press for educative succour for older people.

However, what the new social construction of older age brings is a clinching argument about such provision. This social dimension may be urged from two sides. With work and parenting completed, we are faced with a waste of human experience and ability on a massive and unheard of scale, for many Third and Fourth Age personnel, quite simply, are task-less. They have lost the identity and self-esteem that work certainly, and family-rearing probably, granted them, and a vast potential of human worth is scrapped. Next, in the abandonment of that possible social product we risk individual damage, for it may be pressed that, without the restoration of some purpose or motive in the Third Age, the likelihood of physical, social and mental decline into the Fourth Age is apparent. What is vividly called 'The Fitness Gap' widens: that is, the gap between what people can do and do do is extended as years draw on. Thus, in its broadest sense, education, *inter alia*, has a part to play in that restoration which could bring both a decent social product and an individual betterment.

We will now consider further the First Age of socialisation. Formal education obviously plays a role in this, but, less obviously, not a large part. The socio-economic function of the school in the industrial era has been to act as a corral for children, whose parents' workplace is distinct from the home, until such time — and that date has been deferred later and later over the last century and a half — there is a call for those children on the labour market. What actually happens *in* the school is less important than this, although it may have some bearing on socialisation. For instance, the relation between what one studies at school and how one's career pattern develops is a thin and brittle one. Apropos of good or ill achievement at school, it is well-rehearsed that the effects of family and neighbourhood are mightier than those of the school *per se*. Britain, like other developed nations, has a complex educational system *because* it has an elaborate economy, which for technological reasons, has no place for huge swathes of labour, notably children, and not *in order* to prepare children, as is naively and conversely believed, for so sophisticated an economy. It was necessary to press this seemingly incidental point to make good the claim that 'education', in a systematic sense, should be regarded as less important for children than for older people. And, in terms of resources and given that both cohorts should be equitably treated, it is worth noting that the chief reason why the *proportion* of older people has trebled this century is because the younger proportion has almost halved. There is, therefore, a forceful case for a generational transfer of assets.

The Barriers: Non-participation in Older Age

The chilling factor is that, although by this form of 'status' definition older people have a consummate degree of time available, they are infamously poor users of that time. Their non-engagement with and in constructive pursuits, ranging from the esoteric delectation of educational classes to the homespun matter of a regular walk in the local park, is mournfully well-documented. It is important to realise that this is a general rule, and not one where education holds some special horror for older people. The human waste referred to in the previous section is characterised by this monumental inactivity. Although the use of television may and should be positive in nature, it may be indicative that older people with almost 40 hours on the clock weekly have now by-passed those other telly-addicts, children, as the nation's premier watchers.

The reasons why older people eschew education are the same reasons they deny themselves the benefits of other leisure, recreational and allied pursuits, and educationists need to understand these. There is, more overtly, a series of material barriers, and, whilst very significant, they may be more briefly logged because of their self-evidence. They amount to a set of half-truths about old age. Older people may be regarded as of poor income, poor health and poor mobility, seen in either personal or in transportation terms. For a large, hapless fraction of older people, this is all too sadly true. Many find it difficult to find the money for educational and leisure activities; there are ill-health inhibitors; and, apart from the incidence of disability in older age, this current older generation suffers from the double-bind of representing the nation's lowest usage of the private car alongside a vicious deterioration in public transport. There is also the fact that, although statistically not vulnerable to criminal menace, many older people are reluctant to travel abroad, especially at night, and are not alone among finding many of our urban areas heir to what criminologists call 'incivilities'. Of course there are older people who are extremely rich, who are in good health, who do run cars and who do not feel stressed by the unease of the public thoroughfares, but, all in all, this accumulation of material or environmental issues is a strong one.

Another feature to note is accommodation. A large number of older people live alone or with one other older person, usually, of course, a spouse. Only a very small percentage are in institutional care of any kind, and an even smaller number reside in a house where young children live. This has several ramifications. It underpins the other material setbacks, especially with regard to going out alone or being unable to use or share a household car. From the educational viewpoint, it means that that celebrated feature of successful mature studentship — an encouraging family — is frequently absent. If you live alone, there is no one to bolster you when things go awry, or, more pleasingly, to express delight in your triumphs. Moreover, it is well known that older people are, on balance, only prepared to travel a limited distance for an educational activity.

Living singly or in twos is, in any event, an aspect of what might engagingly be termed the 'privatisation' of society and culture, whereby the silver days of collectivity have been banished, as the cinema becomes the television, just as the laundry becomes the washing machine. This miniaturisation of the social fabric makes the home, as such, much more of a base than it was in the decades when one 'went out' for practically everything. It is difficult to exaggerate the importance of this switch in social practice.

Beyond the more environmental or physical barriers are the less overt but equally telling cultural issues. Like many other depressed or disadvantaged sub-groups, older people believe in their disadvantage. Inculcated with the prejudices and misbeliefs of an ageist society, they play out the negative role in which they have been cast. From an educational stance, they — or many of them — believe that education is about children in schools and has little or no place in the lives of older people; that — the most lethal proverb in the lingo — you can't teach an old dog new tricks; that their 'grey matter' is fast vanishing; and that, whereas a younger person making a slip would speak of a lapse of memory, an older person will claim that his or her memory is 'going'.

Despite the fact that none of these assertions are, as they stand, true, the psychological wall they have built is high and thick. Educationists need to understand more clearly why such assertions are misleading, and how learning habits may be inculcated in or re-stimulated among older people. Furthermore, the question — as older people should constantly be sternly told — is not how well they learn, but that they persist in making the attempt. The process, as ideally, in most education, is more significant than the product.

In combination, these two sets of factors — the one more physical, the other more cultural — explain in greater part why older people are grossly and colossally under-represented in educational activities; and, on Leninist counsel, knowing thine enemy and comprehending why this is so must be an essential halfway step to righting this dreadful social calumny.

The Conventional Answer: The Traditional Didactic Approach

The other side of the coin is what has been on offer. It is only half an explanation to describe why older people, like most citizens apropos the church, demonstrate their admiration from a respectful distance. The other half of the explanation must lie in the impoverishment of the provision, for, plainly, were the offering more attractive, the take-up would be larger.

Basically, there is only one approach. However massaged and packaged, the huge majority of educational offerings are founded in the traditional tutorial-class concept. Initiated in Victorian times from the school base, it has two chief characteristics: it is a teacher or tutor-led group or class of students; and it is located within an institution, normally devised for that sole purpose.

As a Victorian solution to the social problem of displaced youngsters, the school was a brave attempt, and at a time when technology was less in evidence than now, the technical precept of the teacher-class device was equally gallant and not unsuccessful. It continues to be successful for some, not all, children and for some, by no means all, adults. Edward Heath, criticising the Thatcher administration's economic policy, complained that, by a sole reliance on interest rates as a methodology, it was a 'one club' affair. One might join him in his borrowing from the world of golf. Apart from the Open University, the National Extension College and some other excellent proponents of distance teaching, education has a one-club policy. Certainly it works for many, but it is neither suitable for nor attractive to all.

It is against this restrictive singularity of educational provision that one must judge its cumulative effect on older people, beset, frequently, by the sad burdens and sadder values described in the previous section. The great majority of the current generation of old people left school early, having negotiated, even then, one of the shortest phases of compulsory education of any of the developed nations. Their opportunities for further and higher education were small. The actual content and experience was not warm and welcoming, and many older people have an unpleasant memory of their schooling. (Incidentally, we may, unluckily, have a chance to witness something of this experience at closer hand, as the similar vices of that time are revisited upon our coming generation via the iniquities of the national curriculum, a version of which lay like a dead hand upon the nation's children for a century, until, for a brief respite and with much less incidence than its critics contrived to imagine, there was some recognition of the calls of child development.)

It is little wonder that, after years often in stultifying jobs or spent in harsh domestic activity, with what poor skills had been mastered infrequently practised, the degree of functional illiteracy in older age is so high. To the chagrin of vociferous critics of current school standards, it should certainly be noted as over 30 per cent in the over 60s echelon, and some would estimate it as high as 40 per cent. With intellectual confidence shattered, it is hardly surprising that older people have little wish to travel, often alone, often at night, quite longish distances to institutions all too familiar in fashion, in order to join classes where the general method is the same as of yesteryear, and where a mix of vague unease at the institutional surrounding and a slight edge of competitiveness prevails.

The Community Education Solution: Mutual Aid and Non-formality

To repeat, some will find succour in the traditional mould. What we lack is plurality. What we lack is alternative modes, as opposed to attempts (many of them excellent) to reform or enliven that conventional approach.

The 'mutual aid' or cooperative approach, utilised, in its best dispensation, by the University of the Third Age and by allied groups is one such alternative. It has been reasonably successful — there are over a hundred U3As comprising of some 15,000 members as of early 1990 — but it must be stressed that it is only *one* alternative, and the founders of the movement never saw it as the exclusive solution, remaining hopeful that another dozen flowers might bloom, or, to return to the Faldoesque coinage of Mr Heath, the golf bag might grow heavy with clubs.

Out of an amalgam of practial and theoretical arguments and conditions has emerged the concept of self-mobilisation. In terms of its model of voluntaryism, the University of the Third Age has grasped the nettle of mutuality. At its simplest, a University of the Third Age consists of a body of persons who undertake to learn and to help others to learn. Those who teach are encouraged to be students and those who see themselves initially as students are encouraged either to teach or to assist in some other way in the democratic functioning of the agency.

This is education of, to, for, and by the membership. The chief features are that the U3A group is in complete control of its membership, that all stems from matters of personal choice and judgment, with standards for classes and other activities set by the sub-group membership, and with no qualifications sought or awarded. The groups are, therefore, organised on a cooperative principle, in which members give and receive, so that, in the finest examples, there is a learning web of some substance. There is no sense in which this is a second best alternative. Rather is it a preferred option over the didactic dogma of state provision which constantly rests on a single resolution of how education should be negotiated.

It is a shift away from the stronghold of the regulatory principle in British education. In British education, the customer does not become a consumer until, compulsorily or voluntarily, he or she has accepted the programme. The essential characteristic, then, of a U3A or allied group is that it is the creation of its members and that they make the decisions about what subjects should be taught and to what levels and in what style. It follows, too, that many subjects and interests are pursued which would find no place in the narrow ranks of British epistemology. And, as well as putting the lie to the legend that older people cannot learn, they have demonstrated that older people, without formal qualifications, can convene and run groups.

U3A begins from the base that it is neither a state nor a private institution. Several thousand older people have joined a hundred or so groups, without compulsion and with relatively little publicity, and, of their own free will, are apparently pleasantly engaged. In itself that is an achievement, for, having regard for the number of older people involved in the formal education system, that adds quite a percentage to the total. In fact, from one angle, there is no need to explore further than that, but to accept that, with the U3A device, one has found another way of occupying the constructive leisure time of older people. The U3A movement, then, is one of the only mainline examples of non-corporatist and non-conformist formulation in the educational field.

Just take, by way of example, a U3A pilot, in which, nationally, a work kit was constructed based on a television presentation of 'The Pickwick Papers' in the normal BBC1 family spot on a Sunday afternoon, and not, obviously, part of its labelled educational provision. Some sixteen U3A sub-groups underwent the experiment of reading the book, watching the television series and meeting weekly, often in each other's homes, to further their study of the Dickens' novel. The response of both members and convenors suggests that this was reasonably successful, and there has been a loud demand for further provision of that kind. It might somewhat arrogantly be claimed that, rather than being second best, that combination of the ancient art of localised and domestic conversation (as might have been found in the barber's shop or the cobbler's shop or the tailor's shop in centuries gone by) with the modern dispensation of a brilliant television production, supported by nationally and colourfully produced materials, is characterised by excellence. Compare this with the weekly visit to the uncomfortable and draughty classroom in a secondary school, with a second-rate teacher, perhaps trying to get a few more pounds together for his annual trip to the continent, woodenly mouthing a few stale platitudes about the Victorian novel. Of course, this is an extreme and tendentious caricature, but it serves to show that the dogma of the tutorial answer may not always be the best one.

One is rather reminded of the argument at the other end of the life-span that nursery schools were automatically 'better' than playgroups — and the U3A movement is proud to acknowledge its inheritance from that great cooperative venture. It takes some range of vision to appreciate that, educationally, 'there are many ways of skinning a cat'. Mention of the usage of people's own homes and the convening of quite small groups (well under the numbers usually adhered to for adult education) reminds one of the point that highly localised approaches must become more and more necessary, given current social proclivities, particularly as they affect older people. The promotion of street or block-based groups, the decentralised spread of classes as far and wide as possible, the use of mobility (perhaps along the lines of the Playbuses for under-fives), the development of education 'bases' or 'stations' in people's own homes — these will surely form much of the provision of the future.

Because older people, for both good and bad reasons, spend a great amount of time at home, that is where educationists must seek them out, either directly, by home visiting tutors or possibly versions of a kind of 'short distance' teaching, or near at hand, through the provision of small-scale ventures, as close to peoples' houses as possible. We are not going to be able to sustain for long an eminently Victorian solution to our educational quest in the face of the habits of the near twenty-first century and, indeed, the opportunities its sciences proffer. The mountain must go to Mahomet.

The Future: The Professional Infrastructure Required

It is a call for non-formality, and the choice of epithet is deliberate. It is not an innocent and dewy-eyed notion that, somehow, the older laity, like hitherto silenced John Hampdens, will of its own volition, rise and create this new destiny. There is a most important place for the professional educator to facilitate and encourage the movement, but it is a professional educator of a different costume, more befitting the different body of education. Too many communal enterprises in the past have foundered through a self-conscious eschewal of such assistance. Borrowing from another treatise on the same subject and, at the risk of tedium, being unconvinced that there is need to change what we said there, I would suggest three distinctive features for these vital animateurs. They must be barkers for custom, ensuring that education in older age has an enthusiastic populist image; they must be brokers of learning webs, twinning, pairing and grouping busily; they must be boosters of confidence and of latent ability, energisers, not didacts, reassuring older people that education is for them, of them and by them.

There is a wider context for this cause. Each time an older person engages fruitfully, by whatever criteria, in some educational activity, it is, as well as pleasure and more for that person, a positive espousal, in an avowedly ageist society, of a more realistic, authentic and freshly optimistic attitude toward older age.

7 Opportunities Through Open Learning

Robert Leach and Roger Webb

Introduction

Leaners' disaffection and disadvantage were the springboards for the open learning movement. Following the establishment of the National Extension College (1963) and the Open University (1969), the benefits of studying with a range of materials and support systems were increasingly recognised, until in the Manpower Service Commission's Open Tech project it was claimed that 'open learning enables you to study in your own time, at your own pace and in your own place'.[1] Another expression of the aim of open learning is that it is to enable you to learn what, when, where and how[2] you like.

If open learning systems were truly able to fulfil this aim, there would perhaps be no scope for disaffection at all in this type of learning. Indeed, research in this area has concentrated more on the 'barriers as the learner sees them' in terms of physical, time, education/training design and financial barriers, together with lack of confidence and awareness of opportunities,[3] rather than on the more intangible attitudinal barriers which may lead to disaffection. It is also true to say that open learning practitioners have tended to concentrate on the design of learning materials, sometimes at the expense of the consideration of learners' attitudes and expectations. What is probably the leading manual for open learning designers stresses materials production as the key to success. 'Self-instruction . . . depends on materials specially written — or at least specially selected and modified . . . with particular course objectives in mind.'[4] This is a widespread assumption, although another approach suggests that 'study guides' can successfully provide a bridge between the open learner and conventional learning materials.[5] In either case, the focus is on materials.

NEC Research

The National Extension College is a charitable trust dedicated to providing learning opportunities for adults. As both a publisher of learning materials and an organisation that delivers supported courses, it needs to know about the attitudes and feelings of students. The National Extension College embarked in 1990 on two pieces of research into the way that learners respond to opportunities for open learning. One project was designed and undertaken by Roger Webb, and consisted of a survey of NEC students in 1990.[6] The other was a much less ambitious follow-up of two months' enquirers to NEC who did not enrol on NEC courses. This provided further insights which complemented the survey of students.

It can be argued that results of these surveys of potential and actual 'distance learning' students, who normally would not meet a tutor throughout their course, will not throw light on disaffection among open learners in general. However, Rumble's thesis that 'distance learning' relates to means, and that 'open learning' relates to the object and character of learning,[7] suggests that the survey could have significance for all means of open learning. Before a discussion of the survey results, a brief résumé of seven models of open learning suggests that they can all minimise some forms of disaffection, although they have varying success with others.

These models have been generated by a combination of learner needs, provider needs and, in the case of the Technician Training Scheme (model 2), sponsor needs. In general it is difficult to identify which needs are most important. It would probably be fair to say that where a learner need is perceived, it can lead to a new model of open learning as long as it also meets a provider need. For example in the case of FlexiStudy (model 5), a tutor perceived that distance learners would benefit from access to face-to-face tuition. This became possible when the provider, Barnet College, understood that it could use this system to enrol many more students at a relatively low level of resourcing.

This chapter examines briefly a number of models of open learning offered by NEC and other providers, and argues that all the models share features which are designed to empower learners and reduce disaffection. The chapter continues with a description of students' perceptions of one model, together with their aims, social and educational position, and achievements in their open learning courses. In conclusion, we offer suggestions on how the results of this research when matched against essential features of open learning can indicate how disaffection is challenged and often overcome.

Open Learning Models

1 NEC Technician Training Scheme

In this model, students follow a course over a period corresponding to the UK's conventional academic year from September to June. They must attend college on three to four occasions to sit tests and receive instruction, which in the end lead to unit credits in various areas of telecommunications and other electronic engineering. The scheme is attractive to employers as it allows employees to train while continuing to work full-time and it has a low drop-out and failure rate. Of 1,200 students in 1989, for example, 85 per cent passed and 45 per cent achieved a Merit. A recent report[8] noted that:

- outside British Telecom, the main client, the number of trainees enrolled per company was small
- there was high satisfaction with the administration and operation of the scheme
- most companies were already using other forms of open learning.

The small number of trainees in each company indicates both the strength of the scheme in catering for the individual and the weakness that when companies have larger groups of potential trainees they prefer other solutions, for example in-company training or conventional day or block release.

Employer sponsorship means that students are not financially responsible for their course, but does encourage a high success rate, probably because it is tied to career progression. The 'lock-step' September to June programme lacks flexibility, but motivates students to complete work in a reasonable period and in a regular pattern. New means of accreditation will probably encourage a more flexible time frame in the near future.

2 NEC Degree and Professional Study Scheme

The Degree and Professional Study Scheme is a direct private study operation which is popular with students at undergraduate and, primarily, post-graduate level. The model relies more upon the educational planning, delivery and assessment designing skills of the tutors than conventional open learning which may be largely materials based. The personal rapport between student and tutor is very important, as there are no specific course materials and it is up to tutors to recommend books and periodicals and to set suitable assignments. Tutors have a good personal contact with both students and their NEC manager. The range of courses includes ten languages to post-graduate Institute of Linguists levels, a number of post-graduate engineering diplomas, and external degrees from London University.

The system allows for maximum flexibility as students may decide to do as many assignments as they like, as often as they like, and complete the assignments in a way which suits the student after discussion with the tutor. Results, from the Institute of Linguists in particular, are excellent, and 90 per cent marks in examination papers are not uncommon. It is recognised that these results reflect the excellence of the tutors and the high motivation of students. A weakness is that as the system relies entirely on the tutor's choice of materials, then the student has no other academic resource. By contrast, NEC's main distance education system relies heavily on carefully prepared course materials, thus releasing tutors to concentrate on marking assignments rather than setting study programmes and tasks as well. In this sense, students may be more likely to become disaffected and abandon a programme of study in the DPSS system than in the main system if they lose confidence in their tutor. On the other hand, it is always possible to change tutors in either system.

3 NEC's Main System

This system is used for a wide range of general and vocational qualifications and for leisure courses. It lacks the complete flexibility of the DPSS system, and perhaps has a little more bureaucracy, but it allows students to take a wide range of courses and to have contact with tutors through the marking of assignments and use of comment sheets and query cards. Each course is written to include up to 16 assignments (though more can be requested by students who feel they need more practice). The courses include study guides and, for examined courses, revision guides as well as teaching materials divided up into units which may cover two to eight hours' study time. Many courses have a modular structure which allows some choice of coverage as well as natural occasions to pause if a break in studies is required. Each enrolment is valid for up to three years, but there is no time limit for the completion of individual assignments. Thus there is more flexibility than in the TTS scheme, although tutors and students can agree a series of deadlines for assignment completion which may help to create a fruitful pattern of study. Telephone contact is encouraged.

It is this system which all the students in the NEC survey followed, so discussion of its benefits and drawbacks in terms of disaffection will take place later in this chapter.

4 ABACUS

The new range of vocational qualifications, known as NVQs,[9] pose problems for open learning students not in regular employment or regular attendance at college, since they are mainly assessed by on-the-job observation of a student's 'competence' in a range of job-related skills. The evidence of competence can also include written materials and simulation, but it is direct observation over a certain time period which is the main means of assessment. Much of the preparation for taking these NVQs can be achieved through study at home, but hands-on experience and professional interaction with other workers is also important. Thus NEC is now establishing a new system for supporting students on these courses in conjunction with local training centres. In a pilot programme, students work through units of study at home and send in assignments. They also attend face-to-face workshops where they consolidate their learning and gain practical and interpersonal skills. The ABACUS scheme currently applies to Business Administration (office skills) at Levels I and II and Business Administration (secretarial) at Level III. It has advantages in that students may choose the units they take and are free to study in their own time while also having access to face-to-face tuition about every month. The disadvantages so far, apart from the expense, relate to the need to simulate office situations which should ideally be real-life work events. It is expected that a partnership between NEC, the BBC and government any provide video materials to alleviate these difficulties. It does seem that all trainers for NVQs, face-to-face or otherwise, are encountering similar problems in delivering NVQs effectively.

5 FlexiStudy[10]

Like ABACUS, this model offers a combination of distance and face-to-face study, but in a more traditional academic context. Students enrol on courses through their local college, and receive NEC course materials through the post. The assignments may be the ones set by NEC or locally devised. Students send or bring their assignments to the local college for marking, and receive face-to-face feedback on assignments and often additional tuition from the tutor in the college. The system thus allows for local adaptation and a potentially high degree of tutor support, but it depends on the local college's administration being able to see the advantages of this type of open learning and there are times when the pressure of other work relegates FlexiStudy students to a second-class role.

6 Open Learning Units

The same disadvantage may occur if a college has established an open learning unit that is under-resourced. However, at their best, open learning units can cater for any student's needs in terms of the proportion of time spent studying with a tutor, use of course materials and equipment, and choice of learning styles, routes and media. A college's open learning unit is stocked with a number of sets of open learning materials from NEC and other producers. Students may browse and choose their courses off the shelf, and negotiate a learning programme with their tutor. This may coincide with the academic year, but it may well not do so — students may start at any time of year, and the only limiting factor is that most examinations are only available in May–June or January.

In an ideal system, OLU students are able to infill to main courses in the college and have easy access to computer facilities, laboratories and other special-ised equipment. This model probably comes nearest to the open learning ideal of 'what, when, how and where' freedom to learn. Students are able to examine course materials before committing themselves, can have diagnostic interviews with tutors, and have many of the benefits of being a conventional college student as well as those of self-study and distance education. However, it is rarely possible in the UK for such students to receive study grants, and this is the main area where open learning students are disadvantaged with respect to the students attending conventional classes. It may be that government will in the next few years establish adults' right to lifelong training and education, and provide credits which students may use for learning in any mode.

7 Open University

The Open University is the biggest open learning institution in the world, with over 100,000 degree students and a fast-growing population of associate and professional students taking short courses. The usual model encourages students to enrol for courses in February, receive sets of OU course material, watch OU TV and hear OU radio programmes, meet tutors at regular intervals between submitting assignments, attend a summer school, and take an examination in November. The model is like the TTS in that it is 'lock-step' rather than 'roll on, roll off' — students must generally start and finish courses and assignments within a set time. However, also as with TTS, students may choose to take a unit or a half unit, to take one course or more, or to take a year off study. It is also possible to take the courses without attending tutorials, and in special cases without attend-ing summer school. There is no entrance examination — students are accepted as they apply — but many students are advised to prepare for degree-level study be-fore they start (there is a two-year waiting list in some regions of the UK for some subjects) by taking an NEC course or attending college classes. The OU offers a range of support services, including a tutor-counsellor in the first year, access to an educational guidance service, access to senior tutors and counsellors, and frequent tutor contact. The system is sometimes said to be rigid, but there is soon to be much more regional autonomy in the OU which will allow regions to allocate resources more flexibly, and this will enable more students to study what they like when they like. As a large, degree-awarding institution, however, the OU has to be more insistent on timescales and form-filling than the NEC, which is smaller and independent of accrediting bodies.

The Models and the Research: Implications for Disaffection

Each of the above models involves certain essential features of open learning which have implications for disaffection. Hilary Temple has said that 'the absence of involvement in the management of their learning at school is the major factor in the disillusionment which most of the adult population feel for education'.[11] If this is so, then the more control that the adult learner has over the learning process, the more that disillusionment can be conquered. The attached table[12] shows how the continuum of open learning can run from the 'open end' of complete learner control to the 'closed end' of predetermined learning opportunities. The obvious conclusion would be that the more open the learning, the less the disaffection is likely to arise. However, this conclusion may imply that a student has no need of a structure or a support system to guide learning. The three concepts of 'student autonomy', 'dialogue' and 'structure' are centred to open learning.[13] The idea that the first always outweighs the other two concepts is not borne out by the research we undertook, and does not take account of the varying learning styles that students prefer and that are appropriate for particular types of study. It also ignores the appropriacy of different types of tutoring for these students and studies. Penny Henderson[14] suggests that there are seven teaching styles — gardener, guide, coach, modeller, jug and vessel, explorer and shaper — which will each imply different approaches and different points on the continua outlined in the table.

Table 7.1: The Open Learning Continuum

Question	Open end	Closed end	Notes
Who?	Anyone can enrol	Conditions must be met, e.g. age or qualifications	To what extent are any limitations, for the student's sake or for the provider's convenience?
Why?	Student's own decision	Choice is made for the students, e.g. by school/parent	To what extent is the motivation the student's?
What?	Student chooses content of the curriculum	Syllabus is predetermined	To what extent can the student choose/negotiate what is learned?

Table 7.1 (cont.): The Open Learning Continuum

Question	Open end	Closed end	Notes
How?	Many routes Many methods Many media	One route One method One medium	To what extent can the student choose • routes through the content • methods of learning (e.g. case studies, role play, writing, visits) • media (e.g. audiotape, print, illustrations, video, computer)?
Where?	Anywhere	One place only	To what extent are the learning resources portable?
When?	Start anytime One pace Finish anytime	Fixed start Fixed pace Fixed finish	To what extent can the student choose/negotiate • when he or she starts • when he or she finishes • the pace at which learning progresses?
How is the student doing?	Student choice of assessment methods Frequent, full feedback on performance	Fixed assessment methods Infrequent, sketchy feedback on performance	To what extent can the student participate in assessment decisions? How frequent and informative is feedback to the student?
Who can help the student?	Student can choose (e.g. from several teachers) Teacher offers varied help	No choice Teacher in a limited role	What kinds of help are made available? Can the student choose the most appropriate helper/form of help? How broadly does the teacher define his/her support role?
What can the student do next?	Many possible destinations (e.g. jobs, activities, subjects) Process	Only one destination Product	To what extent does the learning lead to other oppotunities? Is the process of learning to learn stressed?

Source: Lewis, R. 'The Open School?' in Paine, N. (Ed.), *Open Learning in Transition*, Cambridge: NEC, 1989, pp. 258–9.

What all the models, and all open learning, has in common, is the search for an effective balance between autonomous, self-directed learning and guidance and instruction initiated by tutors and learning materials. The surveys of NEC students throw light on how students perceive the balance to have been achieved.

Enquirers' Survey

This consisted of a simple questionnaire sent out to all enquirers to NEC (defined as people who requested the NEC *Guide to Courses*) who had not enrolled on a course two months after making the enquiry. The questionnaire is reproduced below.

Figure 7.1: Questionnaire for NEC Enquirers' Survey

We have noticed that you enquired about our courses within the last year but did not enrol. If you would like to help us improve our service, please tick the boxes below and return this questionnaire using the enclosed pre-paid label.

☐ I found a course with another organisation

The course is: ....

The organisation is: ....

☐ NEC did not offer the course I wanted

This was: ....

☐ NEC courses cost more than I was prepared to pay

☐ Other: ....

....

Approximately 5 per cent of the enquirers responded to the survey, an acceptably high figure for a cold canvas of this sort. The responses to the survey fell into four broad categories, each of about 25 per cent of the respondents.

Category 1: 'NEC courses cost more than I was prepared to pay'.

It is noticeable that about 15 per cent of this category crossed out 'was prepared to pay' and inserted 'could afford' or a synonymous phrase.

Category 2: 'NEC did not have a course that I wanted'.

These respondents gave a very wide range of courses not covered by NEC. The only type of course with more than ten responses was Spanish, which NEC plans to run in the near future.

Category 3: 'I found a course with another provider'.

These respondents mainly chose courses at their local college or adult education centre, though about 20 per cent chose Open University or correspondence courses with private colleges.

Category 4: 'I decided not to take a course at this time'.

Most of these respondents gave practical reasons for not studying — ranging from moving house to caring for a relative — and only a very few gave psychological reasons, citing procrastination or laziness!

From the enquirers' survey it is possible to conclude that the major factor creating disaffection is the cost of courses. When most education and training benefits from heavy hidden subsidies, NEC's courses do seem expensive. The next few years may see a change in public perception as more local management occurs in education and training.

On the positive side, there was little evidence of other ways that disaffection prevented people from taking up learning opportunities. In Category 2, the apparent reason for non-enrolment related to lack of appropriate courses. In Category 3, people seemed able to choose freely from the spectrum of courses on offer, whether by open or conventional routes, and to make their choice on the basis of price and convenience. There was no sign of emotional responses to particular modes of delivery having a negative effect. In Category 4, there was again no overt sign of disaffection playing a part in non-enrolment. 'Procrastination', 'laziness' and even more practical explanations such as 'I lost the job which I wanted to do the course for' may all conceal attitudinal reasons for not enrolling, but it is difficult to judge how far this can be assumed. If any strong evidence of disaffection emerges, it must be among the 95 per cent of those canvassed who did not complete the form.

Student Survey

The earlier sections of this chapter described the extensive array of open learning opportunities available. The role of NEC was mentioned frequently. This is partly because NEC is active at a variety of educational levels from uncertificated general interest courses, through publicly examined certificate courses (such as GCSE/GCE), to degree level. But it must also be admitted that the frequent references to NEC also reflect the authors' experiences working with NEC! Thus it is not surprising that data about students and reasons for choosing an open learning experience will also be drawn from NEC. Specifically, this chapter draws on a survey on NEC students conducted in 1989/90. However, before reflecting on the data collected it will be instructive to review earlier perceptions of NEC's student body.

Such perceptions date back to the early 1960s. At that time open learners certainly existed, but they were a disparate group with no known educational or social characteristics and without the direct support of any national institutions. However, it was for this group that NEC was founded, amidst some speculation about who its typical students would be. Michael Young,[15] announcing NEC in 1963, wrote:

> Who are to be the students — or 'members', as we shall call them — of the College? They will be people who need a second chance — those who did not have the education they would like when they were younger and who are not getting it now, people who want to change their jobs or

improve their qualifications in their present careers. . . . We are thinking rather of the people who cannot turn up regularly for ordinary classes, above all of married women, housebound by their children, or those whose jobs keep them travelling, those who are shift workers or tied to a hospital, people who have to study in odd moments of the week if they are to study at all.

This proved to be an accurate description of many of the audiences who benefit from open learning. This was confirmed four years later when Brian Jackson wrote:

Even in a highly-developed educational system like ours, there are still huge numbers of people who do not get as much as they ideally should out of our schools, colleges, and universities, or the work of independent bodies such as the WEA. These are men and women who might have failed under the 11-plus system, or who attended inadequate schools in the past, or who were early leavers, or unsuccessful university applicants in the recent years of severe shortage. They may be adults who, through all the accidents and vicissitudes of life, find themselves in the wrong jobs or discover the excitement of learning only after the schooldays are over. They may be women, who, after the second class educational opportunities too frequently offered to girls . . . find themselves married with growing children, and the possibility of 20 or 30 working years still ahead of them. They may be handicapped, blind or in hospital, or embarrassed by some defect that makes them avoid evening classes. Or simply isolated. Whatever their circumstances, a truly open system of education should have some means of reaching them.[16]

Without stating it explicitly, both Young and Jackson were reflecting on the disaffection of many in society. They were concerned about those who deserved a second chance — and who in many cases never actually had a first chance.

As NEC grew and flourished over the next decade or so one would expect the understanding of the opportunities afforded by open learning to be more widely recognised. After all, during this period the Open University was also founded. To some extent NEC was seen as a precursor for the OU although, ironically, it was to play no formal part in the latter's foundation. It did, however, clearly influence the aims and objectives of the OU. It also influenced many of the teaching methods and student support services. If not exactly growing symbiotically, NEC and the OU did at least grow sympathetically with, for example, NEC providing pre-study, gateway, courses for intending OU students.

Thus open learning was being more explicitly recognised — but the identity of learners, somewhat strangely, seemed no clearer. Indeed, by 1976 Richard Freeman, formerly Educational Director at NEC but then newly appointed as Executive Director, felt that the popular view of its students had become stereotyped. He wrote.[17]

We are a little surprised at the pre-conceptions people have about our students. The typical student is seen as handicapped, living in a remote rural area and doing a shift work job. In fact he (*sic*) is a-typical.

Freeman concluded that these myths would best be laid to rest by a survey of NEC students. Earlier surveys had been used to gather feedback from projects and from students who had studied particular courses but Freeman's 1976 survey was the first systematic attempt to profile the whole NEC student body. He subsequently updated this work in 1984.[18] It is acknowledged that findings from such surveys are specific to NEC's provision and students, but the information collected will be of interest to other practitioners working in open and distance learning — hence their inclusion in this work.

Hence also the need to update — and extend — such information. The information from the 1976 and 1984 surveys required extension because, while providing a useful and fascinating picture of NEC's students, it was largely confined to describing social and educational characteristics. The earlier surveys established who studies with NEC but gave very limited answers to why students enrolled with NEC and no details at all about their experiences while studying with NEC. A new survey was therefore conducted in 1989/90. This survey was designed to update the social and demographic information of the two earlier surveys but extended to explore the experiences of students learning with NEC. The remainder of this chapter is based on some of its findings.[19]

Gender, Age, Occupation and Educational Background

Open learning is often said to suit the educational needs of women in particular. But the 1975 and 1984 surveys indicated that NEC's student populations were fairly evenly split. It was something of a surprise to find that a different picture emerged in 1990: two in three (66.3 per cent) of the NEC student population were women. However, the age ranges, and in particular the median age, of students had changed little: most students were in the 25 to 44 year-old age group with the mean age being 37 years.

The characteristics of the female student population in the 1990 survey differ from those of the female national population. For example, nearly half of the women students (48.1 per cent) were in paid employment for 20 or more hours a week. This is a high proportion when compared to the proportion of working women in the national population: figures published by the Department of Employment in November 1990 showed that the overall figure was 31 per cent of adult women in full-time employment. By comparison significantly more than half of the men (65.5 per cent) were in paid employment for 20 or more hours per week.

Turning to data on occupation, the 1990 survey showed the most common occupations, accounting for 10 per cent or more of those surveyed, to be: armed forces (women 0.0 per cent, men 14.3 per cent), administrators and managers (9.6 per cent, 14.3 per cent), technical (including computing) (8.4 per cent, 10.7 per cent), engineering and allied trades (0.0 per cent, 12.5 per cent), clerical and office staff (50.6 per cent, 14.3 per cent), sales and services (14.5 per cent, 19.6 per cent). The imbalance of clerical and office workers to some extent reflects the gender division in such occupations. However, a comparison with the 1984 survey data is instructive. In 1984 18.7 per cent of women and 5.9 per cent of men were in office based jobs; the comparable figures in 1989 were 50.6 per cent and 14.3 per cent. Significant increases also occurred in those in administrative and management jobs: 2.4 per cent of women in 1984 compared to 9.6 per cent in 1989, and 6.7 per cent of men in 1984 compared to 14.3 per cent in 1989.

The picture that emerges is of more students from administrative, managerial, clerical and office-based occupations — the conventional white collar jobs. The occupations less well represented in 1989 were teachers, lecturers, the professions and the arts, science and engineering.

The picture of social characteristics is completed by considering the highest level of previous education. Between 1979 and 1984 the proportion of NEC students with low prior educational qualifications decreased. However, after 1984 this group increased so that by 1989/90 13.1 per cent of students had no prior formal educational qualifications, another 27.5 per cent GCE/GCSE in one to four subjects, and overall 61.4 per cent had ceased education at a level below GCE A level.

A comparison of some of the characteristics above can be made, albeit in general terms, with other research. For example, a 1982 ACACE report[20] found that continuing education was dominated by young males with higher than average levels of initial education and of higher social class. More recent research on educational opportunities for adults identified that provision for under-represented categories remained marginalised.

> One can search hard (in prospectuses of programmes specifically for adults) for evidence of work targeting specific or 'disadvantaged' categories of students. Courses and other learning activities for groups such as the unemployed, people with basic education needs, speakers of other languages, the elderly and women returners, are often separately listed as specially funded programmes. . . . The 'Catch 22' is that without such special funding such groups might not be catered for, but the availability of special funding provides an excuse for not targeting them within 'normal' programming.[21]

NEC can point back to its inauguration and the targeting of such groups as a primary aim. Now it knows that it is getting closer to fulfilment of that aim. Groups formerly disaffected by traditional educational opportunities are benefiting from developments in open learning such as those offered by NEC. But this is not to say that no impediments remain. The very social characteristics that are related to disaffection with traditional education can be barriers of a more general sort.

Personal Circumstance: The Deterrent of Fees

A common phenomenon (some would say an essential feature) of open learning systems is that they involve part-time (and flexibly-scheduled) study. In turn a phenomenon of part-time study in the UK is that it is only subject to discretionary grants from local authorities. Few students receive assistance with fee payment. It is therefore not surprising that research into factors influencing students' study intentions frequently examines personal circumstances in general — and hardship experienced in paying fees in particular. For example, a survey of Open University students[22] identified that a third of the students felt that finding the money to pay course tuition fees had been 'quite difficult' or a 'severe hardship'. Further, Woodley *et al.*[23] observed more generally that 'three out of ten part-time students . . . feels worse off than before'.

NEC's surveys provide additional evidence of the deterrent effect of fee payment. The enquirers' survey, as mentioned above, found that about 25 per cent cited this as a reason for not enrolling. The 1990 survey identified that 30.8 per cent of women found paying fees was 'quite difficult' or a 'severe hardship'; the comparable figure for men was 22.1 per cent. Another question in the survey pursued this issue in a slightly different way showing that 25.2 per cent of women believed the availability of an instalment scheme was crucial; 17.7 per cent of men held the same view. When other circumstances are taken into account, concern about paying for fees becomes greater. For example, 38 per cent of female NEC students who were not in employment, or who worked for less than 20 hours a week, found fee payment difficult.

There is a concern that applies to all correspondence surveys: it is possible for respondents to list reasons that they perceive as more 'acceptable'. Thus it might be postulated that someone would rather say that they did not enrol because they could not afford the fees than say they did not enrol because they were concerned about the intellectual demands the course would make of them; or because the institutional image presented by the provider was unattractive.

Internally within the Open University there is much dispute about whether or not an increase in fees would actually decrease demand. Further, the assumption that, *de facto*, access is enhanced by having low fees is also challenged; there are those who point out that access is best enhanced by specific targeting of the disadvantaged groups. Proposals that increases in course fees be partially used to bolster the financial assistance fund maintained by the OU have consistently encountered mixed reactions. The ultimate statement, once heard within the OU, of this dilemma is that some OU students regard what they get as cheap at the price while others think it is daylight robbery!

That fee issues are important and that they influence real and perceived disaffection is clear. But there seems to be no panacea — not least because some of the fundamental attitudes of learners may have to change. Richard Freeman[24] put it succinctly when he observed that 'we need to find means of reducing costs to those individuals who are most disadvantaged whilst at the same time promoting the values of learning to the population as a whole; until there is a general recognition that, say, an hour of learning is worth at least as much as twenty cigarettes, participation will always be low'.

Reasons for Choosing Open Learning — And for Choosing NEC

Turning to the positive reasons for choosing open learning, one may wonder if it is a first choice — or a last resort? In NEC's 1990 survey students were asked about their reasons (they were allowed to quote more than one) for studying with NEC. Those quoted by at least 10 per cent of students were: prefer to study in own time (women 53.6 per cent, men 54.9 per cent), prefer to study at own pace (48.2 per cent, 55.8 per cent), prefer to study at home (40.5 per cent, 40.7 per cent), family responsibilities (34.2 per cent, 5.3 per cent), constraints of job (25.7 per cent, 35.4 per cent), no course available locally (12.6 per cent, 13.3 per cent). It will come as no surprise that women remain the principal carers in the family. However, more women were choosing open learning because of job constraints in 1989 than previously; in 1984 19.5 per cent of women quoted this reason; by 1989 the proportion had risen to 25.7 per cent.

The figures above also provide strong evidence that students' reasons for choosing open learning are positive ones. For many the flexibility of time, pace and place are great attractions. Open learning meets real needs, provides unique opportunities and seems to be the first choice for many. The survey also showed that open learning is increasingly chosen freely among a range of alternative opportunities. In 1984 19.0 per cent were studying with NEC because there was no suitable local provision whereas by 1989 this figure had dropped to 12.8 per cent. Examination of the mainstream educational marketplace shows increasing competition (or should it be thought of as opportunity?) for adult learners — but many still deliberately choose open learning. However, the reduction in traditional adult education classes may be another factor.

In choosing open learning, a potential student must also choose with which institution they study. In recent years there has been a significant increase in the number of open learning providers. The Open College was established in 1987 and many local colleges and employers now offer flexible learning opportunities. Against this background, students were asked in 1989 why they chose NEC. A variety of reasons was offered; students were asked to rate each one as being very, quite or not important to them. Many students regarded NEC's institutional status as important, for example 72 per cent of students considered the fact that NEC is accredited by the Council for the Accreditation of Correspondence Colleges to be quite or very important and 67.6 per cent of students thought the NEC's status as a non-profit making trust of some importance.

The flexibility of open learning, especially as applied by NEC, is considered important with, for example, 84.1 per cent of students being influenced by NEC's policy of allowing postponement of a course for a short period if appropriate. Related consumer rights allowing cancellation within 30 days and receiving a refund of part of the fee were considered of some importance by 59.6 per cent of students.

Support for the Learner

The 1989 NEC survey endeavoured to discover how students used their course: what sort of help they received with their studies. It transpired that the overwhelming majority (79 per cent overall) of students surveyed said they studied solely with NEC materials and the appointed tutor. The next highest response was 13.4 per cent who received informal help from a friend or a member of their family. Some 7.6 per cent received supplementary tuition from a formal source but only 0.7 per cent were studying NEC courses in conjunction with an organised scheme offered by another institution.

When the type of the course studied is taken into account some interesting variations are observed. It transpires that only 60.9 per cent of students studying GCSE courses solely used NEC materials and the appointed tutor. It may be that the aim of passing an externally assessed examination spurs students to get a significant level of help from a variety of sources. The disaffection engendered by formal and conventional examinations is beyond the remit for this chapter — but there may be an indication in NEC data that an examination also galvanises students and encourages (or *impels*) them to seek support in their learning.

The information above does show, though, that NEC's provision was the major source of learning for most students. The tutor has an important part to play in alleviating the loneliness of the (long) distance learner. Indeed, the role of the tutor was often referred to in open-ended responses to the survey and many students felt that their progress would have been aided by tutors taking on a more proactive role. 'I felt I need a tutor to talk things through with . . . I feel so isolated sometimes and the college and tutor feel so far away'; 'It perhaps would have motivated me more if the counsellor had . . . become more involved'; 'I would like to suggest that a tutor can be provided who a student can telephone to talk through a problem'. Some seek peer group interaction: 'am doing it on my own and feel it would be more beneficial . . . with a group or a partner'; 'I am sure many people would benefit by contacting/meeting other students with similar interests and subjects'.

The importance of support mechanisms in open learning has often been debated. Care must be taken not to get involved in a debate on semantics, but the notion of the self-directed, but supported, learner is a useful one to have in mind when considering the issues described above. Ross Paul[25] argues that the notion is an important one in that the 'achievement of producing independent, self-directed learners is ultimately (an) important criterion of institutional success'. That distance or open learners can be independent and supported was taken further in a conference which considered independence and interaction. Ronnie Carr,[26] reflecting on the proceedings, sums up the issues: 'any delegate who came to this conference hoping to be given a simple recipe for the ideal mixture of "independence" and "interaction" in distance teaching systems would have been disappointed: no such mixture exists'. This conclusion is supported by the NEC survey. The evidence is that students' needs vary; a variety of mixtures is required. But just as needs vary — so too do outcomes.

Progress on Courses

NEC students were asked to describe what stage they had reached in their particular course. Overall, 61.1 per cent were still studying while 15.6 per cent had completed the course although no examination was involved and 4.6 per cent had recently sat or were waiting to sit an external examination. But of more interest to the context of this book was the fact that 9.7 per cent described themselves as 'resting' — but intending to complete — their course and 9.0 per cent had given up their course.

A surprising picture emerges when previous levels of education are considered. Of NEC students who were resting or who had given up it was found that the highest rate (18.2 per cent) of giving up was among those who already have university degrees. The lowest rate of giving up (5.3 per cent) was among those with GCE A levels, closely followed by those with no previous educational qualifications (7.0 per cent). Students with professional qualifications are more likely to be taking a break (22.2 per cent) while those with no educational qualifications (9.3 per cent) are least likely to be taking a break.

The conclusion that can reasonably be drawn from this information is that NEC is providing learning opportunities for those who otherwise might not have them — and that it is these priority groups who are making the most of the opportunities. Those with low, or no, prior educational qualifications are less likely than most other groups to drop out of their courses either temporarily or permanently.

The 1989 NEC survey therefore asked students to indicate what sort of factors influenced their decisions to give up. The questionnaire allowed students to list more than one factor. In descending order of the frequency with which they were listed the factors were: limited time for studying (21.0 per cent), pressures at work (20.5 per cent), family or domestic pressures (19.3 per cent), health problems (13.1 per cent). A variety of other factors were listed by less than 10 per cent of students.

Gender had a significant impact on the reasons quoted. Family or domestic pressures weigh more heavily on women (23.1 per cent) than men (8.7 per cent); men (13.0 per cent) claim more often than women (5.4 per cent) that the course content was not really what was wanted; men (26.1 per cent) more frequently find they have limited time available for studying, with the comparable figure for women being 19.2 per cent.

Various correlations with other data collected in the survey might indicate those students most at risk of not completing a course. So as not to swamp this chapter with data just two other characteristics are examined. First, correlation with data on students who are not in employment compared to those employed shows that health problems take a heavier toll on those not in employment (18.5 per cent) than those who are employed (7.1 per cent). This might also relate to the age of those surveyed. However, a similar emphasis occurs with those quoting domestic pressures as reasons for resting or giving up: this factor was mentioned by 21.7 per cent of those not in employment and 16.7 per cent of those employed.

The other correlation took previous levels of education into account. It transpires that students without prior educational qualifications (27.3 per cent) are more likely to quote pressures at work as reasons for giving up than students who have previously studied at least to GCE A level (17.5 per cent). It is also noteworthy that despite their greater experience of education those with GCE A levels (12.7 per cent) are the most likely to choose a course that did not provide the content they really wanted.

There can be a variety of responses to the phenomena identified above. But one of them must be to reinforce the role of counselling, especially prior to enrolment. Diane Bailey[27] was writing about work-based open learning but her observations are worthy of a wider application. She observes that:

> Open learning brings together two core life roles for adults, worker and learner, both of them deeply implicated in the individual's self-concept. This conjunction can be a source of energy or anxiety, especially for those who risk self-exposure because they have not studied for a long time. Likewise, women's self-image as workers can be fragile because of the unrecognised nature of women's domestic work and the discontinuous pattern of female employment. Both pre-entry counselling and post-entry support are valuable in recognising and relieving these anxieties and potential role conflict. Such counselling does not have to be an expensive

resource; it can be effectively provided by peer groups and company members.

The last sentence suggests relatively easy ways of providing support when the intending student is, de facto, a member of a group through being in a workplace — but is more difficult to establish for individual students applying 'cold' to an organisation such as NEC. The logistics of making personal contact with disparate individuals can be daunting; the costs will be direct ones and not of the opportunity cost type described by Bailey.

Conclusion

The NEC student and enquirer surveys indicate that many of the messages of the open learning movement are supported by the responses of prospective and actual open learning students. The flexibility of open learning is particularly attractive in that it allows students to study at their own pace and in their own time.

The cost of courses is the biggest obvious barrier to the flexibility that people seek, but there is still a large number of NEC students on low-income levels, and also with previously limited educational attainment. These are the students who appear to be least likely to show disaffection by abandoning courses. It seems that the benefits of open learning outweigh the cost burden for many students, although there are indications that enrolments might rise steeply if costs were reduced.

Other barriers that affect the flexibility which open learners require include the what, where, when and how of open learning. It is probable that the other models of open learning mentioned earlier in the chapter will deal with these barriers in slightly different ways. For example, the DPSS scheme allows more negotiation about what is studied than materials based courses, and models like the OU or Open Learning Unit models allow a flexible degree of face-to-face contact which learners generally (though not universally) want and appreciate. On the whole, though, the various models share most of the characteristics of the one surveyed.

In relation to what is taught, there was little evidence in the survey of concern on this point, but it may well be that students feel inhibited about criticism which might imply that they are unable to cope. It is certain that some people surveyed were resting or had given up because of the course content, but not possible to say how many. The subject content of a course is not very negotiable in most open learning models, any more than it is in most traditional models. The change to this brought about by such initiatives as Access courses to higher education and accreditation by competence, sometimes through prior learning, should help to create a different atmosphere where negotiated course content is commonplace.

The 'where', 'when' and 'how' of open learning were strong attractions for students. Studying at home, or at least away from an educational institution, is important to many students, and so is the idea of study at periods and paces they choose. However, there is also evidence that students would like tutors and NEC to be more proactive in setting and checking deadlines. One student survey respondent commented 'would it be possible to include a time limit?', and another 'I prefer the old system of a structured course'.

There was little specific comment on the 'how' of open learning. Students in the survey praised and criticised course materials, but few considered the mode of delivery except in comparison to traditional study as in school. No-one regretted their choice of open learning, although many would prefer to meet tutors at least occasionally. If NEC could offer varied modes of delivery, with and without deadlines and with various tutor contact options, it is likely that 'how' could be debated more thoroughly. The main choice on means of learning was seen as traditional versus open, with open as the favourite for the individual student concerned at the time they chose to start a course. But there was no sign of a dogmatic insistence on open learning as the only way to study effectively. The 'where' and 'when' of learning seemed to have more importance in students' minds than the 'what' or 'how', at least in response to the survey.

The table on page 96 can give rise to more reflections on the causes of disaffection. All the issues it highlights can show how the more *open* learning can be, the more disaffection can be reduced. It also shows, however, that the closed ends of the various scales also have their place. There can be advantages in joining a course that has selected entry, a pre-determined syllabus, a single route and so on. Different points on the scales are relevant to people depending on their characters, their situations and their aims. If open learning has done anything to banish disaffection, it is by respecting individual differences and providing structures which support students while maximising their self-respect and independence.

Notes

1 Quoted in JEFFRIES, C. (1990) *The A–Z of Open Learning*, National Extension College, p. 1.
2 PAINE, N., 'Introduction' in *Open Learning in Transition, An Agenda for Action*, Cambridge, National Extension College, p. xi.
3 LEWIS, R. and SPENCER, D. (1986) *What is Open Learning*, Council for Educational Technology, p. 25.
4 ROWNTREE, D. (1986, 1990) *Teaching through Self-Instruction*, Kogan Page, p. 11.
5 WATERHOUSE, P.S. (1986) *Supported Self-Study: an Introduction for Teachers*, National Council for Educational Technology.
6 WEBB, R. (1991) *Who are NEC's Invisible Students?*, National Extension College.
7 RUMBLE, G. (1989) 'Distance Learning and Open Learning and the Misuse of Language', *Open Learning*, **IV**, 2, p. 28.
8 JEFFRIES, C. (1991) *TTS Review*, internal National Extension College report.
9 NATIONAL VOCATIONAL QUALIFICATIONS (NVQ's), regulated by the National Council for Vocational Qualifications.
10 FREEMAN, R. (1989) 'Open Learning in the Making', in PAINE, N. (Ed.) *Open Learning in Transition*, National Extension College, p. 38.
11 Quoted in LEWIS, R. 'The Open School?', *ibid.*, p. 256.
12 Taken from *ibid.*, pp. 258–9.
13 MOORE, M.G. (1983) 'On a Theory of Independent Study', in SEWART, D. (Ed.) *Distance Education International Perspectives*, Croom Helm, London.
14 HENDERSON, P. (1989) *Promoting Active Learning*, National Extension College.
15 YOUNG, M. (1963) 'Announcing the National Extension College', *Where?*, No. 14 (Autumn 1963).
16 JACKSON, B. (1967) *National Extension College 1967: four years' works and the future*, Cambridge: National Extension College.

17 FREEMAN, R. (1976) *The Invisible Students*, Cambridge: National Extension College.
18 FREEMAN, R. (1984) *Student Profile Survey 1984*, Cambridge: National Extension College.
19 Copies of the 1990 student profile are avaiable from the National Extension College, 18 Brooklands Avenue, Cambridge CB2 2HN. Copies of NEC's *Guide to Courses* which help to put the survey into perspective are also available from NEC.
20 ADVISORY COUNCIL FOR ADULT AND CONTINUING EDUCATION (1982) *Adults: Their Educational Experience and Needs*, ACACE.
21 McGIVNEY, V. (1990) *Access to Education for Non-participating Adults*, NIACE.
22 KIRKWOOD, A. (1988) *Students Costs and Hardship in 1986*, Milton Keynes: The Open University, IET.
23 WOODLEY, A. *et al.* (1987) *Choosing to Learn: Adults in Education*, Milton Keynes: SRHE/OU Press.
24 FREEMAN, R. (1990) 'Open Learning: Taking Stock', *Open Learning*, Vol. 5, No. 3.
25 PAUL, R. (1990) *Open Learning and Open Management*, London: Kogan Page.
26 CARR, R. (1990) 'Conference Report: Interaction and independence: student support in distance education and open learning', *Open Learning*, Vol. 5, No. 1, Cambridge, September 19–22, 1989.
27 BAILEY, D. (1990) 'Guidance and Counselling in Work-Based Open Learning', in PAINE, N. (Ed.) *Open Learning in Transition: An Agenda for Action*, Cambridge: National Extension College.

8   Disaffection and Distance Education

Alan Woodley

Introduction

In his review of correspondence study in works of literature von Pittman describes the negative stereotypes that abound there (von Pittman, 1988). The proprietors of correspondence schools are usually villains who employ exaggerated or misleading advertising. As for the tutors 'their credentials, competence, and intentions are always suspect'. The lessons themselves 'flow back and forth in an industrial-style model of instruction, with no personal touch or student-teacher interaction'. Such images may seem quaint and dated in the brave new world of 'distance education' pioneered by such institutions as the National Extension College and the Open University. However, this mode of learning is still generally recognised as being extremely difficult and dependent on the motivation and dedication of the student. The Open University's first Vice-Chancellor acknowledged that he had helped create 'the hardest way of gaining a degree known to man' (Perry, 1976) and 'the loneliness of the long distance learner' is a much discussed ailment.

On the face of it then, distance learning is not the most attractive or appropriate route back into education for the disaffected adult. However, if one considers institutions such as The Open University as providers of 'supported open learning' rather than purely correspondence education then one can begin to see how a more flexible learner-centred approach might indeed offer such adults a way back into the system.

Distance education is an extremely wide field. Courses vary in level from higher degrees to sub-GCSE; there are numerous providers both in the public and private sector; there is enormous variation in the types and combinations of teaching media that are used. In this chapter we have tried to assess the actual and potential contribution of distance education for the disaffected adult by looking at one particular programme, namely the Open University undergraduate programme, and asking three basic questions:

   i)   What structural characteristics of the programme would seem to make it appropriate and attractive to the disaffected adult?
   ii) What evidence is there that it has indeed attracted such people?
   iii) What progress do they make as students?

In the concluding section we attempt to draw out more general points and question whether and how the distance education model could be extended and improved to the benefit of disaffected adult learners.

What the Open University Offers to Disaffected Learners

The seeds of disaffection with formal education are usually planted at school. Large numbers of pupils leave with the intention, spoken or unspoken, of never putting themselves in a classroom situation again. For them the classroom is where they are offered irrelevant knowledge and skills, where they are controlled by people for whom they have little respect, and where they are being frequently defined as failures or trouble-makers. Forays back into the field of adult education may re-confirm these views. Often they may find themselves sitting at the same desks!

The Open University undergraduate programme has been designed in such a way that it should be appropriate for and accessible to adults who might not wish to, or be able to, enter conventional higher education courses. In theory at least, several of its features would seem to make it attractive to disaffected learners.

Open Entry
Those who left school with poor qualifications can apply and gain entry on an equal basis. They don't have to go off to gain A levels before rejoining the education 'escalator'.

Study Mode
Because of its part-time nature people can try a degree course without having to make major life changes such as giving up their jobs. Also distance study allows people to study in almost complete secrecy if they so desire. Diffident disaffected learners can easily 'try out' an Open University course without telling friends, relatives and work colleagues and thus avoid the possibility of loss of face if they decide not to continue.

Student Choice
Much disaffection is caused by régimes which tell people what they should learn, how they should learn it and when they should learn it. The Open University has attempted to give students much more control over their own learning.

   i)   Although there is a fixed academic year with dates for assignments and exams, in general terms people are free to study their courses at times and places that are most convenient for them.
   ii) Apart from beginning with a Foundation Course, students are free to choose from a range of 120 courses. These can be taken in virtually any combination and order.
   iii) There is no time limit for graduation. Students can take anything from half a credit to two full credits per year (6 credits are required for a BA degree) or they can choose to have rest years and re-enter the system at some later point.
   iv) Students can live where they like in the United Kingdom. If they move house they can continue to take the same course and they can take their course credits with them.

Student Support
Support is provided locally in the form of tuition and counselling. However, participation is voluntary. The students themselves choose whether to attend tutorials or to seek advice and guidance.

The Curriculum
OU courses are written specifically for adults and are designed to draw on their greater life experience. An OU Foundation Course is more likely to be of revelance to an adult returning to education than is a GCE A level that has been designed for secondary school pupils.

Assessment Strategy
The relative lack of face-to-face feedback from tutors is compensated for by the continuous assessment strategy which takes the form of tutor-marked and computer-marked assignments. These serve to provide regular information to students on how well they are doing and also perform an important pacing function.

Recognition of Prior Learning
Those who have successfully completed a year or more of higher education elsewhere are given exemptions from part of the OU degree course.

Of course, not all distance teaching schemes have the features listed above and some of the features are also to be found in more conventional face-to-face settings. In judging the success of the OU in relation to disaffected learners we are assessing the effects of a particular configuration of factors rather than 'distance education' *per se*. We will return to this topic in the concluding section.

So far we have stressed the 'positive' features of the OU undergraduate programme but there are also some major constraints that might deter disaffected learners. The ones most commonly cited are the sheer amount of time and self-discipline required for successful study plus the lack of face-to-face support from staff and fellow students. Even some of the 'positive' features may have negative aspects. For example, the pacing provided by regular TV broadcasts and assignments can result in people giving up if they fall behind. Rather than attempt to determine theoretically whether the positive aspects outweigh the negative aspects, it is perhaps better to make a judgment based on the experience of the students themselves.

Has the Open University Attracted Disaffected Learners?

The Open University is fond of publicising its most impressive graduates. Thus most readers will probably have come across reports of those who left school at 14 with no qualifications having been told that they were stupid, yet who had gone on to gain a First Class Honours degree with the OU many years later. Such people clearly exist but how typical are they of the average student?

A national survey of mature students that was carried out in 1981 provides us with some data on disaffection with schooling and subsequent participation in adult education (Woodley *et al.*, 1987). The survey covered a wide range of courses and enables us to make comparisons between OU students and those on qualifying courses in other types of institution.

Table 8.1:   The Qualifications Held by Mature Students at the Time of Leaving School

	Open University %	Correspondence %	Universities %	Polytechnics %	Colleges %	Adult Residential Colleges %
None	18	23	8	8	23	50
CSE	3	9	3	8	10	14
O Level	41	37	28	38	42	29
A Level	38	28	59	43	24	5
Other	1	3	3	3	2	1

Note: Columns do not always add up to 100% due to rounding.
Source: Re-analysed data from Woodley *et al.* (1987).

Table 8.1 shows the qualifications held by the mature students at the time they left school. Only four out of ten OU students had left school with A levels or their equivalent. On other correspondence courses (students were sampled from the National Extension College, the NALGO correspondence college and a well-known large private correspondence college and were weighted to reflect the predominance of the private sector) this figure fell to three out of ten. Thus distance education attracted considerable numbers of the less successful school-leavers. However, in comparative terms, this performance was virtually matched by the polytechnics and improved upon by the colleges and the long-term adult residential colleges. It is only the conventional universities that attracted significantly more of the successful school-leavers among their mature students.

Of course school qualifications are not necessarily a good measure of disaffection — there will be disaffected leavers who gained A levels and non-disaffected leavers who did not. However, in the case of the 1981 study we can also look at the reasons given for leaving school by those who were under 18 when they left (Table 8.2). People tended to give several reasons for leaving and so the figures are difficult to interpret. However, it is clear that while many OU students had become disillusioned with school (i.e., the first two categories in Table 8.2), many more had been prevented from continuing by barriers such as the lack of a sixth form, or had chosen to leave because they wanted the money or the independence offered by work. In fact the OU appeared to have the lowest proportion of disaffected students. The figures were somewhat higher for correspondence students elsewhere but once again it was the adult residential colleges with the most impressive figures.

The OU monitors the characteristics of its undergraduates on a continuous basis. Information is readily available on variables such as age, gender, educational qualifications, occupation and ethnic origin. However, while several of these factors are known to be correlated with disaffection, none of them provides a true measure of the extent to which the OU attracts and caters for disaffected adults. Imperfect though it is, we have decided to take educational qualifications held on entry to the OU as the best proxy measure available. For our analysis we will assume that those with low entry qualifications are more likely to have been previously disaffected and we have divided the students into the following three groups:

Table 8.2: The Reasons Given for Leaving School by Mature Students

	Open University %	Correspondence %	Universities %	Polytechnics %	Colleges %	Adult Residential Colleges %
Disliked school	19	30	38	32	20	51
Had had enough studying	20	27	32	27	28	29
Needed a wage to help family	32	28	19	24	26	34
Wanted to earn own living	47	54	42	52	50	51
Parents encouraged to leave	26	26	25	18	25	27
Offered a good job	28	32	26	31	33	15
Had enough schooling for desired job/course	36	37	30	27	38	24
Not got the qualifications to continue	23	27	16	17	18	27
Advised to leave by school/a teacher	12	8	13	8	9	13
School did not provide courses wanted	22	20	22	17	22	22
School had no sixth form	20	23	16	14	23	24
Personal reasons	8	8	11	9	5	7
Other reasons	3	6	4	3	4	2

Note: Columns do not always add up to 100% because respondents could give two or more answers.
Source: Re-analysed data from Woodley *et al.* (1987).

- *Below A level* i.e., those holding qualifications below A level, Scottish Highers, ONCs or some other equivalent.
- *A level* i.e., those with an A level or its equivalent.
- *Above A level* i.e., those holding some higher education qualification such as a teaching certificate or HNC.

In 1990 the proportions of new OU undergraduates in these three groups was 35 per cent, 34 per cent and 31 per cent respectively. In the following section we go on to examine the relative progress made by each of these groups.

Student Progress at the Open University

a) Initial to final registration
Applicants who are offered a place on the undergraduate programme initially register by paying a proportion of the first year tuition fee. After three months on the course they have to decide whether or not to complete final registration. In 1990 some 8 out of 10 (79 per cent) in the 'Above A level' group chose to finally register. This fell to 74 per cent for the 'A level' group and 66 per cent for those 'Below A level'.

b) Course-based progress in a given year
OU undergraduates begin by taking a Foundation Course. Having passed such a course they can then go on to take Second, Third or Fourth Level courses. Figure 8.1 shows the student success rate in 1988 at the various course levels. Those students who had entered the OU with low entry qualifications were somewhat less likely to gain a course credit than those with higher qualifications. This difference was most marked at Foundation level and diminished as they proceeded to higher level courses.

c) Progress over time
Finally we look at progress over time. When undergraduates complete Final Registration in their first year of study they become 'full' students of the University. In effect this means that they can study at their own pace. They can take any number of years off and resume their studies whenever they choose without having to re-apply for admission. This means that it is impossible to measure 'progress' in absolute terms. All one can do is describe the progress made by a cohort at a given point in time and it is clear that the longer the time period covered, the more valid will be the results obtained. For these reasons we have taken the 1975 intake of students and we have followed their progress up until the end of 1989, i.e. over a 15 year period.

We have considered progress over time in two ways. Firstly in terms of credits gained by actual OU study and secondly in terms of total credits gained. The latter includes credit exemptions and advanced standing awarded on the basis of previous study. It is important to consider both aspects when assessing the achievements of OU students. For example, some OU graduates will have gained their OU degree by studying three credits whereas others will have studied four or five credits but will not have graduated yet.

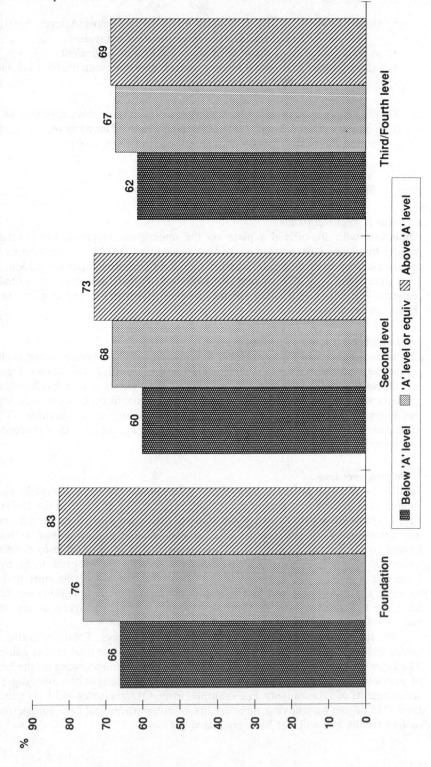

Figure 8.1: The percentage gaining a course credit, analysed by level of course and qualifications held on entry (1988)

Foundation: Below 'A' level 66, 'A' level or equiv 76, Above 'A' level 83

Second level: Below 'A' level 60, 'A' level or equiv 68, Above 'A' level 73

Third/Fourth level: Below 'A' level 62, 'A' level or equiv 67, Above 'A' level 69

Legend: Below 'A' level   'A' level or equiv   Above 'A' level

Table 8.3: The Progress Made by the 1975 Intake by the End of 1989 Analysed by Qualifications on Entry

Credits	a) Credits gained by OU study			b) Total credits gained		
	Below A Level	A Level	Above A Level	Below A Level	A Level	Above A Level
	%	%	%	%	%	%
0	27	20	13	26	18	5
0.5–1.5	19	17	14	17	15	6
2–2.5	13	9	5	13	10	9
3–3.5	8	7	30	8	7	9
4–4.5	6	6	15	5	3	4
5–5.5	5	6	11	2	2	2
6–6.5	17	22	8	22	29	43
7–7.5	2	4	3	2	4	9
8 or more	3	9	1	5	12	14
Average credits	2.6	3.5	3.1	2.9	3.8	5.2
% gaining an Ordinary degree				29	45	66
% gaining an Honours degree				5	12	14

Note: Columns do not always add up to 100% due to rounding.

Table 8.3 shows that approximately three out of ten of those whose qualifications were below A level had gained a degree. The figure for those who held one or more A levels or their equivalent was around four out of ten. Nearly seven out of ten of those in the highest qualification group had graduated.

When we turn to the figures for actual credits gained by study, the picture changes dramatically. Although the 'underqualified' were more likely to leave with no credits at all, almost one quarter of them had gained six or more credits. The figures showing the average number of credits gained by study reveal that the 'underqualified' students gained only half a credit less than those with some higher education qualification. Those with A levels or their equivalent were actually the most successful group when we use this criterion.

If one were to take all those students who gained some credit by study as one's base, the picture would change again. Four out of ten of the 'underqualified' who got past this barrier went on to graduate and their average number of credits gained matched that of those students with some higher education qualification.

Students Who do not Graduate

Gaining a degree is not the only possible positive outcome from OU study. Some students gain a course credit or two, then use them to transfer into a full-time degree course elsewhere. Others stop studying when they have learned as much as they want to. Rather than dismissing such students as 'failures' we must consider why they stopped studying, what benefits they gained from study and what are their attitudes to further study.

In 1990 a postal survey was carried out on a sample of 'dormant' OU students. By 'dormant students' we mean those undergraduates who are not currently taking a course but who are entitled to re-enter the system at any time by virtue of having completed final registration in their first year. For the survey we selected students who a) had entered the OU between 1981 and 1987, b) had taken a course in 1987, c) had taken no courses in 1988, 1989 or 1990 and d) had not graduated. In the following tables we have divided the respondents into six groups. These are our three educational qualification groups further sub-divided into those who gained some OU course credit and those who did not.

The students were asked to say why they had decided to give up, or at least postpone their OU studies. Their main reasons are shown in Table 8.4. The most common reason was lack of time caused by other demands at home and work. Many had decided that another course elsewhere was more suited to their needs and circumstances or were prevented from continuing by 'barriers' such as the cost of OU study, the summer school attendance requirement or by illness. Relatively few complained about the quality of the Open University in terms of its courses and its staff.

When we look at the results for those with low qualifications we see that they were more likely to have experienced the barriers mentioned above and this was particularly true for those who had not gained any course credit. Disaffection with the OU itself was not very common but 17 per cent of the no course credit group were not happy with the OU teaching system (e.g. lack of contact with other students, heavy workload) or with OU and its staff (e.g. dissatisfied with their tutors or the grades received).

Table 8.5 shows that significant proportions of the dormant students felt that their OU studies had produced beneficial effects in various areas of their lives, despite the fact that they had not graduated. For our purposes it is important to note that those with low qualifications who gained some course credit appeared to gain more benefit than their counterparts with higher qualifications. Understandably the levels of benefit were much lower among those who had gained no course credit. However, approximately one in five of those with low qualifications claimed to have derived 'great' or 'enormous' benefit from their OU studies and in general they seemed to gain as much benefit as those with higher qualifications.

If the Open University gives disaffected adults yet another negative educational experience, then the disaffection could be compounded. The dormant student survey allows us to see whether this has happened to any significant extent (Table 8.6). Firstly, very few respondents said that they had given up their OU undergraduate studies for good, thus indicating a positive experience. (Also some of those who did not plan to return will be the ones who have transferred to degree courses elsewhere and won't need to return). Secondly, many had not become disaffected with education in general as indicated by the fact that they had gone on to take further courses elsewhere. (The time between them ceasing OU study and taking part in the survey was 2–2.5 years.) This was most common among those with low qualifications who gained some course credit. More disquietingly, it was rarest for those with low qualifications who had not gained any credit although it is possible, of course, that the barriers that prevented further OU study also prevented study elsewhere. Finally, respondents were asked to say whether they would recommend the OU undergraduate programme to 'people

Table 8.4: The Main Reason for Giving Up or Postponing OU Studies

	a) Some course credit			b) No course credit		
	Below A level	A level	Above A level	Below A level	A level	Above A level
	%	%	%	%	%	%
Could not devote enough time to OU studies	34	44	48	40	53	54
Decided to take a course somewhere else	20	22	15	3	10	1
Prevented from continuing by 'barriers'	15	10	8	26	12	10
Had achieved what was wanted	8	4	3	0	2	0
Could not face any more OU study	6	4	6	1	5	4
Not happy with the OU teaching system	5	7	8	8	2	6
Career changes made OU study inappropriate	3	0	1	3	2	4
Not happy with the OU and its staff	2	2	2	9	0	5
Wasn't getting support needed from spouse, employer, etc.	1	2	1	4	5	5
Other factors	5	7	10	7	8	11

Table 8.5: The Benefits Gained from Study by Non-graduates

	a) Gained some course credit			b) Gained no course credit		
	Below A level	A level	Above A level	Below A level	A level	Above A level
	%	%	%	%	%	%
Good effect on:						
You as a person	77	65	63	55	56	38
Your social life and relations with others	28	22	24	14	9	8
Your family/family life	25	16	13	4	3	7
Your job/career	41	29	39	18	13	16
You as a 'learner'	75	79	67	51	70	51
You as a member of society	36	20	15	33	30	7
Overall benefit*	%	%	%	%	%	%
Enormous	20	15	9	7	1	0
Great	40	31	26	11	18	16
Total	59	45	35	18	19	16

*Note: Where 'Enormous' plus 'Great' does not equal 'Total', this is due to rounding.

Table 8.6: The Attitudes to Education of Non-graduates

| | a) Gained some course credit | | | b) Gained no course credit | | |
	Below A level	A level	Above A level	Below A level	A level	Above A level
	%	%	%	%	%	%
% Who said they had given up the OU for good	6	10	6	10	12	13
% Who had not done another course since OU	56	60	69	75	66	71
% Who would not recommend OU to others	4	4	11	9	0	6

with a similar background to yourself' and again there was an extremely positive response. At least nine out of ten in each of our groups said that they would do so.

Some Conclusions

We have seen that the Open University undergraduate programme has attracted considerable numbers of students who have gained very little in terms of formal qualifications from their previous encounters with the educational system. Furthermore, while progress for them is certainly more difficult, the majority of them appear to value their OU experience and to gain benefit from it.

What is not clear is the extent to which this group, which could clearly be termed educationally 'disadvantaged', should be thought of as 'disaffected'. The survey evidence suggests that very few OU undergraduates left school because they were disaffected with education. Most of those who left early did so because there were concrete, practical reasons preventing them from continuing or because work and independence beckoned. Also, the great majority of OU students, whose median age on entry is 34, have taken a number of other courses in between leaving school and entering the OU. It seems highly likely that it was through participation in these earlier courses that the disaffected adults acquired the motivation and self-confidence to tackle a degree programme.

In Section 2 we argued that the Open University undergraduate programme had several features that might make it accessible to disaffected adults. However, we also noted aspects that might make it unattractive to such people. These include the level at which OU courses start, the cost, the number of years it takes to gain a degree, and the sheer size of the Foundation Courses which require 15–20 hours of study each week over a 32 week period. Distance education courses elsewhere are often smaller, cheaper and more basic, and it is probably significant that the 1981 survey found more disaffected early school-leavers among non-OU correspondence students.

When you begin your first distance education course it represents a great challenge. You are generally faced with a large mass of printed material — both academic and bureaucratic — and the way forward and the rules of the game are not clear. In other educational settings you are usually surrounded by equally bemused students or there are tutors or old hands who will guide you through the first stages. With distance education you are almost always on your own — you have yet to meet your fellow students and your tutor. Even when you meet your fellow students you might find that they all seem to be more knowledgeable than you — they are teachers, bank managers and computer programmers. We stressed earlier that the distance study mode allowed diffident learners to test the water. Perhaps it is not surprising that many never get beyond this point and never submit any assignments for marking.

We also saw earlier that it was the long-term adult residential colleges that seemed to attract the greatest number of disaffected early school-leavers. Now these colleges are perhaps as far-removed from distance education as one can get, but it is worthwhile looking at some of their key characteristics and considering whether they can be replicated in distance education. Three of these key characteristics would seem to be a relevant curriculum, strong student support and a targeted access policy that produces an homogeneous student body. Some of these characteristics can and have been replicated in distance education initiatives such as the following:

i)   The Open University Community Education Programme in Strathclyde.
Under this scheme distance education material on babies and parenting were used with groups of working-class women in inner city areas of Glasgow. The women met regularly and studied as a group. Many used this experience as a spring board into jobs or further courses (Farnes, 1990).

ii)   The University Studies and Weekend College Programme in Detroit.
This programme was designed specifically to attract industrial workers into higher education (Feinstein, 1979). The degree-level curriculum was based firmly in the context of modern, multi-cultural, urban American society. The teaching delivery mode included the use of local TV stations and tutorials held in factories and trade union halls.

iii)   Group Admissions to the Open University Undergraduate Programme.
'Group admissions' have been used in several places in an attempt to ease the transition into undergraduate level distance study for students with low educational qualifications and low self-confidence. A group of students who have studied together on a lower level course elsewhere are encouraged to enrol on the same OU Foundation Course where they will continue as a tutorial group, possibly with the tutor from the previous course (Fielder and Redmond, 1978).

If distance education is to make a significant contribution in the area of disaffected adults then it must not only build on the strengths outlined earlier but also add in the extra dimensions needed in terms of teaching and support. It is important for all distance learners, but particularly disaffected ones, that they know exactly what they are embarking on. This calls for comprehensive and honest course descriptions plus good admissions counselling. Once on a course the students should be able to enlist all the help and support that they want and need, be it student self-help groups, computer-conferencing, phone-calls to tutors, counselling, help with study skills or whatever.

For distance courses to attract and retain disaffected learners they must achieve a delicate balance between flexibility and structure. On the one hand they must offer the returning adult the freedom to choose when, what and how to study. However, there must also be schedules to encourage regular progress and suggested pathways so that learners do not become overwhelmed by the amount of choice available. Successful new distance courses aimed at the disaffected are likely to be short and extremely accessible. Once the disaffected adults have gained the necessary self-confidence they are likely to want to switch into other modes of study. The 'Access modules' being developed by the OU are a case in point. They may be bought off the shelf in bookshops or studied as part of Access courses in other institutions, but in either case it is unlikely that the majority of learners will proceed to other OU courses.

Finally we must mention the role of open and distance learning in industry and commerce. There has been a great increase in these areas in recent years, driven by the growing need for re-training and up-dating coupled with the cost-effectiveness of distance learning. This approach can be highly successful with well-educated and highly motivated workers but what of the disaffected learner? It seems that more shop-floor workers are being offered the opportunity of distance learning, either as a fringe-benefit or as a means of encouraging workers to transfer into other employment or to seek further education — i.e., as a way to reduce the work-force. If this takes the form of sending off workers with a large correspondence course to study at home after a hard day's work it is unlikely to benefit the workers or the employers. What is required are specially written or tailored courses, time off work for study and fully-integrated student support systems. Otherwise the negative stereotypes associated with distance study that were referred to in the introduction will continue to flourish, and justifiably so.

References

FARNES, N. (1988) Open University Community Education: emancipation or domestication?, *Open Learning*, Vol. 3, No. 1, pp. 35–40.

FEINSTEIN, O. (1979) *A Humanities-Based Curriculum for Working Adults*, Detroit, USA.

FIELDER, R. and REDMOND, M. (1978) *An experiment in group admission to the Open University. Teaching at a Distance*, No. 11, pp. 17–24.

PERRY, W. (1976) *The Open University: a personal account*, The Open University Press, Milton Keynes.

PITTMAN, VON V. (1988) *Villainy, incompetence, and foolishness: Correspondence study in fiction*, *Distance Education*, Vol. 9, No. 2, pp. 225–33.

WOODLEY, A., WAGNER, L., SLOWEY, M., HAMILTON, M. and FULTON, O. (1987) *Choosing to Learn: adults in education*, Milton Keynes, SRHE/Open University Press.

Part 3

Outcomes and Achievements

9 Adult Learning and Success

Judith Calder

Introduction

In a formal education context, success has traditionally been taken to mean the satisfactory completion of a course of study or the passing of an exam or test. Course completion rates and pass rates have provided simple and easily understood measures of providers' success in retaining and in educating or training students to a specific standard. Students and trainees, having been given the opportunity to show that they could reach the standards set for them, either measured up to those standards by passing the appropriate exams, or by serving the appropriate period of training, or they were classified as having failed. The very limiting effects of this view of success in relation to the training and education of adults were for many years unrecognised. For a variety of reasons, this situation is now changing. The economic and political contexts within which formal education and training operate have been radically altered. At the same time, our knowledge and understanding of the participation of adults in learning have altered dramatically.

On the economic front, the continuing cycle of recessions in the UK, together with the effects of entry into the European Community, have focused the government's attention on the dismally low qualifications held by our workforce.

The shortages in the trained workforce are likely to be exacerbated by changes in the demographic profile of the country. The proportion of youngsters in the population has been declining and will continue to decline until the mid-1990s. This has led our decision-makers and opinion leaders to recognise the importance of the need to educate and train such previously neglected groups as adults. The need for those who have been rejected in the past as educational failures to have the opportunity to acquire new skills, and to up-date or up-grade existing skills is now more widely recognised.

The political context has been profoundly affected by the market-led ideological stance of the Thatcher, and subsequently the Major administrations. Dramatic changes have taken place in funding policy for different types of education and training provision for young school leavers and adults. The Parliamentary Under-Secretary of State for Education and Science has drawn attention to the fact that over a period of only two years there has been a major shift in the balance of public funding for higher education from grants to fees (Howarth, 1991:12).

Grant-funded, commercially sponsored and self-financing education and training ventures now compete with each other for clients and for resources. Fundamental changes have been and are being introduced in the funding and in the accountability systems devised for the public sector: for FE colleges, for the university sector and for workplace-based training. One effect of these changes has been to draw much greater attention to issues of accountability such as the effectiveness of different types of provision and the efficiency of the providing institutions.

The number of different agencies with a direct interest in the outcomes of education and training for adults has therefore multiplied over the past few years. Three of the key parties are undoubtedly the learners themselves, the providers of education and training and the employers. Employers have an increasingly important but ambiguous role in that not only are they the potential users or 'consumers' of trained people, but they can and do also act directly as sponsors or funders of education and training and they are also developing rapidly as providers of training in their own right. Whether or not a particular learning experience is considered successful can depend very much from whose viewpoint it is being considered. Realistically, therefore, it is necessary to look at the issue of outcomes of study from the different perspectives of the major parties involved — from the viewpoints of the learner, the provider, and the employer. This chapter will examine the variety of ways in which outcomes of study can be viewed. It will also discuss the effects of disaffection with formal education or training on people's attitudes to and perception of success and achievement in learning and training. Finally, it will examine the tension between success as perceived by the different major parties in relation to the particular needs of disaffected adults.

The Learners' Aims

Until twenty years ago, it was commonly believed that the majority of adults stopped learning once they had left school. Having had a short and often largely negative experience of a formal education system which labelled them as failures, it was logical that the vast majority would have no wish either to repeat the experience or to compound it with further confirmation of their lack of ability. The studies of participation in adult education and in training all appeared to suggest that the less successful a person had been at school, the less likely s/he was to take advantage of further education and training opportunities. It was as a result of research carried out in the late-1960s in Canada, and repeated worldwide over the next two decades that it began to be appreciated just how misleading this picture of adult learners was.

It is now recognised that most adults continue with sustained and deliberate learning throughout their lives. Typically, people will spend around five to seven hundred hours a year (or around ten to fourteen hours a week) undertaking deliberate learning activities, but the majority of these activities (for example, learning to drive, learning about indoor plants, holiday French) will have been planned and carried out without the help of a professional educator, and fewer than one in a hundred will be for credit (Tough, 1976:58–73). Education and training which is undertaken in formal structured settings is not an attractive proposition for disaffected adults. In contrast, they are comfortable with the learning that they undertake themselves and which they organise independently, even though it is largely unrecognised and rarely valued by others.

Learners get involved with formal education and training for many different reasons. These reasons may or may not be related to the content of the course. As Houle pointed out some years ago, the learner may want to achieve a specific goal, fulfil a social need, or s/he may have got 'hooked' on learning for its own sake and wish to participate for the sheer pleasure of learning (Houle, 1961). Realistically, there may be elements of each of these different types of aims in a learner's decision to study any one particular course. While it may be that a learner has a simple, well-defined immediate goal directly related to the learning s/he is undertaking, it is far more likely that an individual's goals will be complex and multi-layered. In effect, students are likely to have multiple objectives through which they hope to achieve both short term and longer term aims.

The recognition that learners may have both short term and long term aims is important. Courses are frequently undertaken in the pursuit of an ultimate objective which may take years to achieve. For example, a specific qualification may be a necessary precondition for further training which will then ultimately lead to a particular kind of job. While the actual process of participation in a particular course may be the main objective, as with learners who participate for the sheer pleasure of learning or because of the opportunities for social interaction which it may offer, adults who participate in education or training will more frequently see the course as a means to an end rather than an end in itself.

Providers' Perceptions of the Goals of Education and Training

Providers may be public or private organisations. They may offer second chance, return-to-learning, re-entry to work, initial training, re-training, updating and personal development courses; they may be in-service, company based or open entry; they can be organisations whose prime interest is in education and training, or whose prime responsibility is in other fields, for whom training and education has developed as a necessary service. Providers' assessments of outcomes will depend on their perceptions of their goals and there appear to be four major types of goals which providers hold:

- institution centred
- subject centred
- society/economy centred
- learner centred

These goals are not mutually exclusive in that they may all be held at the same time by one institution. But at any one point in time, different priorities will be assigned to these sets of goals with a consequent impact on the importance an institution gives to different types of outcomes.

Institution Centred

The institution centred goals may receive less public attention than other types of goals but they are clearly important. Institutional goals such as survival, status, and recognition provide the context within which the other central goals of the providing institutions are located. Changes in the funding of public sector providers and changes in government policy have brought the link between student numbers, funding and institutional survival to the fore. Private and voluntary sector providers have always had to operate within these sorts of constraints, but increasing competition for cash limited public funds has led to a greater reliance in the public sector on private funds raised through fee income and fundraising. This in turn makes the financial health and ultimately, the survival of all providers more susceptible to economic recession and more dependent on decisions taken by the individual institutions themselves.

Subject Centred

Education, as opposed to training, has to a large extent been traditionally viewed as being subject centred. The primary aim of subject centred provision is to transmit specific bodies of knowledge to a defined and recognised level. Many providers hold these goals. The problem for learners, however, is that they normally have to show mastery of this body of knowledge to achieve accreditation, regardless of whether or not all aspects of what they have to learn are relevant to their own goals. The government continues to claim support for the idea of scholarship as an aim for higher education but is also concerned that other types of goals should be addressed by providers of higher education. This has resulted in the somewhat ambivalent statement that

> In line with the government's aims, higher education has continued to promote the advancement of learning, and high levels of scholarship. Higher education has also responded to the need identified by the government . . . to take increasing account of the economic requirements of the country . . . [and] . . . to take account of the needs of industry and commerce . . . (DES, 1991)

Two points should be made about this statement. First, that there is a quite clear policy directive that the economic needs of the country take precedence over other needs, and secondly, that the needs of individuals are not highlighted for attention.

Society/Economy Centred

The government's concern that education and training providers should address the needs of the economy has already had a considerable impact on the stated goals of institutions in receipt of public funds. Earwaker, for example, deplored the contents of the mission statements published by the former polytechnics, commenting that, 'In many of these documents, students hardly figure at all' (Earwaker, 1991). He concluded in a rather lively article that:

> Higher education in modern Britain is clearly valued not for itself but for what it can lead to. Institutions of higher education shamelessly declare

without qualification that they exist to serve the needs of the economy. (Earwaker, 1991)

The concern that providers should offer courses and training which meet the needs of the economy was a major factor in the government's decision to set up Training and Enterprise Councils (TECs) in 1990. These were specifically established to 'Customise adult training so that everyone, including unemployed people and people returning to the labour market, have the right skills for the right job' (Employment Department, 1991).

Learner Centred

The British government is not alone in its focus on economic objectives. The chief executive of the Business and Technician Education Council (BTEC) has pointed out that at the transnational level such as the EC, 'the emphasis is put on vocational training to help the individual handle the effects of economic and social change', but that at the national level, member states focus on objectives 'such as creating jobs and building up the economy' (Sellars, 1991). The emphasis given to the individual at the EC level matches well with the learner centred goals of many providers at the local level. In learner centred provision, the emphasis is on enabling the learner to achieve a satisfactory learning experience: 'In general, this kind of course provides a safe learning environment, responsive to the needs of adults, in which students' confidence and skills can be developed' (Lalljee *et al.*, 1989). Such courses as 'Second Chance to Learn', 'Return to Learning' and other forms of Access courses are generally learner centred.

It was pointed out earlier that learners have long and short term goals. This is also the case with providers. The rate of technological change, the political agenda of funding agencies and the need to use training to adjust workforce supply all press providers to meet short term goals. Self-financing programmes are particularly susceptible to the accusation of 'cheque-book' led provision. The demands of scholarship, learning for life, the development of curricula which aim to teach coherent bodies of knowledge, the building up of institutional expertise can all be described as having longer term goals. The steady decline in the funds available to providers for the development of education and training which has these long term goals is a clear indicator of the priorities currently given to them.

Employers' Perspective

From the perspective of employers, the role of education and training is to ensure that a supply of people with the necessary skills at the appropriate level is available for employment when needed; and that they are available in the numbers required at a price the employer can afford. This rarely happens. Changes in employment needs, major reductions in the apprenticeship system, the low amount and lack of flexibility in initial training, updating and re-training provision have combined to make the UK workforce one of the least qualified in the industrial world. In spite of this, the employers themselves have not bridged the training gap. While larger employers do usually have an active training policy for their employees, most medium and small companies, who constitute the majority of employers, do not. Financial constraints, lack of interest by senior management, and indeed, the sheer struggle for survival with which many companies are faced mean that the training needs of their workers come low down on their list of priorities.

Employer as Consumer

The reduction in the number of unskilled and semi-skilled jobs and the accompanying increase in the numbers of jobs demanding new and specialist skills has led to employers experiencing considerable difficulties in recruiting people who have the skills they are looking for. Among the disadvantages to employers of relying mainly on recruitment to acquire skilled staff are:

- costs of recruitment
- time delays while new staff are found and inducted into the company
- staff redeployment problems with the unskilled or wrongly skilled existing staff
- vulnerability to competition by other companies for limited pool of skilled workers

The costs of advertising for and interviewing staff can be substantial. Even when someone with the right skills is found, time will be needed for induction to the company. If no one with the right skills can be found, then there will eventually be pressure to make some sort of appointment, even if the person appointed does not meet all the requirements. At the same time, the need for the redeployment of existing staff who no longer have the skills now required could well lead to redundancies, with all the negative effects on staff morale which this would involve. Competition from other companies for scarce staff is always a problem. Some employers have resorted to poaching staff from other employers but this is a short term and, in the end, self-defeating tactic.

Employer as Sponsor/Provider

For the majority of employers in the UK, training provision is restricted to the initial induction of new staff. While the government is quite clear that the training of employed people is the employers' responsibility, the employers themselves have, in the main, been less than enthusiastic about introducing or extending their training and development role. The percentage of employees receiving job-related training has been growing at only 1 per cent a year and, in 1990, only 15 per cent of the workforce received any form of job related training (HMSO, 1991). The major disadvantages to an employer of providing or sponsoring training for existing staff are cost and the risk of the loss of their investment should an employee leave. In contrast, the advantages to employers of sponsoring or training their own staff are considerable. They include:

- flexibility in staff deployment
- reduced recruitment costs due to staff retention

- higher likelihood of training in directly appropriate skills
- improved staff morale and commitment to the company

The 'in-company' sponsoring and training of staff is seen as a better investment for the longer term. It was to encourage this 'new model of education and training which assumes that companies and other employing organisations will become major providers of learning opportunities' (Jessup, 1991), that TECs were set up. There are 82 employer-led TECs and 22 Local Enterprise Companies (LECs) in Scotland which have now been set up with the express aim of getting employers, and in particular small and medium sized employers, committed to the idea of staff training. Control of the multi-million pound work-related further education budget has been transferred to the TECs to provide them with a baseline of resources for their work. The CBI has also led a successful campaign to persuade the government to adopt specific training targets. In particular, it is intended that all employees should be provided with training by 1996. However, it must be said that the training of adult employees still appears to enjoy a rather lower priority than the education and training of school leavers.

The Nature of Success for the Learner

The measures used by the learners themselves to determine whether or not they view the outcome of their studies as successful appear to be similar both for those who study courses which carry credit and for those studying courses which do not. In interviews with adult learners, certain criteria recur:

- the extent to which their study led to them acquiring or, conversely, losing confidence
- the extent to which the learner experiences any 'enjoyment' or pleasure in the learning or training process
- the balance between the costs of study and the perceived benefits
- the usefulness of the qualification or the skills and knowledge gained
- the quality of the learning experience.

Confidence

Confidence, its acquisition or retention, appears to play a key role in adults' judgments about the worth of a learning experience. The simple lack of confidence felt by many disaffected learners can affect their decisions about the courses which they are prepared to take in quite a fundamental way.

I considered other courses but I rejected them because I didn't want to fail, and I thought if it was something with exams then I would fail. (Student with exam phobia: Calder, 1989)

Among those who suffered from an initial lack of confidence but who nevertheless took the plunge to participate in a formal course, there can be a clear recognition of the importance which gains in confidence can make.

. . . surprisingly with a different attitude and growing confidence the whole thing started to fit into place so I got through it. (OU graduate: Calder, 1989)

The importance for confidence for adults is not just one of enabling people to acquire it, but also of sustaining the confidence where it already exists. Even for those who previously appeared to have no problems, very strong negative feelings about a learning experience can be produced if a loss of confidence is experienced.

> I came here with bags of confidence and I feel that's been undermined in lots of ways. I feel really insecure in as much, after the first week, feeling I wasn't really happy here. I wasn't enjoying any part of it. It was all like a trial, so much to take in and I wasn't relating to any of the other people in the group. (Mature BA Applied social studies student: Hanson, 1989:33)

Studies have shown that major gains are experienced in 'feelings of confidence and self-esteem' (Lalljee and West, 1989), 'ability to relate to other people of diverse backgrounds . . ., self-esteem and self confidence, feeling of accomplishment' (Swift, 1989), 'greater self-confidence and a sense of competence . . . opened up wider horizons, alongside wider knowledge and skills . . . new ambitions' (Swift, 1980). Other personal benefits identified in American studies include both quite specific skills related to their studies such as 'the ability to think analytically' and 'ability to write well' as well as less concrete gains such as 'wider perspectives' and 'increased self-confidence' (Swift, 1991). While such changes may have been part of a learner's original aims in deciding to participate in a course, it is frequently the case that they are seen as unexpected benefits.

Pleasure

The lack of enjoyment mentioned in the extract above is an example of another criterion which perhaps gets taken for granted. An interesting phenomenon is the apparent unexpectedness for some adults, and in particular for disaffected learners, of the sheer pleasure and satisfaction they have gained from what turns out to have been a positive learning experience.

> It was after I had finished and I realised how much I enjoyed this and I had this nothingness, this void because it had finished, and that I had enjoyed learning . . . I had found it very rich and stimulating and I didn't see what else there was for me to do because of not being able to do exams and things. . . .

> You just get a certificate of participation. I was quite pleased — I was looking through my assignments the other day. It was quite enjoyable. I'm actually thinking I'd like to do something else but I can't make up my mind what. Another thing is all the cost again . . . I like the idea of the discipline, the self-discipline of actually getting down to do it. (Woman whose schooling was 'a total disaster': Calder, 1989).

Costs

The costs of study are measured by adults in terms of time and of effects on personal relationships as well as in economic terms and can take on great importance when desired outcomes are not achieved. The course itself may have been completed successfully and the credit awarded, but adults often appear to judge the success of a course against the achievement or lack of achievement of the longer term primary aims. The greater the investment which an individual makes, whether economic, emotional, or of time, the greater the disappointment if the planned or hoped for outcomes do not materialise.

> A very frustrating experience causing family difficulties and not providing any form of job on graduation. I rather regret the time and money involved. (Swift, 1980)

> There are lots of cries about shortages of skills and where people are required . . . but there are no follow-ons from it. They're saying, we'll train people, we'll provide people with a new area of skill because society needs a skilled workforce in a variety of areas and it's as though they're training them and then they're coming through the golden gates at the end and saying 'What do we do from here?' [but] there's no follow-up . . . I never expected anyone to be waiting at the other end who would take me by the hand . . . it's not a disappointment but I think in a sense it's a waste. It's a waste of resources because if there are thousands of people with a wish to do something and been given a level of skills and they're not being put to good uses, it's a terrible loss. (OU graduate working as clerk in local government: Calder, 1989)

Usefulness

The question of the usefulness of a particular learning experience or of a particular qualification is frequently raised by learners.

> I didn't see the point in getting myself a bigger letter at the end saying I've done this and the other because it's of no interest to nobody, not even me. No, when I, when we get a problem, I go through it in that little course and I find out all the pros and cons of the particular subject. (Retired tradesman with technical qualifications doing a home study 'Governing Schools' course: Calder, 1989)

> I've done about a third of the course . . . I shall probably do the computer marked assessment just for my own satisfaction. No one will be at all interested in whether I finish or not. I hope I get to the end of it, but I may not because I'm pressed for time. But I would tend to skim read the bits I'm not interested in. (Businessman with degree: Calder, 1989)

The recognition of a learner's efforts by the award of a qualification can mean a great deal to people, especially to those who have experienced only failure in the past. However, the award of a credit or a qualification does need to be seen as distinct from the studying of a course or the undertaking of training. For example, just as many 'traditional' adult education courses are followed by adults with vocational goals in mind, so some courses whose topics covered appear to render them unsuitable to be assessed (for example, courses which are designed to help adults to cope with particular life demands, such as parenting, bereavement, looking after elderly relatives, handling redundancy and so on) may also be used by some of their students for vocational purposes. In practice, records of attendance and certificates of participation can often be used in support of job applications or applications for further training where either the content or the experience of participation in organised study is seen to be relevant. Similarly, courses which were specifically designed for vocational purposes may actually be studied by learners who only intend to use them for personal development.

Examples abound of students for whom success is not tied in with the formal recognition of a particular level of skill or understanding of a certain area of knowledge but to other goals; for example, the retired man who studies computer programming in order to keep his mind active, or the widow who joins a literature class in order to have some proper discussions on serious topics (Calder, 1989). For such students, success is tied to the achievement of aims, the nature of which only the individual student may be aware. While the learner herself and, perhaps, her teacher will be aware of the extent to which she has been successful in achieving her personal aims, the institution through which she is studying is unlikely to have any mechanism for recognising such achievements. To some extent, 'personal' successes such as those which are not formally recognised may account for the dissonance which can occur between teachers' perceptions of the success of a certain type of provision, and the authorities' perception.

Quality

The quality of the learning experience, although not in itself an outcome, does appear to affect people's perceptions of the usefulness or of the nature of what they took away with them from their studies.

> The local county council ran a five week course . . . it wasn't long enough, just evenings. They don't go into it deeply enough. There were too many people — there were probably sixty-odd people — now you can't go into a subject with that number of people because one or two hogged the floor . . . so we didn't learn anything really. (Retired electrical retailer: Calder, 1989)

Quality is very much a subjective measure, as indeed are the other criteria used by learners which have been discussed here. When adult learners assess whether or not a course or a formal learning opportunity has been successful, they draw on a complex and personal set of criteria which they use to judge their experiences and their outcomes to date. A learner's assessment of the worth of any particular course will change with the passage of time. After the short term goals are passed, the longer term goals will loom larger. For disaffected learners in particular, the effects of a positive learning experience may be lost if their longer term goals prove more elusive than anticipated. Contrariwise, the value of a learning experience to an individual may not become apparent for some considerable time. The question then for learners' perceptions of the value to them of the outcome of an education or training experience is not only the terms in which they value it, but the point in time at which they do the valuing.

Providers' Perceptions of Success

One result of the increasing competition for funds between providers in the public sector has been the growing move towards the adoption of performance indicators as a way of providing quantitative measures of outcomes. This is by no means a purely British phenomenon. David Bethel has described the financial driving force behind the spread of performance indicators over the OECD countries (Bethel, 1990). Performance indicators are sets of quantitative information about an institution which can be used by the institution's own management or by external agencies to assess how successfully or how badly an institution is performing. These are increasingly seen as important by the funding agencies, both as a way of comparing the performance of different providers, and as a way of increasing the efficiency of the providing institution itself by enabling it to evaluate its own performance. However, in order to assess an institution's performance, decisions must be taken about what is to be assessed and by what criteria.

In 1988, the CVCP had identified 54 different indicators of performance, the majority of which were indicators of financial performance (Sizer, 1990). The academic performance criteria relate to entry qualifications, throughput of students, and employment destinations (CNAA, 1989). It is, however, clearly recognised that the criteria which a providing institution uses to assess its performance will reflect its own aims, whether these are of extending access, specialising in certain areas of knowledge or skills, achieving good academic results or making a profit; which is not to say that these aims are mutually exclusive.

Of more concern, perhaps, is the paucity of criteria which relate to teaching quality. Crooks has pointed out that the only performance criterion of teaching quality recommended by the CVCP Working Party on performance indicators was the acceptability of the graduates in employment. She reports that:

> They were unable to find a satisfactory measure of teaching quality although they say 'we are convinced that there is a need for universities to undertake formal appraisal of teaching as a matter of good practice'. They see the use of student questionnaires on the content and presentation of courses as an important element in this analysis. (Crooks, 1987)

However, as Sizer comments, 'Publishable institutional teaching quality performance indicators are even further on the horizon than publishable research outcome measures' (*ibid*: 24).

In general, however, the government is aiming to measure institutional success in terms of quality assurance.

> The aim of quality assurance is to provide goods or services that satisfy customer expectations by ensuring that they conform to specifications . . .

This is in contrast to quality control, in which it is accepted that there
will be deficiencies amongst the items produced but that inspection and
testing will prevent the majority from reaching the customer. (Grover,
1991)

This description of the aims of quality assurance clearly raises the issue of just
who is the customer whose expectations are to be satisfied? The issue is complicated
by the presence of a variety of regulatory and monitoring bodies in addition to the
funding bodies, and the users of the provision. In the government White Paper on
further education, for example, it proposed that quality assurance be maintained
by the colleges themselves and through monitoring by examining and accreditation bodies, and by external assessors. The same emphasis on self-monitoring was
apparent in the White Paper on higher education, with institutional quality control
mechanisms being checked by a separate quality audit unit. External judgments
would be provided by quality assessment units which would monitor general
trends in quality across HE. The startling absence of any discussion of what
actually constitutes quality must be of concern.

Educational quality is very much a subjective issue, but by ignoring such
subjective aspects as the perceptions of the actual learners themselves and going
for the technically easy 'neutral' measures of success and performance, providers
and funders risk major errors of judgment about which courses should most
appropriately be provided for whom. The dangers of the pure 'efficiency' model
have already been bitterly debated in the USA. Franke-Wikberg reports that:

In the present political climate these simplified measures can be used in
a seemingly neutral way to legitimize the fact that certain groups will be
excluded from higher education. (Franke-Wikberg, 1990)

The concern is very much that the needs of disaffected learners are forgotten by
providers and by sponsors in their assessment of outcomes. Individual teachers
and trainers may be able to identify individual or group successes with learners
who bring a variety of problems with them. However, it remains very difficult
for providers or sponsors to acquire the evidence they need to make similar judgments at the institutional level without setting up special reviews and evaluations.
It is imperative that providers collect and synthesise evidence from learners and
tutors as well as using neutral throughput and outcome assessments. Otherwise it
is clear that special schemes may be at risk during a period when evidence of
institutional success is so economy centred rather than learner centred.

To a considerable extent, the problems associated with identifying and
measuring success is a methodological one. Indicators of success such as throughput figures and costs, which can be easily measured, are more likely to be used
than subjective judgments or complex indices based on student feedback. However,
there are signs that the inadequacies of the measures discussed so far are being
recognised. For example, attempts are being made to measure the more subjective
elements of learning outcomes. In the UK, Lalljee, Kearney and West have reported some success in this area with learners on 'Second Chance' courses. Using
standard psychological questionnaires to assess changes in participants' feelings of
confidence, self-esteem and feelings of control, they claim to be able to produce
statistically meaningful and valid scores. Similar work has been carried out in the

USA. The research emphasises that providers of courses for adults which are credit bearing should find out about and take into account the learners' perceptions of what the outcomes were from their studies (Swift, 1991). Assessment instruments have already been developed which attempt to measure gains among students in a range of what are termed 'personal growth and ability' areas which include aspects such as evidence of increased participation in community activities and voluntary organisations (Swift, 1989).

Employers' View of Success

Measures which employers use to assess the outcomes of education and training provision depending on whether the employer is looking at outcomes in relation to the recruitment of new staff, or in relation to staff training, re-training and updating. For the majority of employers, particularly small employers, the ease or difficulty of staff recruitment is the primary measure of the success or otherwise of education and training provision. Success in staff recruitment derives in the main from:

Availability of trained people
This is often based on the number of applicants for different types of jobs and the number who are assessed as suitable for interview. Unfortunately adults who have recently completed training or acquired a new qualification are frequently sifted out at this stage because they do not fulfil the initial selection criteria with respect to age, or expected career path.

Relevance of skills or knowledge
Common measures include the possession of appropriate qualifications and time served in a recognised capacity. For an adult who is trying to change careers, their previous experience may well be seen as irrelevant, even though their qualifications are in an appropriate area.

Level to which staff are trained
Again, the level of the qualifications and the status of recognised job experience are the key criteria. Adults who are trying to make the jump between manual or clerical to managerial or professional levels may find structural barriers even within their own companies which prevent this kind of movement.

Quality of training
It is important to the employer that the skills or knowledge held by the employee are reliable and up-to-date. Qualifications provide one form of guarantee of quality, as does whether or not the person's experience is recent. Employers need to be assured that qualifications are subject to some form of quality control mechanism.

Success is seen in similar but rather different terms by employers who are considering the question of whether or not to engage in the updating and re-training of existing staff. There must usually be clear financial benefits, so in theory the two questions which employers ask in relation to education and training for their employees should be:

1   whether it is worthwhile financially to engage in the sponsorship of education and training?

and, if the answer to the first question is yes,

2   which form of provision is the most cost effective?

Attempts have been made to quantify the benefits of funding or sponsoring education through the use of measures such as increases in production, decreases in cost, or in increased participation rates, either in the employing organisation or in society (Weisbrod, 1962). In his review of efforts to develop cost-benefit analyses for training, Blomberg identified some of the benefits for employers as being:

* increases in the productive value of the worker
* greater retention of workers in the company
* more discipline among workers
* fewer hazards in the workplace (Blomberg, 1989)

As Blomberg points out, corporate training may be specific or generalizable in nature, but regardless of which type it is, the aim of training is to increase employee productivity and organisational profits (*ibid.*, 1989).

One recommendation which is made in relation to cost-benefit analysis of employee training programmes concerns the period of time over which the benefits should be measured. For increased earnings, it is suggested that a ten year time period should be taken in relation to assessing the value of any training (Gay and Borus, 1980). For training which focuses on management succession, Blomberg cites evidence suggesting a three to four year period (*ibid.*). Other suggestions include the remaining amount of time spent in that job, or the remaining working life of the worker. This contrasts with the six month period after graduation which the CVCP Working Group use as one of their major student related Performance Indicators.

This touches on what is recognised widely as a problem area for employers in that the employee may well be the main beneficiary of any training. The more generalizable the training is, the more 'portable' will be the value of that training, leading to greater job mobility for the individual, with increased status and pay, but to greater turnover of staff for the employer unless the company recognises the greater worth of the employee in some way.

Even where the employer accepts that it is of commercial benefit to invest in education and training, the question of which form that provision should take still arises. A recent survey among medium and large companies about management education training concluded that the most important criteria for selecting a particular course or for deciding whether or not to sponsor a particular employee were:

* course content
* method of delivery (i.e., face-to-face, open, distance learning)
* reputation of the course provider (OBS, 1991).

When it comes to deciding whether a particular course or period of training was successful, the answer will, to a considerable extent, depend on who is doing the asking. The identification of an individual worker's training needs may be the responsibility of his or her line manager, the training officer (where there is one), the worker or some combination of the three. Similarly, when it comes to determining the success or otherwise of the course or of the training, the conclusion drawn may well differ among those involved, assuming that there is at least some feedback from the learner or from the trainer or training organisation.

The discussions about the criteria which employers use in determining the success or otherwise of training do make the assumption that employers' decisions about training and about recruitment are based on rational grounds. However, as with other humans, employers share the shortcomings of their society in terms of prejudices and misconceptions. Racism, sexism and ageism are all represented in employers' attitudes to the training of adults and to the recruitment of trained adults. For example, quite clear evidence exists which shows the reluctance of employers to recruit mature graduates. Woodley compared the employment situation of mature graduates with young graduates six months after graduation. He concluded that, 'Compared with those who went straight from school, those who entered university in their thirties and early forties were twice as likely to still be seeking their first job' (Woodley, 1991). These were not isolated conclusions. The Association of Graduate Career Advisory Services (AGCAS) has published its own report drawing attention to its concern that in spite of acknowledged shortages of skilled staff, anyone who does not fill the stereotype of the school or college leaver is likely to find it difficult to step on to the ladder or to make major job transitions which do not conform to the norm (AGCAS, 1991).

Conclusions

Disaffection is not a static state. An individual may be disaffected with education and training because of early experiences which have not been resolved. They will therefore enter their current studies with a jaundiced or negative view of the experience they are going to undertake. Others with happier experiences may begin their current studies or training with some anticipation of pleasure, but may become disaffected as a result of either the process or the outcome from the process of organised education or training in which they have just participated.

> I have not yet received the opportunity to test skills/ability relevant to the possession of a degree . . . I lost my job, and in applying for others I do not even get interviews. It does not seem to help me get another job, not even a low grade job. Losses: job, prospects — with resultant cynicism. . . . Consequence: Catch 22 situation and unemployment . . . It (studying with the OU) gave me false hopes. The result of six years application to getting a degree has made me feel embittered. (Swift, 1980)

> I've got a bit of a problem because I've certainly got more qualifications although that's no guarantee of anything nowadays in the present employment situation. I've got problems with my age particularly. . . . I mean the government says you've got to up-date your skills and you've got to reorientate yourself to the market which is changing at such a speed . . . but then if you go away and do that and come back in ten or

twenty years time and say 'here I am with my up-dated skills' and you don't feel there's any way you can get back into the system. You're an up-dated person but you're getting older so 'sorry we want people with those skills twenty years younger' so it seems that people are getting obsolete simply by their age in a sense. (Calder, 1989)

At the same time, disaffection may be experienced as a result of a particular type of provision, and may apply only to that form of provision, or it may be a recurrent problem for an individual learner. Certainly the reason for a person's disaffection will strongly affect their perceptions of the outcomes of their studies. A specific problem, such as exam phobia, may well be put in perspective by participation in a course which uses a different form of assessment (such as continuous assessment). The problem will still be there, but recognised for what it is, rather than as a general disaffection with education. A problem with the teaching may be specific to a particular type of provision (such as discomfort in or irritation with large groups) or may be a recurrent problem for the learner (e.g., sensitivity to criticism). Here again, the option for the learner is to learn to recognise what the causes of the problem are so that he or she can select learning opportunities which are likely to avoid or at least minimise the potential for further disaffection.

It is clear that there is some dissonance between perceptions of success between the learner, employer, provider and sponsor. At the present time it could be argued that the major clients of publicly-funded providers are the funding agencies, and that it is their criteria rather than those of the learner which such providers seek to meet. It also appears that employers' concerns can best be met if they themselves act as providers, or if they directly fund another agency to undertake this task. However, the potential for a conflict of interest between the learner and the 'employer as provider' is considerable. Such conflicts make the spread of disaffection more rather than less likely.

These differences between how the major parties involved in the provision and use of learning opportunities perceive success are exacerbated by the relatively primitive measures developed to date as formal measures of outcomes. There is an appreciation among providers of the potential of learning as a facilitator of change, at the personal and community as well as at the societal level. However, this understanding does not yet appear to have been incorporated in any widely-recognised outcome measures. In other words, there does not yet appear to be a way of reflecting the diversity of aims which the main parties involved in the learning process all hold. At present, the major performance indicators appear to reflect the concerns of major government funding agencies and of the providers who see these agencies as their clients. The outcomes which map onto the concerns of employers and of learners tend not to be represented. Statistical information on the outcomes for adults of formal study is so limited as to be almost useless for policy or strategic planning purposes. At the same time, ways of identifying and evaluating the successes of different forms of provision for adults, and particularly disaffected adults do exist, but are as yet methodologically complex to apply. Measures which take a longer term view, and which acknowledge and reflect the diversity of aims held by the main parties involved in the extension and support of adult learning and which attempt to measure the extent to which those aims are achieved are urgently needed.

Judith Calder

Bibliography

ASSOCIATION OF GRADUATE CAREERS ADVISORY SERVICES (1991) *Messages from Mature Graduates*, Central Services Unit, Association of Graduate Careers Services, Manchester.

BETHEL, D. (1991) 'A Global Urge to Appraise', *Times Higher Education Supplement*, 29.3.91.

BLOMBERG, R. (1989) 'Cost-benefit analysis of employee training: a literature review', *Adult Education Quarterly*, Vol. 39, No. 2, Winter 1989, pp. 89–98.

CALDER, J. (1989) 'A study of the relationship between deliberate change in adults and the use of media-based learning materials' Unpublished D. Phil. thesis, Oxford.

COUNCIL FOR NATIONAL ACADEMIC AWARDS (1989) 'Towards an educational audit', *Information Services Discussion Paper 3*, March 1989, CNAA, London.

CROOKS, B. (1987) *Indicators of performance at the Open University, with particular reference to the teaching quality*, Student Research Centre/IET Open University, Milton Keynes.

DES (1991) *Education and Training for the 21st Century*, HMSO, Cm 1541, London.

—— (1991) *Higher Education: A New Framework*, HMSO, Cm 1536, London.

—— (1991) *Training Statistics*, HMSO: London.

EARWAKER, J. (1991) 'Boo to the Barbarians.' *The Times Higher Education Supplement* 29.3.91.

EMPLOYMENT DEPARTMENT (1991) *Training Enterprise Councils*, Pamphlet issued by the TEC Branch, Sheffield.

FRANKE-WIKBERG, S. (1990) 'Evaluating Education Quality on the Institutional Level', *Higher Education Management*, Vol. 2, No. 3, November 1990.

GAY, R. and BORUS, M. (1980) 'Validating performance indicators for employment and training programmes', *Journal of Human Resources*, No. 5 pp. 29–48.

GROVER, R. (1991) 'Quality Assurance in Higher Education', *Teaching News*, No. 27 Spring 1991, Oxford Polytechnic.

HANSON, A. (1989) Mature Graduates speak for Themselves, in mimeo, Lancashire Polytechnic.

HOULE, C. (1961) *The Inquiring Mind: A Study of the Adult Who Continues to Learn*, University of Wisconsin Press, Madison.

HOWARTH, A. (1991) 'Market forces in Higher Education', *Higher Education Quarterly*, Vol. 45, No. 1 Winter, 1991, pp. 5–13, Oxford.

JESSUP, G. (1991) *Outcomes: NVQs and the Emerging Model of Education and Training*, The Falmer Press, London.

LALLJEE, M., KEARNEY, P. and WEST L. (1989) 'Confidence and Control: a Psychological Perspective on the Impact of "Second Chance to Learn"', *Studies in the Education of Adults*, Vol. 21, No. 1, April 1989.

MILTON KEYNES AND NORTH BUCKS TRAINING AND ENTERPRISE COUNCIL (1991) *Prospectus 1991*, Milton Keynes.

OBS (1991) *Open Business School Management Development Study 1991*, Prepared for the Open Business School by MAI, Open University, Milton Keynes.

PHILLIPS, M. (1991) 'Bigger holes mean net loss', *Guardian*, 19.4.91.

SIZER, J. (1990) 'Performance indicators and the management of universities in the UK, A summary of developments with commentary', in DOCHY, J., SEGERS, M. and WIJNEN, W. (Eds) *Management information and performance indicators in higher education: an international issue*, Van Gorcum, Assen, Maastricht.

SWIFT, B. (1980) 'What Open University Graduates Have Done', SRD Series No. 23. Institute of Educational Technology, Open University, Milton Keynes.

SWIFT, J. (1989) 'Liberal studies programmes and the adult college graduate: Assessment of the outcomes', *International Journal of Lifelong Education*, Vol. 8, No. 3 1989, pp. 197–20.

TOUGH, A. (1976) 'Self-planned learning and major personal change', in SMITH, R.M. (Ed.) *Adult Learning: Issues and Innovations*, ERIC Clearning House in Career Education, Northern Illinois University, pp. 58–73.

WEISBROD, B. (1962) 'Education and investment in human capital', *The Journal of Political Economy*, Suppl. pp. 106–123.

WOODLEY, A. (1991) 'Access to What? A Study of Mature Graduate Outcomes', *Higher Education Quarterly*, Vol. 45, No. 1 pp. 91–108.

10   A Society of Opportunity

Peter Raggatt

I . . . hope . . . to build a society of opportunity

(John Major, 29.11.90)

The Thatcher decade formally ended with John Major's election as leader of the Conservative party in November 1990. It was a decade of change for education and training, marked by a deluge of acronyms and new programmes. It was a poor Monday when the government was unable to announce a new initiative or to confirm that last week's pilot was now to go national. Bad publicity was a sure catalyst for action and there was a steady re-modelling and re-launching of schemes making serious evaluation problematic.

New government departments and agencies entered the arena. The Department of Employment took a substantial stake in education and training through the Manpower Services Commission. Initially focusing on training for adults and young people who had left school and college in 1982 it was charged with introducing and managing curriculum reform in schools through the Technical and Vocational Education Initiative (TVEI) and later assumed responsibility for 25 per cent of further education funding. The Department of Trade and Industry's speciality was 'enterprise', contributing to curriculum innovation in schools through Understanding British Industry (UBI) and to the re-education of teachers through Teachers into Business and Industry. The Department of Education and Science, chastened by these incursions into its domain, proclaimed the economic purposes of education and launched its own initiatives, PICKUP, the National Curriculum and GCSE, to name but a few.

Amidst this welter of activity was an overriding imperative: education and training must be geared towards serving the needs of the economy. Within that the vocational education and training system formed an important sub-set and reforms were set in process that are now beginning to affect other parts of the system.

This chapter examines that reform, briefly summarised as the introduction of competence-based qualifications, and assesses whether and how it may increase opportunities for adults, particularly those adults who missed out on the 'window of opportunity' at 16–19, and whether it will influence the take-up of new opportunities. It takes a broad view of disaffected adult learners, including those whose experiences with the educational system have been unhappy and ended in failure and those who simply believe that 'qualifications' are not for them. The chapter will begin by discussing the rationale for the new system and the principles underlying the change. It will then discuss its implementation and the need for procedures that will facilitate and support adult participation. It will conclude by re-assessing the reform in the broader context of social policy.

Reform

Origins

The driving force for the reform of the education and training system is economic. It is convenient to see its origins in a speech by the then Prime Minister, James Callaghan, at Ruskin College, Oxford in October 1976, though this was merely the most public critique of the perceived irresponsibility of the education system. The speech asserted that education should give a much higher priority to serving the needs of industry. It ushered in a period of curriculum and structural change in education that has been summarised by the term 'the new vocationalism'.

The substantive analysis that was to emerge over the next few years was, of course, more complex than that offered by Callaghan. It showed that the changes taking place in the economy were structural and permanent rather than temporary consequences of a cyclical recession induced by the rise in oil prices. The significant changes were products of increased automation in which capital replaced labour, and decentralisation of labour-intensive mature industries — for example clothing, footwear and motor manufacture — and of heavy industries such as iron and steel manufacture, to countries where labour costs were lower. These industries moved to Third World countries and, in some cases, to the European periphery. Both developments, automation and decentralisation, resulted in a decline in industrial employment in Britain.

These changes in the industrial economy gave notice that competition for world markets was now global, Britain was facing unprecedented international competition. Moreover, it was increasingly apparent that the opportunities for growth lay in the high technology and knowledge-based industries, in computing, information technology, business and financial services, all of which required advanced specialist skills, and in service industries such as hotels and catering, leisure and recreation. The future economy, it was argued, would need more people with managerial and professional skills. The direction of the shift was self-evident and the scale is substantial. Studies in Denmark and France, for example, indicate that from 1985 to 2005 the proportion of the workforce in varying degrees of managerial responsibility will double. In France this involves an increase from 17 per cent of the workforce to 34 per cent. More generally there have been powerful arguments that have emphasised the importance of enhanced communication and interpersonal skills providing the foundation for a more adaptable and flexible workforce.

Even more compelling than the immediate changes in the structure of the economy was the recognition that change was likely to be continuous and rapid. There was a need for a new approach to vocational education and training (VET), one in which adults had access to continuing opportunities to improve and develop new and advanced skills.

The additional element in the emerging analysis was the implications of the demographic changes in the latter part of the 1980s. These had for the most part been obscured, as indeed had the other changes, by the recession and the very high levels of youth and adult unemployment in the late 1970s and particularly in the early 1980s. Looking ahead, however, it was clear that the numbers of young people entering the labour market were set to decline by about one-third. Increasingly industry would have to recruit from the non-waged adult population, notably women, ethnic minorities and the long-term unemployed. This would necessitate new opportunities for training, particularly so because many adults in these groups have been disadvantaged in their access to education and training and lack basic skills. The scale of the problem has been revealed in a study involving all the 12,500 children born in one week in 1958. This has shown that six million adults, 13 per cent of the population, have basic problems with reading, writing, spelling or simple arithmetic (ALBSU, 1987); at least 300,000 of those cannot read or write at all in practical terms. Extrapolating these figures the Manpower Services Commission, which helped to fund the project, estimated that three million of the workforce are functionally illiterate.

Other member states in the European Community face similar difficulties in developing and upskilling their workforce but a brief comparative review indicates that Britain's problem is particularly acute. First, we start from a lower base line. As late as 1988 only 47 per cent of Britain's 16–18 population was in full-time education or training with a further 7 per cent in part time education or training; in France some 71 per cent of 16–18 year olds were in full-time education in 1987 while in Germany the figure for full-time and part-time education and training was 90 per cent. Second, as a recent European Commission survey of the community labour market has shown, in Britain only 38 per cent of the workforce has a vocational qualification (44 per cent males and 24 per cent of female workers); in France 80 per cent of the workforce has a recognised qualification, in Italy the figure is 79 per cent (reported in Education, 8.6.1990, p. 550).

The analysis of Britain's shortfall of skilled labour and the need to reform vocational education and training did not spring fully formed into the policy arena in the late-1970s but the main thrust is apparent in the approach and in-house papers of the Manpower Services Commission (MSC) (see Ainley and Corney, 1990). It is clearly evident in the highly influential *A New Training Initiative: a consultative document* (NTI) published by the MSC in 1981. This proposed a permanent, national and comprehensive training programme for all young people and stressed the need for a flexible, adaptable workforce capable of responding to the unpredictable challenges of technological and industrial change.

Principles

The government quickly endorsed the NTI and the three major national training objectives for the future of industrial training. For our purposes two have particular significance:

> to develop skill training including apprenticeship in such a way as to
> enable young people entering at different ages and with different edu-
> cational attainments to acquire agreed standards of skill appropriate to the

jobs available and to provide them with the basis for progress through further learning;

to open widespread opportunities for adults, whether employed or return-ing to work, to acquire, increase or update their skills and knowledge during their working lives. (Department of Employment, 1981, p. 3)

The associated programme for action set a target date of 1985 for recognised standards (of competence) for all the main craft, technical and professional skills to replace time-serving and age-restricted apprenticeships.

The NTI provided a blueprint for the reform of VET. It introduced the concept of standards of occupational competence, access for adults and progres-sion to higher levels of skills and knowledge. More than any other government document in the decade it was manifestly framed within a human resource de-velopment model in which the human resources developed through education and training are perceived as an investment.

Development

Over the next few years the competence-based approach was developed through the Youth Training Scheme. Confirmation that the government was committed to a system of vocational qualifications based on agreed standards, rather than time serving, was apparent in various publications, for example in the White Papers *Training for Jobs* (DE/DES, 1984) and *Working Together: Education and Training* (DE/DES, 1986). The latter endorsed the *Review of Vocational Qualifica-tions in England and Wales: A Report of the Working Group* (MSC/DES, 1986). The latter listed a number of weaknesses in the existing arrangements which had par-ticular significance for adults. These included: the many barriers to access to quali-fications and inadequate arrangements for progression and the transfer of credit; assessment methods which were biased towards the testing of knowledge rather than skill or competence; and insufficient recognition of learning gained outside formal education and training.

Working Together also announced that a National Council for Vocational Qualifications (NCVQ) was to be set up, charged with developing a framework of National Vocational Qualifications (NVQs) based on standards of occupational competence defined by 'effective and appropriate industry bodies' by 1991 (later postponed to December 1992). The framework was to embrace levels of awards up to and including higher levels of professional qualifications with the first four levels covering the range of achievement up to and including Higher National awards and their equivalents. The magnitude of the task set for NCVQ may best be understood by noting that no other nation has attempted before to define standards of occupational competence in this way and for the whole of its workforce.

The National Council was established in October 1986. It defined an NVQ as:

a statement of competence clearly relevant to work [and which] should incorporate specified standards in:

— the ability to perform in a range of work-related activities

and

the underpinning skills, knowledge and understanding required for performance in employment.

Higher level NVQs involve a greater breadth and range of competence, increasing complexity of competence, the ability to take individual responsibility, to plan and organise work and to supervise others. Thus an NVQ at:

Level I indicates: 'competence in the performance of a range of varied work activities most of which may be routine and predictable'.

Level II indicates: 'competence in a significant range of varied work activities, performed in a variety of contexts. Some of the activities are complex or non-routine, and there is some individual responsibility or autonomy'.

Level III indicates: 'competence in broad range of varied work activities performed in a wide variety of contexts and most of which are complex and non-routine. There is considerable responsibility and autonomy, and control or guidance of others is often required' (NCVQ, 1991).

The actual occupational competences are defined by lead industry bodies working with the Employment Department/TEED. Initially presented as 'employment-led' bodies they are best regarded as employer-led bodies as is clear from *Employment for the 1990s* (DE), the White Paper on the future of employment and training published at the end of 1988:

Standards must be identified by employers. Thus we need a system of employer-led organizations to identify and establish standards and secure recognition of them, sector by sector, or occupational group by occupational group.

NCVQ works with Awarding Bodies, advising them on the construction of NVQs, and accredits the award as an NVQ. Each NVQ is an aggregate of units of competence — each of which is concerned with a work function — and each unit is an aggregate of associated elements of competence. Units can be individually assessed and accredited. Competence is assessed against performance criteria in a relevant range of contexts, working conditions and situations. Work on defining occupational competences and NVQs has proceeded rapidly and by October 1990 more than 30 per cent of the working population were working in areas covered by the 240 NVQs that were available. By the end of 1992 about 1000 NVQs will be available covering occupations involving some 80 per cent of the workforce.

Key Provisions

In developing the new system the National Council made two key provisions: it provided for workplace assessment and for the Accreditation of Prior (Experiential) Learning (APL).

Workplace Assessment

Strongly encouraged and supported by the MSC and its successors, (the Training Commission, the Employment Department — the Training Agency and the Employment Department — the Training, Education and Enterprise Directorate) it stressed the assessment of performance in the workplace: 'As a general rule assessment of performance in the course of normal work offers the most natural form of evidence of competence and has several advantages, both technical and economic' (NCVQ, 1989).

Lead bodies and awarding bodies moved rapidly to implement this provision. Lead bodies for the hotel and catering, retail, clothing, and those for some other industries, stressed the need for assessment to be undertaken in realistic working situations. In many instances this meant that assessment had to be conducted in the workplace itself. This shattered the near monopoly that educational organisations had typically enjoyed over the delivery of vocational qualifications, effectively privatising their delivery. Any company is now able to negotiate with an awarding body to become an assessment centre for NVQs.

A large number of companies have been approved as assessment centres. In the retail industry many of the big chains now deliver Level I and Level II NVQs in retailing. They include Marks and Spencer, Boots the Chemist, WH Smith, Mothercare, Do It All, Sears Menswear and Milletts. In-company assessors, normally the candidate's supervisor or line manager, assess the candidate against performance criteria as specified in the national 'Standards'. The candidate's competence is assessed through observation supplemented as necessary with oral questioning. Similar arrangements have been adopted in the hotel and catering industry. Hotels, industrial catering units and other centres are approved by the Hotel and Catering Training Council (HCTC) and candidates are assessed by front-line assessors. In this case there is also a multiple choice knowledge test which is set by City and Guilds which, with the HCTC, is the Joint Awarding Body. [Authors note: In 1992 the Joint Awarding Body arrangement ended. City and Guilds and HCTC are now both accredited by NCVQ to award NVQs.]

This measure, of work-based or workplace assessment, and the accreditation of individual units has dramatically enhanced the access of adults to vocational qualifications. By placing the emphasis on the assessment of performance in the workplace, NVQs have opened the way for the inarticulate, the hesitant and even those lacking literacy skills to gain a footing on the qualification ladder, with whatever effects this may have on their motivation for progression to higher levels. What matters is that the candidate performs consistently on the job to the occupational standards established.

At the lower levels of NVQs competence can often be assessed by observation in the workplace. Such other evidence of competence as may be required in, for example, the NVQ Level II in Retailing is obtained by oral questioning. There is no need for candidates to provide written evidence. This may be particularly helpful for those disaffected adults whose experiences with educational institutions have been unrewarding or hostile, serving simply to vaccinate them from further contact and thus from qualifications. Now they will be able to gain recognition for individual elements and units of competence within their workplace (provided that it has been approved as a registered assessment centre by an awarding body).

The encouragement that accompanies such success may provide the confidence necessary to work towards the full NVQ.

The second provision, which may well have an even greater impact on opportunities for adults lacking in qualifications and reluctant to participate in education or training, is the accreditation of prior (experiential) learning (APL). This is a process through which competent but unqualified people can receive recognition and credit for their prior learning/achievement. Consider, for example, Sharon, a woman who left school at sixteen with no qualifications. Now 35 years old with three teenage children she has for the last seven years looked after the invoices, orders and VAT returns in her husband's small business. Her husband recently died and she needs to find work. But despite having looked after all the paperwork for the business Sharon has no qualifications and seems destined for casual, unskilled work. Indeed, this is where she starts, working for a contract cleaner at the Town Hall. While there she notices an advert for a position in the accounts office. The authority has an equal opportunities policy and provides an APL service as part of that policy. Leaflets on APL are available alongside the jobs vacant display board. Sharon takes one home with her, reads it that night and decides that it's worth following up.

The next morning Sharon turns up at the Personnel Department to get further details about the job and to find out how APL can help her. She describes her experience, her interest in the vacant post and her lack of formal qualifications. Her experience seems to correspond well with the job specification and the Personnel Officer outlines the APL process and arranges an appointment with the APL adviser a few days later. At that meeting Sharon again outlines her experience and with the adviser, who has been briefed about Sharon's interest in the accounts job, looks at the units of competence for a Level II NVQ which is listed as a relevant qualification. Sharon quickly picks out elements of competence that seem to match her experience. She's confident that she can meet many of the standards described. Her problem is proving it without a job.

Sharon and the adviser select one of the elements of competence: 'Prepare and despatch quotations, invoices and statements' and discuss how Sharon can provide evidence of her competence to satisfy the performance criteria for that element. These include:

a) All preparatory calculations, using agreed information, are correct
b) All quotations, invoices and statements are prepared correctly and despatched to correct recipients/destinations
c) All copies of documents are filed/distributed correctly

Talking this over with the adviser she realises that she still had a file of documents at home — quotations, invoices and statements — which provide direct evidence of her competence. She can also get a letter from the accountant who audited the business and from two suppliers confirming that they always dealt with her. She also has VAT invoices with transport charges and providing a cash discount facility. She suggests these as evidence. This is agreed as a good starting basis. The adviser uses this discussion to point out key features in the APL process — the need for the candidate to prove the authenticity of the evidence, i.e., that it is her own work; that the evidence always needs to be valid, i.e., it matches the competence being assessed; that there needs to be sufficient evidence of competence, e.g., for this element the documentation Sharon brings must include manual and computerised processing of invoices. Together they agree how Sharon should proceed to collect the necessary evidence. Sharon leaves the meeting with a copy of the units of competence and performance criteria for the NVQ, an Action Plan and a month to develop a portfolio of evidence.

On her return the assessor reviews the evidence that Sharon has produced. There is no difficulty in deciding to recommend that Sharon be credited with some units of competence but the assessor is less confident about others and asks Sharon to undertake some tests in the office. Sharon performs competently and is signed off for those. At the end of the APL process she still needs three further units before she can be awarded the Level II NVQ but none the less she is appointed to the Accounts Department. Three months later her workplace assessor signs off her last unit and in due course the awarding body forwards her NVQ — by which time she is thinking about working towards a Level III award, having realised that her business tasks and her voluntary work have enabled her to develop a number of organisational and management competences.

In combination with workplace assessment APL has the power to transform the relative proportions of qualified: unqualified workers in this country. But this is the potential. The reality, however, rests in large measure with employers, a group better known for their reluctance to invest in training than for facilitating opportunities.

Criticisms

The new system emphasises outcomes. It clarifies what is required of candidates seeking vocational qualifications, enabling them to trace their progression towards competence. It can make qualifications accessible to many adults who were previously eliminated at an early age and had little or no opportunity to participate in the VET system or to obtain qualifications. In doing it it should help to motivate many individuals who have been marginalised by their educational process. The NVQ system of qualifications and public specification of occupational competence also makes clear to employers what the holders of qualifications can do and eliminates one of the major criticisms which employers made of the previous system — that candidates achieving a vocational qualification may 'know' but can't 'do'. On the surface, then, it seems to have a lot going for it, but before we turn to its implementation and to what is actually happening it is important to record some significant criticisms of this new system.

The first concerns the principle of a system of qualifications based exclusively on the concept of occupational competence which is operationalised in employer-led, sector specific lead bodies. Employers' principal concerns are with the ability of workers to perform competently in the confines of the job — as a process operator, a sales assistant, a machinist and so on. The focus for the national standards is on what workers should be able to 'do'. The performance criteria provides the template for assessment. In so far as there is reference to knowledge and understanding it is justified *only* in terms of the individual's ability to do the job competently, i.e., knowledge and understanding are defined and valued solely in relation to employers' perception of need. It is context-bound, known and understood by the workers in the occupational sector and unlikely to be transferable to other situations or working contexts.

There are two problems with this. First, there must be some doubts about whether employers can define their needs effectively, even with the help of

Employment Department staff. Most of the evidence suggests that they take a very task-orientated approach to competence and a short-term view of need (see, for example, CBI, 1990). The narrowness of the sector specific NVQs produced for Levels I and II tends to confirm this criticism. The issue here is whether employers appreciate the effects of technological change on working practices in the most productive and efficient companies — the development of interdisciplinary multi-skilled work teams, new approaches to process control, the processing of information in new ways and so on. These developments lead inescapably to a broader view of occupational competence than that manifested in many current NVQs. In this broader view communication and interpersonal skills, literacy and numeracy and other skills are important components of *occupational* competence.

The second problem is essentially an extension of the previous point. The emphasis in national policy has been on the need for a flexible and adaptable workforce, one which is capable of accepting change and re-training as and when traditional industries decline and new ones develop. The emphasis has increasingly focused on defining core skills or generic competences which are broadly transferable between situations and occupations. They include a primary group of problem solving skills, communication skills and personal skills with a secondary group comprising information technology, the application of mathematics and foreign language. It is proposed that all NVQs should incorporate core skills from 1994. This can, however, only occur if individual lead bodies accept the argument and are prepared to re-write their standards.

Core skills have been cited here in relation to horizontal mobility, i.e., the mobility *between* occupations, but they are also key factors affecting vertical mobility, i.e., progression to higher levels *within* an occupation. Research currently in progress suggests that there is a big jump in the cognitive expectations embedded in Level III NVQs and in the form that assessment takes. There is, for example, much greater use of written assessments in which the candidate's knowledge and understanding of theory, principles and concepts will provide inferential evidence of competence. It is probable that many adult learners who were unsuccessful at school will lack the skills to express themselves adequately, particularly in those occupational sectors where the Level II NVQ requires no reading or writing — despite its proclaimed equivalence to five Grade 3 GCSEs.

The argument outlined in the previous three paragraphs may be briefly summarised: the NVQ reforms may sharply increase the numbers of qualified workers in British industry but will do little to increase competitiveness or to stem the decline in Britain's share of world markets. More pertinent to the issue addressed in this chapter is that, as presently constructed, NVQs though offering a route to a vocational qualification for disaffected learners, coming perhaps through ET, do not empower those learners by supporting the development of a broad range of transferable core skills which would enable *them* to make choices about their future.

The contrast with the approach used by our industrial competitors is sharp. No European vocational qualification is as narrow in scope as a Level I NVQ. There is nothing comparable, for example, with our Level I NVQ qualification (Prais, 1989). In Europe vocational qualifications, uniformly, require a broader understanding of principles and concepts in the vocational area (as well as practical abilities) and a corresponding breadth in training, including achievements in the native language, mathematics, social studies and, possibly, a foreign language. The contrast is between training directed, on the one hand, towards highly specific skills and, on the other, to more general skills and abilities which may provide an extended foundation for an occupational area. In Germany the trend is to increase both the general education component of vocational qualifications and the length of shared time in training for related occupations. For example, in the metal working industries the training regulations covering a range of qualifications for forty-two occupations have recently been revised; the new regulations define six skilled occupations which share a broad-based foundation lasting for one year. After this training is progressively differentiated according to specific occupational clusters and leads to sixteen qualification profiles (Raggatt, 1988).

A third area of concern is assessment. There are very considerable difficulties in guaranteeing that the standards (the specifications of occupational competence) are being consistently interpreted and applied in the multiplicity of workplaces that are, and may be, engaged in assessment around the country. Assessment practices vary widely. In no case is there a requirement that assessors are competent in the same terms as prescribed for NVQs. Some lead bodies and/or awarding bodies specify that the assessors are trained but none of the training needs to be competence based nor do training programmes focus on the principles and practices of assessment for competence. The criteria for approving assessment centres varies widely, as does the development of suitable procedures for verification — for checking that an assessment centre is doing what it agreed to do. The credibility of the NVQ system and thus the value of the qualifications gained will rest in very large measure on the development and maintenance of an effective system of assessment of consistent quality (see Raggatt, 1991, for a detailed discussion of this point). There are now positive signs that some of the issues are being tackled. For example assessor and verifier competences have been defined and it is probable that awarding bodies will increasingly require assessment to be undertaken by competent and qualified assessors.

Realities

It is, of course, still early days in the development and implementation of the NVQ system. Many employers, particularly the smaller ones, have never heard of NVQs or the competence-based approach to vocational qualifications. NVQs are, however, now becoming better known through government training schemes — all ET and YT trainees must work towards NVQ qualifications — the publicity given to large companies that use NVQs and through the adoption of NVQs as the main qualification for the occupational sector. This last example is true of the care sector which is introducing NVQs for the wide range of care workers in the NHS and in residential, day and domiciliary care. This huge investment is, in part, a product of the radical reform in nurse training and the consequent need for qualified workers to take over activities previously undertaken by student nurses.

Access

Policies on access to NVQs vary widely among private and public sector organisation. The retail trade which employs more people than any other sector provides a particularly instructive example of the way in which the potential of the NVQ system can be realised and how employers act as gatekeepers, controlling access to opportunities and qualifications of adult learners.

Many employees in the retail trade are female and part-time, fitting their work around other responsibilities. They are not well paid. NVQs, which can be delivered through the workplace, could provide a significant opportunity to improve their qualifications and life chances and, in doing so, would promote equal opportunities. But it requires support from employers who may work to a different agenda. Some companies have adopted NVQs on a large scale, for example, in 1990 Boots the Chemist introduced NVQs for all its new full-time sales assistants. In other instances companies allow access only to young trainees. We can also expect to see training programmes increasingly selectively incorporating the competences specified by lead bodies, as their work and that of NCVQ becomes better known, but without providing assessment towards NVQs. This may provide a better trained workforce but would not add to the stock of qualified workers.

The Boots approach is interesting. NVQs were introduced as part of a new corporate policy in which a central role was attributed to a human resource development strategy in which all staff would have an opportunity to develop their potential and careers. The company had become increasingly doubtful that young people would provide the main source of recruits. For some years the company had been increasingly dependent on women returners and part-time staff and with the sharp demographic decline already reducing the numbers of young people leaving school, the company believed that it would not recruit sufficient numbers of young workers. The introduction of NVQs into the mainstream staff development programme has had major consequences. First, it has given a high profile to NVQs. It is not just a scheme for young people and therefore in danger of being marginalised but ensures that a 'critical mass' of people are involved in working towards the Retail Certificate. Secondly, the visibility of training leading to a qualification for new full-time and part-time staff has encouraged existing staff to join the programme. The evaluation of the stores involved in the pilot programme was strongly positive, noting that staff morale had benefited and staff turnover was substantially lower than in other stores over the same period. This evaluation has helped to confirm the company policy.

Set against this is the approach of another large retailing company with branches in all major towns. The company restricts access to NVQs to young recruits, which is important for its corporate image, but has no plans to extend this opportunity to adults. Adult recruits are trained in company procedures and are allocated to a work station. They are given additional training as necessary to the company. The company believes that a full-scale training programme leading to NVQs would be expensive in assessor time, documentation, record keeping and so on. Not surprisingly the visibility of NVQs is low, few of the sales assistants know about it and the demand for access to the qualification is consequently very low.

Similar examples can be offered in manufacturing industry. On the positive side is Courtaulds Grafil Ltd, Europe's largest producer of carbon fibre (see Unwin, 1991, for a more complete account). In 1988 the company faced a problem that will affect many other companies. The machinery being used for production was increasingly sophisticated and in order to use it to best advantage skilled process operators were required. The company decided to introduce a competence-based training programme based on the proposed NVQs for this sector. Labour turnover dropped and the Chief Executive declared that the programme made a major contribution to workforce morale and motivation and improved the perceived status of the operatives.

The company is clearly satisfied that the introduction of NVQs is paying off but it is equally clear that the workforce is benefiting. The immediate bonus is increased pay — the workers get an extra £10 per week for a Level I NVQ and £20 for Level II — but the longer term benefits are the new opportunities to progress from low skilled, poorly rewarded jobs to higher levels. Such a congruence of perceived benefits — to both companies and to workers — is vital if the NVQs are to become widely available.

The principle of part accreditation is another feature of NVQs which has substantial potential for access. It also provides further insights into the ways in which employers can act as gatekeepers to opportunity. This is, perhaps, most easily illustrated through a brief consideration of developments in the care sector. NVQs in care are delivered in multi-site organisations. For example, a health authority will be approved as an assessment centre. The authority will deliver assessment in a variety of often highly specialised care facilities. In many of these sites health care assistants can only achieve a limited number of units of competence. If they are to achieve the full NVQ they will need to move to another unit. The commitment of managers to a well-organised and supported system for delivering NVQs is essential. There is little hard evidence on this to date but there is some indication that managers intend to allow access to NVQs in relation to the number of qualified workers that are needed [personal research]. It seems likely that there will be growing number of health care workers who hold part NVQs and will be unable to complete the qualification because assessment facilities are unavailable.

Progression

The NVQ system is based on a ladder principle. Completion of an NVQ at one level is a suitable foundation to progress to the next level. This may be more problematic in practice than in theory. Where assessment is in the workplace access will be controlled by the availability of supervisory level assessment opportunities. It may also be affected by the substantial jump in cognitive and intellectual demands between levels which has been reported in a number of occupational sectors and seems most evident between NVQ Levels II and III. There is some evidence that 'easy' and 'hard' routes to Level II NVQs are developing. The former is concerned solely with the competences and is awarded by a number of awarding bodies; the latter, regarded as a value added NVQ, is concerned with common skills and integrated assessment as well with the individual competences and is awarded by BTEC. The latter is regarded as providing a better preparation for Level III and for future managers.

There is also the worrying development of Outcome Related Funding (ORF) which has been introduced by Training and Enterprise Councils. ORF is essentially a payment by results process. Training providers participating in government funded training schemes, for example YT, are paid only a proportion of the training costs of each participant. The current level of payment is 75 per cent. The remainder of the fee (25 per cent) is paid if the trainee achieves a Level II NVQ within a specified period.

Two consequences are already evident. First, managing agents are becoming selective about the trainees they are prepared to accept. They choose the most able, the ones that seem most likely to achieve the NVQ in the given time. Adults and young people who have learning difficulties, who lack confidence or require extra support are omitted. Second, there is some evidence of an increased emphasis on pushing candidates through as fast as possible, of 'paring provision to the bone' in the process and narrowing activity to instrumental needs. It is too soon to estimate how pervasive this is but it clearly puts considerable pressure on the quality of NVQs and increases the importance of an effective quality assurance system.

Three developments may encourage employers to change their current indifference or opposition to NVQs for adult employees. The first is pressure from adult workers themselves. Will they accept being left out when there is provision for young employees to gain qualifications? Second, and adding to the potential power of adult employees, is the problem of the demographic time bomb that employers will increasingly face. Unable to rely on a steady supply of young people looking for jobs, they may seek to improve the working conditions and training opportunities for adult employees. The effects of this are muted at present by economic recession. The third is the influence of government schemes, particularly those such as Employment Training and Youth Training which require that all participants should work towards NVQs. The last year has, however, witnessed a sharp reduction in funding of these schemes and a cut of around one-third in the numbers of adults participating in ET. There is also the work of the Training and Enterprise Councils (Local Enterprise Companies in Scotland) who will be promoting training and the use of NVQs with local employers.

In the longer term, as NVQs become better known, it seems likely that training programmes leading to national vocational qualifications will be a feature in recruiting policies, particularly in areas where there is competition for labour. This may well be associated with an employer-based APL service, possibly in association with a local college of further education.

AP(E)L

To date most APL activity has been college-based. The national APL project supported by the Training Agency and by SCOTVEC ended in 1989. A number of colleges are now taking this forward independently and there should soon be useful evidence about the costs and effectiveness of APL and its use in different occupational sectors. It will be particularly important to monitor the take-up of APL according to gender, ethnicity and age and to compare the numbers of units of competence accredited to individuals from different social groups. APL is a potentially powerful mechanism for delivering equal opportunities. We need to see whether it fulfils its potential, and that will be affected by the way in which subsequent learning is organised. This could be problematic.

APL is an individual process. The initial assessment, normally based on a portfolio of evidence, leads to an action plan. Action plans will be unique and will require a system that provides individual routes to NVQs. This involves considerable commitment by organisations. The dominant system in colleges is based on learning (or instruction) in groups. Changing to a learner-centred workshop system in which individuals pursue their own pathways to NVQs will be a difficult and demanding process for colleges, and will require a major staff development programme. At first glance, companies will be far better placed to organise individual learning and assessment. This is to overlook the considerable demand on the resources required to undertake initial assessment, plan individual programmes in relation to operational needs, brief mentors and assessors and to maintain and review individual records.

There is some evidence of growing interest by employers in the public sector. The Economic Development Department of the City of Birmingham, for example, is supporting APL within a skills updating provision programme. Funded through the European Social Fund this is targeted at women who do not fulfil the criteria for Employment Training. Northamptonshire, too, is initiating a pilot scheme for its employees.

In the private sector the Training and Enterprise Councils (TECs) will have a particularly influential role to play and it is encouraging to see that the South and East Cheshire TEC is strongly promoting APL with employers in its region. The Employment Department (TEED) is also promoting APL in an initiative involving twenty TECs.

Training Credits

With few exceptions employers have been extraordinarily reluctant to invest in training, whether for managers or for shopfloor workers. The reasons for this are complex, involving cultural and structural issues and go beyond the scope of this chapter. It is, however, worth noting that training is essentially long term in its rewards and this puts it in conflict with the short-term perspective that many employers are virtually forced to adopt to meet the financial expectations of their bankers and shareholders or to avoid the predatory embrace of asset strippers or of the receiver.

Throughout the 1980s a number of government policies have emphasised the needs of employers who have in almost all respects done rather well. YTS, for example, enabled many employers to use public funds for training apprentices — in many instances YTS simply displaced existing company apprenticeship schemes — or it provided a publicly-funded means of selecting staff. The competence-based reform of vocational qualifications put, as Lord Young proclaimed, 'employers in the driving seat'. Employers dominated the lead bodies and the early standards of occupational competence were narrowly defined, concerned with specific skills which provide little opportunity of horizontal mobility to other occupations. They lacked any core or transferable skills component.

The introduction of training vouchers may give individuals more power. Ten pilot schemes were being introduced in TECs in April 1991. The people involved, all of whom will be on ET or YT schemes, will each receive a voucher which can be used for training. The choice will rest with the individual. They will be able to use it for college courses or with private training providers. They will also be able to use it for the occupational area of their choice though, no doubt, it will relate closely to the action plan they develop with their adviser. This points up a serious difficulty in seeking to help underpowered adult learners, they often do not know the system well enough to make informed choices and are all too easily guided by those with power.

Summary

Throughout the 1980s there was a major emphasis on changing the VET system to bring it into line with the perceived needs of employers. The development of

NVQs was one part of that programme. The early NVQs show a number of deficiencies, particularly in their preoccupation with a very narrow definition of occupational competence. The recent emphasis on transferable skills is more encouraging and may increase the opportunities for adults to achieve qualifications enabling them to progress to higher levels within the occupation or to move more easily to other occupational sectors. APL offers a kick start to previously unqualified but experienced and capable adults and workplace assessment potentially makes assessment readily available. Access is, however, controlled by employers whose interests may not coincide with those of workers and trainees. Stronger guarantees are needed to ensure that assessment will be available on demand and that all who seek to become qualified will have a chance to do so before we can convincingly contend that Britain is a 'society of opportunity'.

References

AINLEY, P. and CORNEY, M. (1990) *Training for the Future: the rise and fall of the Manpower Services Commission*, London, Cassell.

ALBSU (1987) *Literary, rumeracy and adults*, London, ALBSU.

CBI (1990) *Towards a Skills Revolution — a youth charter*, London, CBI.

DE (1981) *A New Training Initiative: a consultative document*, London, HMSO.

—— (1988) *Employment in the 1990s*, London, HMSO.

DE/DES (1984) *Training for Jobs*, London, HMSO.

—— (1986) *Working Together: Education and Training*, London, HMSO.

MSC/DES (1986) *Review of Vocational Qualifications in England and Wales: A Report of the Working Group*, London, HMSO.

Education, 8.6.1990, p. 550.

MAJOR, J. (1990) Speaking immediately after his appointment as Prime Minister. Reporter in *The Guardian*.

NCVQ (1991) *Criteria for National Vocational Qualifications*, London, NCVQ.

PRAIS, S.J. (1989) 'How Europe would see the new British initiatives for standardising vocational qualifications', *National Institute Economic Review*, August 1989.

RAGGATT, P. (1988) 'Quality control in the dual system of West Germany', *Oxford Review of Education*, Vol. 14, No. 2. pp. 163–186.

—— (1991) 'Quality assurance and NVQs', in RAGGATT, P. and UNWIN, L. (Eds) *Change and Intervention: vocational education and training*, London, Falmer.

UNWIN, L. (1991) 'NVQs and the man-made fibres industry: a case study of Courtaulds Grafil Ltd', in RAGGATT, P. and UNWIN, L. (Eds) *Change and Intervention: vocational education and training*, London, Falmer.

11 The Assessment of Prior Learning: Relating Experience, Competence and Knowledge

Linda Butler

In this chapter, which looks at relating experience, vocational competence and academic knowledge to accreditation through the process known as the Assessment of Prior Learning or APL, the tone and purpose is pragmatic rather than philosophical. The chapter covers, what the Assessment of Prior Learning is, how it is done and how far practice is established. It also covers how far, if at all, APL offers new ways and means for adults to obtain credible recognition for what they have learned outside formal education and training. This issue is addressed specifically in relation to women's access to accreditation.

Terms

In its most comprehensive and widely-used contemporary sense, the acronym APL refers to the assessment of all prior learning, certificated and uncertificated, formal and experiential, intentional and incidental, which is brought forward at the time of assessment for credit towards a vocational or academic qualification.

The term APL is used in this comprehensive sense throughout this chapter and therefore includes such practice as APEL, where the E stands for experiential, and APA, the Assessment of Prior Achievement. APEL commonly refers specifically to the assessment of learning which has been acquired through experience rather than through formal education. APA is the increasingly preferred term used in NVQ (National Vocational Qualification) assessment, reflecting the current emphasis of these awards on observable outcomes rather than underpinning knowledge or academic learning.

The APL Matrix (Figure 11.1) shows how formal, experiential, intentional and incidental learning can configure into an APL profile for potential accreditation. It is the essence of APL that competence or knowledge which one individual has acquired experientially and incidentally may have been acquired formally and intentionally by someone else. As an example of how APL works, a candidate for a National Vocational Qualification (NVQ) might have existing typing qualifications; s/he may have undertaken further uncertificated training in word processing; and s/he may have developed additional competence over some years in working in paid or unpaid work. All of this could potentially count towards credit for an RSA NVQ Level II qualification in Business Administration.

Figure 11.1: The APL Matrix

	Intentional Learning	Incidental Learning
Formal Learning	e.g. typing qualification	e.g. training to maintain the office photocopier
Experiential Learning	e.g. learning by mentoring and observation how to service a meeting	e.g. acquiring time management skills as a way of dealing with office pressures

Equally, a candidate for a Master's degree level credit for prior learning might put exactly the same range of sources forward in a claim for credit. She might successfully have completed one year of a degree course in drama; gone on to a variety of further formal but uncertificated educational experiences; and attained recognition for the quality of her/his work as a producer or playwright.

The Appeal of APL

APL has wide appeal at least superficially as an education and training concept. First, equating adults' experience with vocational and academic awards appears to offer a new way of redressing inequalities in access to formal education or training opportunities, whether from school or work. Second, and more positively, APL sits comfortably with the liberal education tradition that people are capable of acquiring both additional and quite new competence and knowledge in adult life. Third, the adult learner acquires national economic significance as the UK seeks to retrain and upskill its paid labour force in response to internal and European labour market pressures. The comparatively recent rise and rapid promotion of APL in vocational education and training programmes is certainly linked with Employment Department targets, for example that by the year 2000, a minimum of half the employed workforce should be qualified to NVQ Level III or its academic equivalent. Fourth, APL appears to offer the possibility of increasing education and training efficiency. The argument is that accrediting the competence or knowledge that people already have, and building from that shorter and more individually relevant learning programmes, might motivate larger numbers of participants, as well as lead to lower per capita costs.

Underlying Principles

In all APL undertaken for accreditation, whether vocational or academic, the onus is on the candidates themselves to prove to their assessors exactly what they have learned from their uncertificated formal education or training and from their experience. Merely going through an uncertificated course or through several years

Figure 11.2: Acceptable Evidence for the Assessment of Prior Learning in NVQS

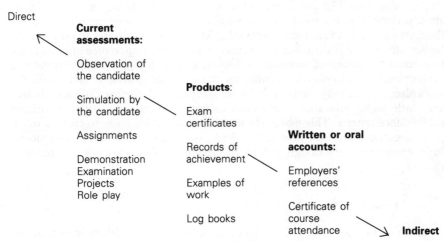

of apparently relevant experience is not enough to demonstrate vocational competence or academic learning: what counts is what has been learned rather than what has been experienced.

The nature of what is acceptable achieved learning is closely prescribed. In the NVQ example discussed earlier, the candidate would have to provide evidence of competence in all the units and elements of the award, against the award's specified performance criteria and range statements (see Chapter 10 for a discussion of NVQs), exactly as in a conventional NVQ assessment. The nature of the proof of learning is similarly closely prescribed. Where the candidate wishes to use APL to support a claim to competence, say, for example, for a complete unit of an award or for several elements of different units, s/he would have to offer evidence within the definitions of acceptability defined by the National Council for Vocational Qualifications (NCVQ) and by the awarding body itself. Thus, for example, the candidate's typing qualifications would have to be sufficiently recent, the uncertificated training would have to be appropriately endorsed, and the competence gained from working practice would also have to be evidenced. There is also a predisposition towards direct rather than indirect evidence, as shown in Figure 11.2. Evidence of candidates' prior learning in the form of the assessment of their current competence is more acceptable than evidence in historical form or as endorsed by others.

In the Master's degree level credit example, the candidate would have to offer evidence within the definitions of acceptability defined by the Council for National Academic Awards (CNAA)'s Credit Accumulation and Transfer Scheme (CATS) or as defined by a local CATS scheme (see Chapter 12 for further information about CATS). Thus, for example, this candidate's year's study on a degree programme, uncertificated courses and learning from paid work would all be subject through a CATS procedure to verification, matching against existing course offerings, and evaluation by independent assessors to determine what, if any, level and amount of credit was due.

There are some important differences of principle between APL practice in further education (FE) and higher education (HE). The assessment of performance, preferably in the workplace, is emphasised in FE competence-based qualifications such as NVQs, and underpinning knowledge is of lesser importance. In higher education it is the other way round. This greater importance of knowledge impacts on the nature of acceptable evidence, so that in higher education indirect evidence such as examination certificates and evidence generated away from the workplace, is generally likely to be more acceptable. A further difference is that very little higher education is currently expressed in outcomes, with associated performance criteria. This makes the matching of an APL claim to credit a much more negotiated business than with NVQs, even more so since HE institutions have autonomy in the design and award of degrees NVQs are not negotiable in this way.

How it is Done

At all levels of vocational and academic accreditation, the APL process is essentially the same, involving broadly the steps outlined below.

1 Potential candidates are provided with basic information about the APL procedure, how it can help them and what (if anything) it will cost them.
2 Candidates are helped to review their prior experience, either individually or through a workshop. The outcome of this review is a profile of the vocational competence or academic knowledge they are likely to have.
3 Profiles are matched to the qualifications or courses in which the candidates are interested.
4 Potential sources of evidence to support an individual's claim to APL to part or all of the award are identified.
5 Candidates are helped to generate a portfolio of evidence, on their own, in a workshop, or by working closely with a counsellor.
6 The evidence is assessed, using procedures acceptable to the awarding body.
7 Credit is awarded, or a further assessment plan is developed where the evidence submitted is not adequate for an accreditation.
8 In the light of the assessment, any further education or training required to support the candidate towards a complete award, or a further award, is planned.

Equally, the key staff functions in APL, which are advising and assessing, are essentially the same at all levels of vocational and academic credit. The APL adviser (also referred to as a counsellor or mentor) helps the candidate to reflect on experience, select a suitable route to assessment and develop a portfolio. S/he needs no special subject expertise but is expected to build up a supportive relationship with the learner. The adviser is viewed organisationally as a guide and advocate for the candidate.

The assessor, on the other hand, reviews and assesses the evidence to ensure it is genuine and sufficient, and designs appropriate assessments where the evidence submitted falls short of requirements. The assessor is viewed organisationally as a subject expert and the 'gatekeeper' to credit, that is, s/he maintains control over

Figure 11.3: What Evidence is Valid?

Sue Hitchcock is a home computer enthusiast. She is a candidate for a Level 2 NVQ in Business Administration. She wishes to claim an APL-based credit for a unit on 'Computer Applications: Database' because of her hobby and offers a collection of computer programs from her own database as evidence.

Comment: The evidence provided is unlikely to be sufficient. Although competence-based awards emphasise learning outcomes a product like a computer program needs supplementing by observed performance. Without this there would be no guarantee that the products were entirely the candidate's own work, or that she could exercise them in a business environment.[1]

---

[1] *Source: Developing Competence. The Effective Trainer Series.* National Extension College, 1990.

allowable evidence, as laid down in the awarding bodies' guidelines. The case study at Figure 11.3, quoted from a trainer's manual, is an example of how this control operates. The assessor would probably question the candidate further, or ask her to do a demonstration in this case.

APL Without Accreditation

In its commonest current manifestation, APL has assessment for accreditation as its primary outcome. However, there is a longer-established form of APL which has as its primary outcome individual self-awareness and confidence-building. It is worthwhile at this point contrasting this older form of APL with the newer one.

The older form of APL is usually practised with students perceived by the receiving institution to be personally unconfident or unused to formal education and training. It has commonly been offered, for example, in Adult Basic Education and in Access to Higher Education courses aimed at women. It involves only step 2, and perhaps some of steps 3 and 8 of the process described earlier in the section 'How it is Done'. Traditional APL may be offered over a few days or several months, as an option or integrated within a course. It may or may not be called APL.

Characteristically, this APL without accreditation is:

   i)   client-led. In particular, descriptions of individuals' competence and knowledge and supporting evidence are designed by the student with help from the tutor

  ii)   centrally concerned to enable students to acknowledge whichever of their own achievements will help them achieve their personal goals

 iii)   as much about the educative process, such as developing self-awareness and direction, as it is about product, which could be a portfolio or a CV

  iv)   centred on a counselling and enabling relationship.

By contrast, APL for accreditation is characteristically:

   i)   institution-led. Competence standards are described and determined by national industry lead bodies and these standards form almost verbatim the content of the new vocational awards; and academic standards are described and determined by national or local awarding bodies

ii) centrally concerned with meeting external measures of evidence
iii) primarily focused on the outcome of accreditation
iv) centred on an advising and assessing relationship.

Barriers to Practice

APL for accreditation has been practised in the UK from about the second half of the 1980s, and in its unaccredited form for several years longer. So far, it has achieved little more than marginal status in either form.

Traditional APL without accreditation, may be described as marginal. First, because it is almost always reserved for those students perceived to have problems fitting into the mainstream offerings of the education or training institution, rather than made available for all students. Second, any course which does not attract accreditation but which is run in institutions whose main business is accreditation is by definition marginal. Traditional APL practice fails to attract accreditation in two ways. It does not attract accreditation in its own right, not even for a completed course or for a portfolio which has taken months to assemble and write; and neither does it act as the carrier of the student's claim to credit, in the way that the new APL does. At best, it acts as the carrier of the student's claim to access. In effect, APL without accreditation is a means of 'warming up' students to the ways of institutionalised formal learning. It is not a means of accommodating the institution to the student.

The new APL, with accreditation, is potentially much more of a challenge to institutional control of what is deemed to be valued learning. It seems to be the means by which vocational competence and academic knowledge acquired outside any education or training institution is accepted to have, and is awarded, exactly the same value as competence and knowledge acquired within the institution. Accredited APL is, as already noted, offered in higher and in further education. In higher education, it is reasonably described as marginal practice, since APL rarely crosses the divide into the older universities practice. Its acceptability to the former polytechnics is limited; not all of them offer it, nor all the departments among those institutions which do.

APL for credit in further education awards has only begun to emerge with the establishment of NVQs. Despite Employment Department national programmes in the late 1980s and early 90's and the continuing encouragement offered by the NCVQ, APL is still at the time of writing viewed with caution by the further education awarding bodies and has been very slow indeed to penetrate into college and training centre practice. It also appears that the demand so far from individual clients for accredited APL is very limited. Even when carefully marketed, APL has attracted lower numbers of enquiries than anticipated, and there is a high non-completion rate amongst those clients who do enrol.

How far, then, if at all, does the new APL offer ways and means for adults to obtain credible recognition for what they have learned outside formal education and training? In the rest of this section, seven barriers to the accreditation of prior learning are discussed.[1] Each is illustrated with reference to women's access to vocational and academic credit for the competence and knowledge they acquire from undertaking unpaid work in the home, community and in volunteering. Women over 25 years old are the largest under-qualified group in the adult population, and the group therefore to whom effort to improve access to credit might most properly be addressed. This group is also the most likely to be undertaking a large amount of unpaid work, instead of, or in addition of, paid work. Six million women between 16 and 60 years old work full-time in unpaid work; among large sectors of the population, one in two women and men undertake some form of voluntary work; and 1.2 million women and men in the UK give care to an elderly or disabled person for more than 20 hours per week.

Identification

Women themselves, as well as educators, trainers and employers, may not realise that their life experiences outside formal education and training provide opportunities to learn. This barrier is a particularly high one for women, in a socio-economic and cultural environment where unpaid work, especially in the home, is perceived to be trivial and low-skilled. That women themselves understand their unpaid work to offer no opportunities to learn is verified by the common reports in the literature of access of women who describe themselves as 'Just a housewife' who have learned 'Nothing' in their last five years in unpaid work in the home.

But how far do women's educators, trainers and employers realise that unpaid work provides opportunities to learn? Fieldwork undertaken for the NCVQ in 1989 revealed the almost universal assumption in FE that the new vocational awards were solely related to paid work, despite the clear and frequently repeated central message of the NCVQ that competence is acceptable for accreditation irrespective of the mode, duration or location in which it is acquired,[2] just as knowledge which may count towards higher education credit may be so acquired. In HE, it was not possible at the time of writing to identify any examples of unpaid work in the home, community or volunteering being offered as the basis for a claim to HE credit. There is no research in the UK on the extent to which employers identify unpaid work as a means of providing opportunities to learn competence relevant to their requirements.

Articulation

Women themselves, as well as educators, trainers and employers, may not be able to see the relationship between the competence and knowledge acquired through prior learning and that needed in education, training or employment. The barrier of articulation is critical in access to accreditation for women. APL philosophy and practice needs to be robust enough to override deeply-held sexist beliefs that women's work, especially their unpaid work in the home, is a 'vocation' and thus so different from the external vocational worlds as to make the competence and knowledge acquired in each quite distinct and non-transferable; or where transferable, to have lower value in the paid work world or in formal education than in the home.

The history of attempts at articulation are not encouraging. As discussed earlier, access courses aimed at women do use traditional APL, that is, APL without accreditation, to encourage women to re-evaluate the competence and knowledge they may have acquired in their unpaid work; but in failing to offer accreditation, these educators and trainers can be said to reinforce the very message that learning from unpaid work has no value outside the home. Even, the term 'Women Returners' implies that such individuals are returning either to learning or employment and that therefore what they have been doing in their unpaid work lives involves neither of these.

So how far are the component parts of the new APL for accreditation able to articulate fairly the relationship between unpaid work and vocational competence or academic knowledge? There is no doubt that competence-based awards, such as NVQs, do offer the basis for articulation in FE provision, since such awards lay out in detail exactly what candidates should be able to do and how they should go about proving it. As already noted, these awards are about performance to standard, not about the mode, duration or location of learning and so should be readily useable in unpaid work settings. This potential for articulation is not necessarily convincing for women themselves, who can be so alienated from their unpaid work competence that they dismiss as patronising any attempt to make such links.

Educators and trainers working with women from unpaid work report that their own major articulation problem is working with the strongly commercial and industrial workplace biased language of the new awards. Such tutors need to feel very confident of their ground to undertake the translation task required to show the equal application of the standard in question to the unpaid workplace, for example, to read 'home' for 'organisation'; or to challenge ill-defined and exclusive requirements which act as barriers to those in unpaid work, for example, that a candidate should be able to work to the demands of a business environment, without a definition of what a business environment is and precisely what its demands are. It is almost certainly the case that not one industry lead body took account of the articulation between paid and unpaid work settings in writing any of its occupational standards, which standards are the basis of the whole of the new awards system. Such guidance as is offered has come only as an afterthought by the NCVQ and some of the awarding bodies.

Assessment

Even where educators, trainers and employers accept that prior learning is relevant, accreditation may be limited because of difficulties in determining the scope and quality of the learning. APL has been greatly aided by the development of NVQ and awarding body and CATS systems for measuring and evaluating prior learning. However, procedures are by no means completely established; for example, some awarding bodies have not yet (1991) issued APL evidence guidelines, and there are no nationally agreed guidelines for APL in HE. Additionally, even where procedure is established, practice may not be. Prior learning comes in every sort of variety, and the tendency so far by advisers and assessors has been to act cautiously in the face of this variety, particularly in respect of unpaid work, rather than to develop the new procedures in a permissive and inclusive way. Few assessors have so far developed assessment procedures which accommodate unpaid work, for example by identifying potential community-based substitutes for paid workplace supervisors or by developing ways of compensating for the limited historical evidence of competence which may be available in the home (few women keep records of what they do). This last point illuminates a more fundamental problem, which is that awarding bodies' APL guidelines are themselves biased towards paid work settings.

Even if these practice issues can be resolved in ways which are inclusive of unpaid work, it is still the case that unpaid work is widely stereotyped as low-level and trivial. Such credit as derives from learning acquired in unpaid work is likely to reflect this underlying bias. It is understood that there have so far been no examples of degree level credit deriving from unpaid work in the home. However examples of degree level credit for learning acquired in voluntary organizations are beginning to emerge.

Knowledge Gaps

Because prior learning may not have been supervised within a formal programme, the competence and knowledge acquired is unlikely to cover completely the topics taught in a formal accredited programme. The embedding of APL in further and higher education is to a considerable extent dependent on accompanying fundamental changes to the organisation's offerings and systems. Perhaps the largest of these is the modularisation or unitisation of learning programmes, as well as their more open availability, for example, as part-time courses, distance learning packages or through drop-in workshop facilitation. All these changes greatly support the task of identifying and providing whatever 'top-up' education or training may be required for an individual who begins her search for accreditation through APL. Progress towards modularisation is limited and patchy; for example, it is much more common in the former polytechnics than in the older universities, while in further education it tends to follow the progress of NVQs, so that some departments will be modularised and others will not. With institutions very unlikely to offer APL across the range of their provision, even strong candidates for APL can find that they have little alternative but to take a full course.

Financial

Educators and trainers are reluctant to spend time and money on APL unless there is a related benefit, such as more students. APL is widely acknowledged by institutions to be an expensive process. As it has evolved so far in the UK, it requires individual and sometimes lengthy attention from the APL adviser and one or more assessors, to determine exactly what accreditable competence or knowledge is claimed, and to track closely its verification and assessment. APL has not been notably successful so far in either further or higher education in bringing in more students. It is therefore currently a low-incentive option for institutions, a cost (advising and assessment time), rather than a source of income (courses sold). However, in higher education, these costs may well be passed on to the individual in paid work or her/his employer, with the argument that the costs are potentially offset against the benefit to both sides of a shorter programme for the completion of the qualification. In further education, the practice of passing on the cost to the individual or employer is not established, so that the institution bears it all.

It is widely claimed in both sectors that it is in many cases cheaper for the individual, in time and money, to undertake a full course rather than seek credit towards some of it. There is something of the self-fulfilling prophesy in this claim, lying as it does, suspiciously close to institutions' own interests. APL is now such a highly advised and assessed process — one might almost term it such a highly policed process — that few candidates obtain much credit for their APL. A more liberal response towards accrediting prior learning might make the process more attractive to more candidates, so reducing the unit costs of advice and assessment and bringing in more students for 'top-up' learning. The question has to be asked how far established institutional interests wish this to happen. The provision of APL as a full-cost recovery service in either further or higher education is likely significantly to deter women in unpaid work from using it.

Policies

Awarding bodies and others may have regulations or informal policies which discourage the award of credit through APL. For higher education institutions, the award of credit through APL may require a change in regulations, as it may for further education awarding bodies which are required to make their awards open to APL in order to attract NCVQ approval. Many bodies have not yet made these changes and even where they have done so, delaying tactics such as failing to publish APL evidence guidelines may be used. Similarly, discouraging informal policies take the form of the over-exacting interpretation of APL regulations, or operating a local system which actually subverts the more liberal intention of the awarding or validating body. Such subversion has already appeared in respect of the relatively tiny amount of credit sought for unpaid work.

Beliefs

Some educators and trainers, as well as employers, fear that the acceptance of APL will mean lowering standards, particularly where APL leads to the accreditation of competence or knowledge acquired by women in unpaid work. The concern that APL carries with it the lowering of standards appears to be based on the notion that experience may be traded in, without verification or assessment, for an award for which other candidates may have studied for a year or longer against conventional assessment. In vocational education and training, the specific concern expressed is that inept practitioners will gain qualifications and so bring all such awards into doubt. In higher education, the specific concern is about buying degrees. Since the notion on which these concerns is based is mistaken, the high level of control exercised over access to credit through APL requires a different interpretation.

What appears to be at play here is a sense of threat that APL could close down courses, by making them unnecessary, or turn educators and trainers into little more than examiners, since by definition candidates have acquired much if not all of their prior learning without formal teaching, including in the case of unpaid work, in settings heretofore considered quite irrelevant to the acquisition of competence and knowledge. Accredited APL thus poses a profound challenge to education and training institutions' position of power as the prime repository, generator and judge of valued competence and knowledge.

Conclusions

In the alleviation of adults' disaffection towards formal education and training, APL appears to be a good idea currently hi-jacked by vested professional interests and inertia. It is therefore in all its infrastructure and practice also marred by sexism in respect of the accreditation of competence and knowledge acquired in unpaid work.

Potentially, as we have discussed, APL offers a promising bridge between experience and competence and knowledge and between vocation and vocational. Its relevance to women's unpaid work is subject to current research and development programmes which will perhaps lead to some reform and liberalisation of existing systems and procedures. In the meantime, practice across the whole of APL could be improved if the education and training establishment, from lecturers upward, were more able to come to terms with APL as an ally to their provision. Assessment offered with a genuine respect for candidates' prior learning is likely to be a great motivator to those candidates' subsequent take-up of formal education and training. In this case, less could mean more.

Sources of Further Information about APL

1 The National Council for Vocational Qualifications. 222 Euston Road, London NW1 2BZ
2 The CNAA Credit Accumulation and Transfer Scheme. 334-354 Grays Inn Road, London WC1X 8BP
3 The Employment Department Training, Enterprise and Education Directorate. (0742-593220). Moorfoot, Sheffield S1 4PQ.

Notes

1 The barriers discussed are adapted from information provided in 1989 to the author by Dr Ruth Ekstrom, Educational Testing Service, Princeton University, USA.
2 This unpublished research was conducted by the author for the NCVQ.

12 Credit Accumulation and Credit Transfer

Geoff Layer

Adults, Education and the Need for Change

The Context

Post-compulsory education has come under increasing pressure to change over the last decade. Reductions in public spending, the decline in the number of 16–18 year olds available for further and higher education, and a strong political wish to relate post-compulsory education more closely to the needs of industry and business, have, as we have seen in earlier chapters, been some of the major reasons for this.

As a result, both further and higher education have looked more closely at the cost of conventional courses, and have experimented with potentially cheaper alternatives, such as open and distance learning. The needs of mature and disadvantaged students have been taken more seriously, influencing the design of some courses and the type of institutional support offered. Special 'Access' courses have mushroomed, and college crèches are no longer a rarity.

The Problem

While many of these changes have been valuable to the adult student, they have left intact the linchpin of the educational system — the discrete course into which the student must fit. Conventional courses do not always suit adult learners, however, who characteristically have a wider range of needs and commitments than their 16 or 18-year-old counterparts. They may bring with them experiences of work and previous study. They may be planning to study while continuing in employment, or while caring for children or elderly relatives. Acquiring a further qualification may be an immediate goal or form part of a long-term plan for self or career development. Not surprisingly, adults wanting to return to education after a number of years outside the system, often fear a mismatch between their own needs and traditional provision, believing 'education is not for us' or 'we don't fit'.

At the National Association of Educational Guidance Workers' Conference in 1990 one of the workshops considered an adult's view of a traditional Higher

Education Institution. They concluded that for most adults, higher education is about:

- Predetermined courses
- Predetermined sequence of study
- Predetermined duration
- Predetermined attendance
- Predetermined location
- Predetermined demand-led entry criteria
- Predetermined assessment

Many of these features can equally well be found in further education. They represent the course-based 'core' of the traditional system, and they can all lead to adults being 'turned off'. It is too close to the school experience. They may have welcomed or accepted it then but now they and their lives have changed. Many need to develop confidence in their ability and a sense of control over the choices they are making before they can fully utilise what education has to offer.

A Strategy for Change

Further and higher education have developed many strategies which are intended to redress this image, and hopefully significant changes in the participation rate of adults will result. One type of development that is beginning to lift the barriers of traditional provision is that of credit accumulation and transfer.

Schemes which are similar in concept and overall design exist in both further and higher Education. Known as Credit Accumulation and Transfer Schemes (CATS) in higher education, and Open College Federations (OCF) in further education, the schemes are separate and different operationally but share a number of common features.

Schemes based on this principle can act as powerful catalysts for change, and enable educational institutions to respond more effectively to adults and their needs. No schemes guarantee this; they only allow institutions who want to change to do so. The amount of change depends on the nature of the driving force behind them, and the willingness of the participants. However, the successful introduction of such schemes necessitates major institutional change as they challenge course structures, academic year patterns, student support processes and structures and, in some cases, staff attitudes. Inevitably these schemes are developed alongside existing provision and therefore two systems operate in parallel, the traditional, course-based system and the more flexible credit accumulation system. This generates a degree of tension in institutions, particularly as each may be making different demands on finite resources. For example, a greater commitment to educational guidance required by a flexible structure may appear as a disproportionate investment of resources until the scheme is embedded into the institution.

Credit Accumulation and Credit Transfer

The main forms of credit accumulation and transfer schemes fall within the two broad categories previously mentioned:

    i)   Open College Federations (OCF)
    ii)   Credit Accumulation and Transfer Schemes (CATS)

Open College Federations

These are groupings of FE and Tertiary Colleges working with other partners to create a local system of accreditation. This accreditation means that a whole range of learning provision can be given a credit value which people can then use to seek progression within the education system or employment. This accreditation is normally directed towards forms of provision that did not previously carry any accreditation. This accreditation system normally sits alongside the standard provision of the colleges.

The Open College movement began in the mid-1970s when David Moore, then Principal of Nelson and Colne College, created with Lancashire Polytechnic and Lancaster University the Open College of the North West (OCNW). The original focus of this Open College, like many of the early moves, was to provide alternatives to traditional O and A level courses, thus offering a more widely accessible route to higher education. The OCNW was enormously successful and was responsible for the development of other Open Colleges in the country.

This initial development was taken a stage further in 1981 with the creation of the Manchester Open College Federation which provided an accreditation service spanning four levels, from adult basic education to preparation for higher education. This was primarily a credit accumulation system which enabled adults to achieve credit for a form of learning which had previously carried no formal recognition. The four levels adopted in Manchester have gradually been developed and amended collaboratively with the expansion of such federations and the review and evaluation of practice. These levels now form the basis of the Open College movement and are becoming more generally recognised and accepted nationally. Such a system could not be successful without significant staff development implications, enabling teaching staff to ensure that previously unassessed learning was assessed and that the learner was empowered to have control of their own learning.

The Open Colleges that developed in the 1980s were designed to fit local scenarios, some developed with educational guidance services, some providing access to higher education, and some, on the Manchester model, providing credit for learning. It is not surprising that the significant involvement of polytechnics in many of these Open Colleges assisted in the implementation of credit systems in higher education. Two notable examples are the Polytechnics of Liverpool and Sheffield, where David Robertson and Roy Bailey were prime movers in the development of the Open Colleges of Merseyside and South Yorkshire respectively.

The Open College Federations have joined together within the National Open College Network and have agreed broad aims, credit levels and definitions of credit. The aims are perhaps the most important step and can generally be represented as:

- to improve the quality of available provision
- to facilitate access, and in particular, progression through existing and new provision

- to encourage change in organisations in the interests of learners
- to improve the flexibility of available learning opportunities.

These aims are all directed at the needs of the adult learner and evidence shows that adults do want to receive recognition for what they have learnt.

> People on the Manor actually asked for credits . . . the idea met with a very high level of enthusiasm. People want their achievements to be recognised, they want something to show for it and something with currency value.

> I think the credits are a really great idea for someone like me who left school without any qualification, because by receiving them it will give me a sense of catching up slightly on what I've missed and restore some confidence in my own ability.

Credit Accumulation and Transfer Schemes

These schemes are found in higher education and generally exist within the guidelines of the Council of National Academic Awards CAT Scheme. Most of these schemes are replacing the existing form of higher education provision in those institutions adopting them. Open College Federations and CATS come together at the point of entry to higher education, although the Open College Federations are not designed with the primary purpose of preparing people for higher education.

In order to understand fully the opportunities opened up for adults by credit accumulation and transfer it is important to look at the evolution, principles and practices of these schemes. The national development of these schemes has primarily been contained either within local education authorities for Open College Federations or within HE institutions for CATS. Two exceptions for this trend have been in Merseyside and South Yorkshire, where linked Open College Federations have developed alongside CAT schemes in Liverpool and Sheffield City Polytechnics.

The development of credit accumulation and transfer in higher education dates back a number of years and is shown in practice through modular programmes. Much of this early work was aimed at 18-year-old school leavers and is based on routes of study leading to a qualification. A major source of influence in such developments has been the curriculum design and delivery found in the USA, which is based on a well-developed and understood credit-based system. This system enables students to transfer from one institution to another with credit, and to count that credit towards the degree they are seeking. This credit system also gives the students flexibility in the composition of their programme. Recent moves in the USA seem to be placing more restrictions on exactly what can be included in the programme leading to a degree. It tends not to be an open choice of any unit that is available (what is often referred to as a 'cafeteria' system) but to require a core and some electives.

The major push in the development of CATS in higher education was a report by Peter Toyne to the DES in 1979. Toyne defined credit accumulation and transfer as:

Essentially a process whereby qualifications, part qualifications and learning experiences are given appropriate recognition (credit) to enable students to progress in their studies without unnecessarily having to repeat material or levels of study, to transfer from one course to another, and gain further educational experience and qualifications without undue loss of time, thereby contributing to the maximisation of accumulated educational capital.

This was followed by the introduction by the CNAA of a central CAT Registry and guidelines for CATS. The success of this move is undoubtedly far greater than was envisaged when the Registry was set up. Indeed so successful has the development been that the need for such a Central Registry in its current form must now be questioned as it may have already served its purpose. The pace of CAT developments is such that since 1988 nearly all polytechnics have developed an institutional CAT scheme, or have plans to introduce one in the near future, and a smaller number of universities have entered CAT agreements with the CNAA. This rapid expansion means not only that all these institutions can carry out the same functions as the CNAA CAT Registry but that they can improve on that service as they deliver the learning programmes and the necessary learner support. The CNAA CAT Registry may now need to concentrate more on the dissemination of good practice and the maintenance of an accurate database.

All these institutional CAT schemes are based on broadly similar principles, although the actual implementation varies. To understand fully the significance of introducing such schemes, institutions have been forced to debate a variety of issues relating to curriculum design. Emerging from such discussions is a general agreement on the following principles:

- any form of learning, wherever it takes place, which is assessed at an appropriate level can be awarded credit
- compatibility with the CNAA credit tariff system is essential to an accessible transfer system
- individuals should be able to negotiate a programme leading to an award, and this should not be dictated to them.

The need for compatibility with the CNAA credit tariff system is important. It ensures that adults within an institutional framework know that they can take their credit to another institution and that it will mean something to that other institution.

The adoption of such principles can lead to major changes in the education opportunities offered to adults. However, adoption of the principles is not sufficient. It is the implementation of such principles that lead to change. Adoption of the principles alone can mean that the learners are left unsupported and lacking direction within a large and faceless institution.

The Sheffield Experience

An example of the cultural change that can take place in higher education is illustrated by the developments at Sheffield City Polytechnic. The polytechnic had developed its curriculum along the lines of individual sector-based courses serving the needs of a particular vocational body and group of students. The courses were structured in a very rigid manner with little flexibility and no common elements. In 1986 the Academic Board introduced a common curriculum structure by deciding that all degree courses should be made up of 18 units. One unit was equivalent to one-sixth of the assessed curriculum of a full-time student. This common structure led to the implementation of a CAT scheme in June 1988 which:

- included all the polytechnic's provision
- enabled the award of credit for prior learning
- placed the responsibility for negotiating a programme on the student
- allowed the student to negotiate the pace of learning
- introduced a new award called the Combined Studies programme which covered all the units in the polytechnic, coherence was to be determined by the match between the negotiated programme and the student's stated needs.

In effect, the CAT scheme over-rode all course regulations in the polytechnic and said to the student 'this is what we have, what do you want?' This was obviously a major culture change for staff and students but the interest expressed in the scheme by staff and prospective students was enormous. Significantly, the vast majority of people using the scheme are adults who want to return to some form of education, change direction or improve career prospects.

The following case studies show how the flexibility can be used to enable adults to utilise their experience and to negotiate programmes that fit their needs and timescales.

Sarah

Sarah left school at 16 and trained to be a nurse and then a midwife as well as completing a Diploma in Nursing. Under agreements between the CNAA and the English National Board for Nursing, Midwifery and Health Visiting, Sarah had credit towards a degree. Sarah is now a midwifery tutor and wishes to achieve a degree. She is unable to study full-time and has therefore negotiated a programme building on the credit she already has for courses she has completed, allowing her to claim credit for her prior experiential learning and to study units at the Polytechnic that fit her work and family commitments.

Sharon

Sharon left school at 18 with two A levels and joined the Civil Service working in what is now the Department of Employment. As a person with a heavy work load who undertook a variety of in-service training with her employer she was unable to attend classes at the polytechnic on a day-release basis. Sharon, therefore, negotiated credit for her in-house training and mixed that with units at the polytechnic to achieve a qualification.

Chris

Chris left school in 1983 and now works for Sheffield City Council in its Joint Transport Policy Unit. Chris wants to achieve a degree based on transport policy but there is no such degree in the area. He has therefore negotiated a programme mixing together units from a variety of polytechnic courses and work-based projects which are jointly supervised and assessed with his manager and the polytechnic. This will enable Chris to achieve the degree he wants and make maximum use of his work experience.

How do the Schemes Work?

The two schemes of credit accumulation and transfer operate on similar principles, although in higher education there is the advantage of a well-established peer review system of validation and accreditation. The Open College Federations have attempted to work collaboratively through the National Open College Network. This has enabled the member federations to agree a credit transfer framework based on a common definition of a unit of credit. There are no limits placed on the number of units that a provider may offer within a programme. The individual is awarded credit for units successfully completed and does not need to complete the whole programme to gain accreditation. In effect, the two systems are pursuing the notion of unitisation of the curriculum and enabling the student to build a programme from the units they wish to follow, although many restrictions may exist in the form of co- and pre-requisites.

Both systems are based on definitions of credit and level of achievement. The levels are important in the curricula design as it places the learning within a framework of progression. The systems collectively aspire to measure the level of achievement in respect of the anticipated learning outcomes. Considerable effort is still required to achieve this goal and the systems tend to measure the level against a benchmark within an existing system. This is particularly the case in HE where three levels are used which equate to the year of study of a full-time degree, with level one equating to year one and level three equating to year three.

The units of credit are also defined in each system with an increasingly common use of language. In the Open College Federations the unit of credit is based on the concept of notional time-based learning, with one unit of credit equating to 30 hours of learning opportunity. In order to determine the amount of credit, therefore, the notional amount of time involved in the learning process is assessed and then awarded a credit-rating. The CNAA framework is arrived at by working backwards from the degree and calculating the credit-rating of each unit in relation to the full degree. Within this framework, the honours degree is worth 360 credits, and the full-time degree year 120 credits. Units are divisions of 120 or 360. This is often referred to as being a 'degree centric' approach, paying little attention to the structure within the degree. This comment ignores the fact that when higher education institutions develop CAT schemes they introduce definitions of a unit of credit in order to implement the scheme. Such definitions are primarily for internal consumption, to facilitate curriculum design and the accumulation of credit. The following features of a unit of credit are widely accepted in CAT schemes in HE:

- a full-time student normally achieves an honours degree in three years and this usually equates to 360 credits
- in one year such a student would usually achieve 120 credits

- a full-time year is notionally made up of 30 weeks which means that each week is notionally worth four credits (the minimum size for a unit of credit within the CNAA framework)
- each week is notionally made up of 30 hours of directed learning and therefore a unit of four credits is equal to 30 hours of directed learning.

The use of 30 hours of directed learning as a credit marker is therefore used within both the Open College framework and that of higher education. Liverpool Polytechnic has attempted to bring the two schemes into closer alliance by moving away from direct comparison with the CNAA framework and stating that the minimum unit of credit is 1, and this equates with 30 hours of directed learning. A full-time student, therefore would typically achieve 30 credits per year and 90 credits for an honours degree. This scheme is still compatible with the CNAA framework as all that is actually now required is a currency exchange rate which in this case is that '4 CNAA credits = 1 Liverpool Polytechnic credit'. Similarly, the currency exchange rate with the Open University is one based on the contribution of the unit size towards the award and there is an on-going dialogue between the CNAA and the Open University on the actual mechanics of that exchange rate.

The major advantage of the Liverpool scheme is that within one significant geographical area the unit of credit is defined in a broadly similar way which can only facilitate flexible curriculum design across the colleges and the polytechnic. The credit-based schemes, therefore, bring greater opportunities to the adults in Merseyside by ensuring that the Open College and HE work together.

The nature of such collaboration depends entirely on the commitment of the organisations concerned to deliver an integrated, accessible programme for adults. The existence of credit-based schemes only facilitates the cooperation, it does not guarantee it. Another example of such collaboration is in Sheffield, where the Tertiary Colleges and the Polytechnic have agreed on a curriculum structure which enables adults to achieve credit from both the Open College and the Polytechnic and to have guaranteed progression to the later stages of programmes at the Polytechnic. This means that an adult following a particular learning programme with the intention of entering HE will take some units which have an Open College credit rating and some that have a CATS credit rating, thus integrating the curriculum and facilitating progression. This is achieved by the colleges providing parts of the Polytechnic's courses within an agreed framework.

What Real Benefits do the Schemes Provide for Adults?

The schemes offer major advantages to adults because they break down the curriculum into segments which can either be packaged into a programme or undertaken as individual segments. In HE the latter are still regarded as credit-bearing and can be used towards an award, which may be a degree or an intermediate award. Similarly in the Open College framework the segments are credit-bearing and can be collected as the programme develops. There is not, however, the accepted framework of awards into which such credit can easily fit, and this has to be negotiated with a course-validating body where appropriate. This is a major disadvantage of Open Colleges, and there is an obvious need for the Open College movement to negotiate recognition of its accreditation by a whole range of validating bodies in order to fully empower the adult to use the credit they have achieved.

The value of Open College credit may be limited to gaining entry to courses until the validating bodies such as BTEC, RSA and City and Guilds recognise the credit within their approval structure. This will hopefully happen soon. The development of NVQs and the demands of the adults with Open College credits may well provide the necessary impetus for such change. Already the Unit for the Development of Adult Continuing Education (UDACE) has published a development paper looking at future links between Open College Networks and National Vocational Qualifications.

In the HE framework the nature of the credit is addressed in a different way. The actual amount of credit that can be utilised will depend upon the nature of the programme the individual wishes to follow, and on the distinction between general credit and specific credit. General credit is the amount of credit an individual has gained within the framework, whereas specific credit is the amount the individual is able to use against the programme they wish to follow. The specific credit rating would normally be smaller than the general credit rating. Many adults who wish to achieve a qualification as quickly as possible will be able to negotiate a programme which meets their needs and maximises the use of their general credit, for example:

- a student who has successfully undertaken a unit in history with the Open University will have that unit recognised for general credit with an institution. If the student wishes to use that credit towards a degree in engineering physics the institution will determine the amount of specific credit against that particular degree. The amount of specific credit may be substantially smaller unless there is an element of general elective choice within the degree
- the same student may wish to use the credit against a general humanities degree, in which case the student may be able to devise a programme of study which ensures that the amount of specific credit will be the same as the general credit rating. The student will therefore have maximised the possible use of credit and will have shortened the period of study towards the degree.

As the curriculum is necessarily divided into units to achieve such schemes, teaching staff have been required to assess the value of particular segments of the curriculum in relation to the whole course, or in some cases in relation to learning outcomes. Through this kind of analysis, staff have developed their skills of curriculum design, and in particular, recognise the relevance of a wider variety of learning styles and approaches. These skills are then further developed through the delivery and on-going review of the curriculum. The different starting points of the learners, their different routes of study, and their diverse goals all place new demands on staff accustomed to a narrower framework.

This is particularly the case with the accreditation of prior achievement, either through:

- the Accreditation of Prior Learning (APL) where the learning has been undertaken in some formal context and been assessed, or

- the Accreditation of Prior Experiential Learning (APEL) where an assessment is made of what the individual has learnt from the experiences they have had.

Both these processes are difficult and time-consuming for institutions, but for adults they represent an opportunity to have their learning recognised and to make sure it counts. These processes are more firmly embedded within HE, primarily due to the role of the CNAA and the Open University in developing databanks and assessing forms of learning. The most difficult of these processes is APEL, and a range of strategies have been adopted to assist the adult to make the claim for credit. One of the most common is to work with the adult, helping them to identify their experiences and to document what has been learnt through the compilation of a portfolio, and finally to assess that learning. The existence of a credit-based curriculum makes such assessment much easier as it can be assessed against segments of learning which carry a value.

Another advantage of the credit-based curriculum is that the opportunities for adults to study part-time are enhanced. In addition to the part-time courses that exist, individuals can take the segments of full-time courses and build them into a programme.

How Can the Schemes be Utilised by Groups of Adults?

Adults entering such schemes and able to benefit from them will vary enormously in their background and expectations. Many will be wanting to re-enter the world of education, and the schemes provide the flexibility to meet their immediate needs while they fully consider further progress. These adults will come from a range of backgrounds and the only common issue is the desire to return to education. There will also be groups of adults who are employed in the same or similar organisations and are attracted by a scheme flexible enough to meet both their own personal aspirations and those of their employer.

The needs of those employed in the Health Service are a good example, particularly nurses and the professions allied to medicine. These professions represent major sections of the workforce, and in order to practise in such a role individuals must undertake a specific qualifying programme. These programmes differ between the professions but they are all capable of providing an individual with credit towards a further educational programme, in many cases towards a degree. The English National Board for Nursing, Midwifery and Health Visiting, for example, approves a number of qualifying and post-qualifying courses. Many of these courses now have a credit-rating towards a degree and the newly-introduced qualifying programmes (Project 2000) are to be validated at the level of a Diploma in Higher Education. The individual course credit-rating given to the ENB were assessed by the CNAA and published in 1989. The award of such credit-ratings immediately empowers thousands of adults employed as nurses to enter degree programmes with credit. Whilst this possibility has existed prior to such credit-ratings, the flexibility of the CAT schemes has led to an upsurge in interest. This is primarily due to the fact that the form of study can be negotiated, a very important factor when you work long and irregular hours, and because substantial credit can be given towards a qualification through the Accreditation of Prior Learning.

In order to examine the possibility of a structured approach to such a massive demand, the CNAA and the National Health Service commissioned a feasibility study of a Bachelor in Health Studies degree based on credit accumulation and transfer for nurses and professions allied to medicine. This study reported in September 1989 and further work has since been undertaken. The feasibility study looked at a multi-faceted approach to such a development with the possibility of employers, employees and higher education negotiating a collaborative programme based upon:

- taught units of study
- Accreditation of Prior Learning
- Accreditation of Prior Experiential Learning
- work-based learning.

This would enable the development of a relevant programme which would recognise prior learning and utilise current working, thus reducing the period of study towards a degree. Any adult undertaking such a programme will require significant guidance and counselling as will the line-managers involved. The advantages of such a scheme are that it enables a large number of adults who come from a similar background to negotiate an appropriate programme of learning with colleagues, and to develop the peer-support structures which support the learning process.

Such schemes of credit accumulation and transfer are not only concerned with the curriculum experience within educational institutions. Many of these schemes enable institutions to work with a range of employers to facilitate the award of credit for work-based learning programmes. Most of these programmes are aimed at adult employees who, in the majority of cases, would not have re-entered education without such opportunity.

In the economic climate of the 1990s, many organisations recognise the importance of having a well-trained workforce that is adaptable and highly skilled. These organisations invest in training and welcome the additional advantage that educational recognition gives for recruitment and retention. The South Yorkshire Open College Federation has carried out work with a range of organisations to accredit basic training in presentational, interviewing and selection techniques, for example. The accreditation gives the individual recognition for the learning that has been achieved and formal recognition within the education system.

A different example of adults being able to use the learning gained in the workplace is that of collaborative programmes. This is where programmes are designed which draw on workplace learning alongside open learning packages and some units or modules. If successfully completed the programme leads to a qualification. Such programmes provide those adults with educational qualifications they would not otherwise achieve. This is highlighted by the programme developed by Thames Polytechnic and the Woolwich Building Society which leads to the award of a BA in Business Studies.

These programmes place different stresses on the adults involved as by definition they are not part of the educational institution culture, but this is not significantly different from the experience found within open learning programmes. The support required for adults following these programmes needs to be more structured and open. In many cases the adults involved in such programmes are those who believe in self-reliance. A major element of the curriculum is therefore the kind of group activity which brings the participants together and promotes team building and mutual support.

What Changes are Implied for Institutions?

A Student-Centred Approach

In order to develop flexible and effective education provision based on credit accumulation and transfer it is important that institutions take fully into account the needs of students studying in such a manner. Many of them are adults and post-16 education has a mixed history of providing appropriate opportunities for mature students.

Student Support Factors

In developing such frameworks the student support factors need to be fully considered and then integrated into the system. The support factors that require immediate attention are:

- pre-entry guidance and negotiation
- post-entry guidance and counselling
- student-tracking systems
- staff awareness
- academic support
- peer-group support.

Many colleges, polytechnics, and universities will justifiably claim to have all these services and to provide particularly for mature students. But do they provide for students who are not following a standard package of course provision? The answer is probably not because the development of such services will have been based, quite properly, around their existing provision. Once adults arrive following a very different programme, the system is challenged. Unless the challenge is taken up, the adults will become marginalised, and all the hard work invested in attracting the adult back into education will have been wasted because they won't come back. All the above support systems can be provided fairly easily with the appropriate resources, except for staff awareness and peer-group support. Yet these are two of the major factors which are vital for the comfort of the adult.

Pre-entry Guidance and Negotiation

The provision of pre-entry guidance and information has become much more widespread in the 1980s, particularly through the development of Adult Guidance Services. Many of these, such as the Rotherham Educational Guidance Service for Adults, were funded through education support grants. However, much of their work is related to guidance and advice in respect of course-based systems, and any radical re-appraisal of the curriculum through CATs must ensure that such services are fully informed. Providers and guidance workers must be more aware of the skills needed for study on a unit or module as opposed to a course. The guidance may be very different because of the combination of units. The guidance worker also needs to be significantly more aware of the opportunities available, because they are more varied. It may be the case that in order to provide the appropriate level of guidance there must be a close partnership between guidance services and educational providers.

However, once the adult is in the college pursuing a programme of study further guidance will be needed to negotiate and re-negotiate further programmes. This is very different from the conventional notion that a student embarks on a set course and pursues it to the end. The students are in charge of what they are learning and they need guidance to achieve their aims and objectives. That guidance process must empower them to negotiate and not just lead them back into a closed delivery system.

Peer-group Support

The development of peer-group support is obviously very difficult in such schemes, as by creating flexibility, the standard peer-group support mechanism — the course — disappears, because the students are not all doing the same thing. Indeed, in some cases there may be only one person taking a particular combination. That student, and other small groups, face the danger of becoming very isolated. Those following a more conventional route will create their own student groupings which may well exclude the student maximising the flexibility. Any group work undertaken out of the classroom poses additional pressures on students utilising the flexibilities of CATs, as they will have a different timetable. This is, of course, exacerbated for adults who have other pressures in their life which limit their flexibility. This obviously needs to be addressed by teaching staff in the design of such activities, and by the students themselves in negotiating timescales and priorities with their colleagues. Because such students have to work much harder at creating peer groups, these tend to be more supportive, more structured and more active, all of which enrich and facilitate the learning experience for the student.

One example of peer-group support at Sheffield City Polytechnic takes the form of a specific society within the Students Union, initiated by a group of students, and the publication of a regular newsletter distributed to appropriate students. This has led to the formation of a number of small groupings of adults which fit around not only their curricular needs but their personal requirements as well.

Staff Awareness

Staff awareness is a key element in ensuring that an adult is made to feel part of the programmes and not just somebody allowed to sit in. Whilst as at any institution there will be differing views amongst the staff concerning the value of any change, it is vital to ensure that the non-believers understand the system and know how to respond to a differing clientele. One way of achieving this is through the use of structured staff development sessions and the production of comprehensive handbooks to help staff understand what is happening. There will still be a number who will claim not to know. This process should not be underestimated either in respect of its importance or its difficulty, particularly at a time when there is substantial change taking place in higher education coupled with expansion and declining resources. The handbooks and the detailed procedures that are developed need to ensure that all staff are made aware through user-friendly means, of relevant issues and processes. The institution should continually address particular aspects of the development as it affects different parts of the institution. This process of staff development will need to be sustained for a few years until such change is firmly embedded in the curriculum.

The development of such schemes also requires changes within the administrative process. Adults tend not to be too concerned with the administrative system until it does not provide what it should for each student. Adults, quite rightly, expect the system to be worked out and to reflect what they were expecting.

Mapping Progress

The introduction of any scheme of credit accumulation and transfer will lead to some change in an institution's curriculum. The significance and the pace of that change will be determined by the institution's commitment to such change. However, one issue that will and should be fully debated is that of the monitoring and evaluation of the scheme. This will enable the impact of the development to be measured and should enable the quality of the student experience to be evaluated. This challenge has yet to be taken up effectively by institutions for a number of reasons, not least that it tends to be courses that are reviewed and not the student experience as a whole.

Many of the schemes introduced into higher education are required to undergo rigorous internal reviews within a relatively short timescale, normally two or three years. The intention of such reviews is to support the embedding of the schemes into the institutional profile. These reviews often concentrate on a number of key factors including:

- staff development, measured by awareness and involvement in the process
- quality of the student experience, measured through student feedback
- recruitment strategy, measured through reference to strategic plans
- student performance, measured through analysis of results and destinations which must develop criteria appropriate to such flexibility.

The Open College Federations, which act as course accrediting bodies and not providers, tend to be reviewed by their supporting LEAs on a regular basis. These reviews, by definition, are not as extensive, as they do not systematically consider the student experience. This is seen as a function of the providers' quality assurance mechanisms. It is questionable, though, to what extent the Federations can monitor their impact until they can fully consider student experience within the learning context, by comparisons with other students in the colleges.

One of the criteria referred to as appropriate for evaluation is that of student performance. The success of the students on any scheme is a major factor in highlighting performance. An analysis of a report at Sheffield City Polytechnic of the students who entered a student negotiated programme of study in 1989/90 is revealing in identifying the achievement of the students. In this scheme 176 students were enrolled, of whom 77 per cent were mature students: 66 per cent of the students successfully completed that year's programme, 3 per cent failed and have left, 15 per cent have used their credit and changed their programmes to follow specific courses and 16 per cent have withdrawn for a variety of reasons and many will return. It soon becomes clear that the performance indicators that an institution may use to assess the quality of its provision may have to be reviewed to take account of student progress through such flexible schemes. One significant factor has been the number who have used the scheme to gain confidence, knowledge, understanding and skills. They have then been able to consider fully what type of programme they wish to follow and they have negotiated entry to such programmes, normally with specific credit. The scheme is therefore being used as a vehicle for access which is one of its major aims. This raises the important issue of guidance for students entering the scheme and those on other programmes. The days of following a narrow course programme for a fixed period of years may be over, but it is important that institutions do not ignore the support and guidance needs of any such changes.

Conclusion

Clearly significant progress has been made in starting the process of institutional change which is necessary not only to widen participation in education but to provide appropriate curricula and support systems. It is very easy for organisations to stay the same and insist that any adults wanting to come back into education must do so on the system's terms and conditions. This is particularly the case in higher education, where demand for places is buoyant. The commitment to access is such, however, that even the slowest moving organisations are starting to adopt the principles of credit accumulation and transfer. This is seen as a means of creating flexibility and providing a service to the large number of adults who wish to re-enter education but to remain in as much control of their lives as possible, a standard adult reaction.

It will not be long before every institution in the country will be able to provide information and guidance on the flexible service they provide, along with its many advantages. The cultural change is such, however, that merely changing the framework of provision is not enough. In order to make real opportunity available the whole ethos of our institutions must change and we must all treat adults with the same respect we would expect elsewhere. This means that all staff must be fully aware of all that is available. Reception areas must be more welcoming and impartial guidance must be available. Support structures must reflect the diversity of the student population, which will increasingly have to have a higher proportion of adults with more varied requirements.

Such developments cannot be achieved through piecemeal change; it requires a fundamental review of strategic plans, and delivery systems that can cope with the effect of the change. Tinkering with the system will not do. Promising adults a product which is not delivered will lead to greater disaffection, and they and their friends will have been lost to education forever.

Bibliography

BALL, SIR C. (1990) *More Means Different: Widening Access to Higher Education*, London, Royal Society of Arts.

CNAA (1990) *Going Modular*, London, CNAA.

LAYER, LYNE and MCMANUS (1989) *Feasibility Study on a CAT Scheme for Post Basic Award for Nurses and Professions Allied to Medicine*, London, CNAA.

NATIONAL ADVISORY BODY FOR PUBLIC SECTOR HIGHER EDUCATION (1987) *Report on Continuing Education*, London, NABPSHE.

ROBERTSON *et al.* (1990) *The Integrated Credit Scheme*, Liverpool, Liverpool John Moores University.

RABAN, COLIN (1990) 'Student experience and CATS', Unpublished, Sheffield, Sheffield City Polytechnic.

LAYER, G and RABAN, C (1988) *Credit Accumulation and Transfer Scheme*, Sheffield, Sheffield City Polytechnic.

UDACE (1989) *Open College Networks*, Leicester, UDACE.

UDACE (1990) *Open College Networks and National Vocational Qualifications*, Leicester, UDACE.

UDACE (1991) *What Can Graduates Do?* Leicester, UDACE.

WATSON, D *et al.* (1989) *Managing the Modular Course*, London, SRHE/Open University Press.

13 Informal Learning Opportunities and their Contribution to Overcoming Disaffection

Marian Lever

In this chapter I shall attempt to share with you the experience of the last ten years of working in an informal adult education project which has as a main aim the removal of barriers to learning. Rather than present a theoretical model of educa-- tional strategies, I shall describe the application of those strategies in a practical setting, an attempt to overcome the barriers created in disaffected learners by their previous experience so that they become motivated and confident students responsible for their own progress. First I shall give a brief description of the project so that you will be able to judge how applicable our experience is to your own situation. Secondly, I shall clarify what I mean by disaffection and some of the effects this can have on adults' participation in structured learning opportunities — even informal ones — and relate this to the types of disaffection observed within the target groups for the project. I shall explain the rationale behind the targeting of particular groups and outline the educational style adopted by the project and the objectives set, including how we validate the learning in a non-accredited course. Finally, I shall identify the areas in which we feel that we have been successful and those areas which still create problems; I shall also identify those aspects which are peculiar to Strathclyde and those which could be used in other areas.

The Strathclyde Open Learning Experiment

The Strathclyde Open Learning Experiment (SOLE) was set up in 1981 and is a collaboration between Strathclyde Regional Council and the Open University. The project aims to make community-based flexible learning opportunities more readily available in Strathclyde. We attempt to recruit adults as returners to education and to give them the confidence either to continue or to make an informed decision to stop. The learning opportunities on offer within the project are local, resource based and free to the participants. The resources we use are Open University study packs from the Institute of Continuing Education. Although the packs were written initially for individual learners, whenever possible we work with groups of learners so that students both support each other and have an audience with whom to rehearse their learning. Group leaders are recruited from many spheres — education, social work, health, from the communities in which the groups meet and from the groups themselves.

Expectations of Adult Learning

Statistics show that most adults do not take advantage of organised learning once they have completed their initial full-time programme. As children one of our main activities is the acquisition of as many skills and as much knowledge as we need or as the opportunities allow. But once we leave full-time education we have had our turn; leaving school is a rite of passage into adulthood. Not only that but education is often seen by the participants as a series of tests, many of which they fail. At each stage of secondary education the processes of accreditation mean that fewer people proceed to the next level because of academic failure, parental pressure or personal decision. Most of us leave school with a long mental list of things that we failed to achieve as well as a certificate listing those we did achieve.

This does not mean that adults do not learn once they leave school. We all continue to learn new skills, new facts, to absorb new ideas because we need or want to know them. But we do not learn many of these in organised classes; rather we teach ourselves. So it is not the ability to learn which is the barrier but the motivation or perhaps the lack of it. Disaffection is at the root of this rejection of the formal structured approach and creates many of the barriers to participation that many in outreach education work to overcome. Disaffection, in this context, is a mixture of anger, estrangement and inadequacy. Anger arises from the memories of failure, boredom or opportunities lost. This reinforces the feelings of inadequacy which come from being labelled so. This feeling seems to be stronger in women, many of whom recount stories of being undervalued as learners. Finally there is a feeling of estrangement from a system which seems irrelevant to everyday life and leaves so much to be found out later. All of these factors affect the perception of chances of success in adults' thinking about learning and therefore contribute to their reluctance to undertake formal classes of study.

The main feature of disaffection that we have observed in our students is that of inadequacy. Low self-esteem has been reinforced in them as far back as they can remember. In the early stages of many groups we do a series of exercises to recall both good and bad experiences of learning. Good experiences are usually bland and generalised but bad experiences are recalled vividly. And the message remembered is not that the processes were poor but that the student was unable to learn. This inadequacy is often reinforced by parents, in the case of women by references to the inappropriateness of learning to the assumed life role of wife and mother.

The Rationale for the Targeting of SOLE Participants

The SOLE project is funded by Strathclyde Regional Council and the main target groups are necessarily those set by them. The council operates a policy of positive discrimination in favour of disadvantaged groups as part of the effort to overcome the problems of multiple deprivation. This policy is outlined in the Social Strategy for the Eighties. It is, firstly, an area-based policy. Certain places within the region are defined as Areas of Priority Treatment (APTs) and they receive positive discrimination in terms of staffing and resources. They also qualify for special funding under the government Urban Aid funding mechanisms. This is very important in a non-statutory service such as adult education. The educational ethos is one of empowerment using community development approaches and the resource-based group learning which we promote is ideal for achieving this. The council also defines our target groups in terms of personal characteristics such as unemployment, lone parenthood, ethnic minority membership and adult returners, especially women. These priority groups are common to all outreach adult education projects. Our aim is to overcome the alienating effects of disaffection as quickly as we can so that the participants can enter main stream provision.

The Educational Ethos and the Objectives of the Project

Our objectives within the project are fourfold and simple. They are in no order that implies priority, for each group decides its own. At the end of the course the students:

- will have gained an appreciation of the knowledge content
- will have developed their own self-confidence and self-esteem
- will have developed their study skills
- will have enjoyed learning so that they include study, if appropriate, in their plans for the future.

Our methodology is also simple. We offer local resource-based learning to people, most of whom meet in areas of priority treatment in groups which include special target categories. We use student-centred approaches in terms of subject definition, practical arrangements and other issues commonly decided by the tutor. For example, in an attempt to overcome the reluctance of our client group to study we initially offer topics which are familiar and can be seen to be useful. If your definition of learning is that of a process of childhood which seems to have little relevance in adult life (how much hard-won, school-learned information do you actually use?) and at which you were not particularly successful then it is easy to see how it is given a low priority. Not only should the learning be familiar and useful but according to our objectives it should be an enjoyable experience and so we use learning groups. The group members provide for both the social and support needs of each other. As well as the knowledge and skills that our students acquire during their studies they also make some good friends. Often the successful learning that takes place is as dependent on the support that students offer each other as on anything the group leader does apart from encouraging this process. Recognising yourself as a learning resource for other students in the group is a step on the road to developing self-awareness and self-esteem. However, in order to energise the potential support that comes from group study students have to be recruited in the first place and at this stage the lack of confidence and the diffidence with which disaffected students approach study has to be overcome. Many barriers are perceived by the student and as many as possible must be removed to encourage participants. I will deal with the simple barriers first. These are the ones commonly recognised and for the removal of which most open or flexible learning systems have been designed. They are, of course, time, place and cost. Pacing and content are more complex in the mixed ability groups which we feel are an important support to vulnerable beginner-learners and will be dealt with once the easier problems have been 'solved'. When people have low expectations of what study can add to their lives because of disaffection, the simple barriers are sufficient to deter them from taking part.

Time

Even if a disaffected learner does identify a learning need it is probable that the course has already started or will not start for several months, by which time the need to study and therefore the motivation will be lost. We try not to recruit group members for any outreach course unless we have identified the resources and the group leader so that the course can start as soon as the participants wish and the practical arrangements can be made. Although an initial meeting may be at a time set by the leader — we have to start somewhere — once the icebreaker exercises have been completed the group sets about deciding on the most convenient time for meetings. In fact, the group is involved in as much of the practical organisation as possible. For this reason there is no typical pattern of group meetings. Although many prefer to avoid Monday or Friday and mornings seem to be more popular than afternoons there are evening and weekend groups. It depends on what suits the group and for this purpose the group leader is as entitled to a say as the other members. So we remove the barrier of timetables by allowing the group to negotiate its own.

Place

Many of the venues used by formal education are large and daunting buildings. It is not that the people inside are unfriendly and unhelpful but to someone who lacks self-confidence the entrance hall can be an intimidating place. Besides, these venues are often remote from the students and whilst easily accessible to the car owner they can require complex journeys by public transport. Again the organisational task of getting to the class is a real barrier, especially for a student who is not very sure of motivation or skills. SOLE groups meet in the most convenient local venue. Many groups meet in the local school, especially if there is a crèche provided. However, nurseries, clinics, community centres, social work offices, church halls, residential homes, village halls, pubs and even students' homes all provide the venues for our groups. What matters is that the place is convenient to the group, large enough for them to meet in and is welcoming in atmosphere. As the group chooses the place of meeting this removes another barrier to the disaffected learner. Almost all of our venues are available free of charge which reflects on how we are able to overcome the next barrier — that of cost.

Cost

When learning as an adult is given a low priority, then spending money on a course is another disincentive. Adults have many and varied calls on their budget and spending on themselves, especially for women, is given a very low priority indeed. So our courses are free to the participants. We have over the years built up a large resource of Open University packs using a variety of funding methods and therefore we can operate a course material loan service so that packs, however acquired, remain as a resource in the local community. This efficient use of the packages whilst creating management problems has enabled us to remove the cost barrier from our learners.

The other cost element is the tutor. Whilst some of our group leaders are paid usually on part-time contracts many of them are workers in related fields who have identified working with a group as a way of carrying forward their own work agenda. So, for example, teachers work with groups of parents as part of their strategy to increase parental involvement and health visitors fulfil part of their health education remit in this way. Even more encouragingly in the context of disaffection some of our group leaders are former students who demonstrate their new found confidence and self-esteem by working with a group themselves. So we try to counteract the low self-esteem and lack of motivation in our students by giving them as much control over the practical arrangements as possible. Elements such as the pace of the course and the contents can also create barriers to the involvement of disaffected learners.

Pacing

We use group delivery for the benefits it gives to hesitant learners in terms of support and yet to work this method demands a lock step approach which is an anathema to many proponents of flexible learning. 'In a place and at a pace' is a slogan often used for a delivery mechanism which we apply in other areas. It is well known that the pace of learning varies between individuals and for each individual at different stages of the course. Besides, disaffection and its demotivating effects are not the result of lack of ability but rather of a complex and unsatisfactory learning history. A pace which is too challenging just reinforces the low self-esteem and the 'I can't do that' feeling described by several of our students. How do we balance the need for the group as a whole to feel a sense of progress and achievement with the need for individuals to feel in control of their learning and not overwhelmed by too much content? First, we do encourage the group to set its own targets and we foster an atmosphere in the group which enables the raising of problems. Often when one person identifies a difficulty in completing the work others will also come forward. Knowing that you are not the only one with difficulties does reduce the tension. As each student has their own study pack for the duration of the course the gaps between the meetings in part allow for different rates of study and for particularly vulnerable students it is possible to arrange one-to-one support. Another strategy we use is to build in opportunities to assess progress regularly so that learners recognise their own success. Study is a complex of skills just like any other; feeling in control and able to make progress gives increased confidence which in turn leads to increased competence and so the skills develop.

Content

One of our aims throughout the project has been to involve the learners in choosing what they study. The negotiated curriculum sounds a fine principle but in the context of the disaffected learner it is difficult to achieve. How can you start to discuss the content of a course with people who have largely discounted education as a process with relevance to them? Our strategy has been to offer a range of courses initially so that learning is back on the agenda and to negotiate at a later stage. We have developed a range of workshop activities to enable groups to analyse and assess their skills, attitudes and beliefs and to identify their own targets for self-development. The 'New Directions' pack again is a flexible resource to be used as the group demands.

Recruitment

Obviously in the early stages of working in a particular area much effort goes into recruiting group members but that intense effort cannot continue for too long, especially with a region the size of Strathclyde. So the process must be one which sustains itself over time and encourages learners to volunteer. We use local publicity about successful groups to recruit new students. Word of mouth is the most effective way of overcoming that reluctance to use high status materials, even if its the 'Well if she can do it I'm sure I can too' that underpins the approach. In fact we now have students so confident about their relationship to materials-based learning that they become involved in the process of pilot testing new materials. And some groups even define their own learning needs, research them and write packs themselves so that other groups can learn too.

Assessment in Non-Accredited Courses

In this section I want to address some of the issues involved in assessment within formal adult education. For learning to be recognised as taking place we need some measures of behavioural change. We also need to validate the learning for the students to recognise their own progress and growth, yet we are not involved in any external accreditation and validation scheme which would set targets and measures for us and define competence. Such links would be inappropriate for us, working as we do largely in the area of life skills. For us to have a pass/fail system would pass on messages to our students that they are, for example, unfit parents or unhealthy. And yet this way of measuring progress is the one with which our students identify. So we compromise.

In terms of challenging disaffection it is important to build potential success in for all our learners and to give them measures of success early on and several times during the course. This keeps motivation high and fosters confidence in their ability. We do this by means of the multiple choice quizzes that accompany the courses, but we offer support to those who answers context questions incorrectly and encourage those who omit the activity-based ones to attempt them in future, as experiential learning is more effective. Students can resubmit if they wish. In this way we tread the difficult path between rubber stamping everyone and thus devaluing the achievement and reinforcing failure for some as the cost of success for others. Tutor support is crucial in this process. So there is a system of feedback during the course and our observation is that students prefer this to be applied from outside the group even in the initial stages of returning to learning. Success is something that students find hard to assess for themselves initially, although our ultimate aim is for the learners to identify their own learning as they become more self-confident.

Having successfully completed a course our students look for some mark of that success and we have, with the support of the Open University, developed a series of certificates which we award at presentation ceremonies. There are local variations, of course, in the form the ceremonies take, but they all involve local recognition of students' achievements and publicity for the students in their success. I started in this project ten years ago with a belief that learning was its own reward but I have come to understand how important external recognition of achievement is — to all students. I have learned through attending hundreds of presentations and talking to successful students how important these events are in reducing the effects of disaffection. For many of our students the opportunity to acquire these markers of success has been lacking and has contributed to their alienation from the system. They value the recognition and this in turn reinforces the growth in self-esteem and confidence. The presentation ceremonies are an important ingredient in overcoming the negative feelings about learning.

There are other measures of change that we identify. Students often become more aware of their self-presentation as they grow in confidence. They become more willing to express their own opinions rather than just accepting what they read. They accept that there can be more than one correct answer. All these mark increasing awareness of their own self-worth.

We are experimenting with different methods of assessing learning too — all with the aim of moving from external to self-assessment. Some groups now identify learning objectives for themselves and performance criteria for successful completion. 'This is what we want to get out of this course and this is how we will know when we've got it.' Other groups undertake this task as individuals — more of a challenge for group leaders trying to keep a joint learning process going but more useful for the individuals. Whether individual targets are disclosed to the whole group or just to the leader depends on the confidence level in the participants. All of these strategies rely on the individuals being able to frame objectives in advance. For less confident students we invite them to evaluate at the end by identifying the topics they have found most helpful and why.

Our most complex attempts to enable students to assess their own learning needs and ways of filling them as a prelude to self-assessment of learning surround the New Directions pack. In this pack the results of the various self-assessment exercises feed into a self-portrait. This self-portrait identifies strengths and areas to be worked on. Once the latter have been identified then an action planning exercise is undertaken and the student can move on with clearly expressed learning needs and a method of assessing their own progress towards the goal. So we aim to encourage increasing confidence in the student in terms of their achievements and in their own ability to judge success and failure.

The Achievements of the SOLE Project

In this section I would like briefly to identify the successes and otherwise of the project and to indicate where what we do may be applied elsewhere. I find it helpful to consider a series of tensions between opposing elements. For example, there is a tension between the high status materials that we use and the lack of self-esteem in our learners. Many people consider the materials middle class in outlook and intimidating to the learner. We have been successful in overcoming the barrier. Our recruitment figures demonstrate that. Sometimes we do it by subterfuge, setting up workshops at which learners first interact with the material and enjoy it and then learn where it comes from. Often it is the known local face suggesting the course that removes the fear. Whatever the method used, once the learners are involved and successful then the high status of the materials operates as a positive force in developing self-esteem. As for middle-class bias, that is often interpreted here as Englishness and this contributes to group cohesion. This is, of course, a feature which is not applicable everywhere! But the reinforcing effect of the status is.

We have seen that the materials do attract learners fairly easily if they are presented in a low key way. But that does not mean that they are accessible to everyone and we do not want to recruit learners to fail. We are currently experimenting with ways of presenting these materials in Strathclyde in ways which enable post-literacy students and members of our ethnic minority communities immediately to join groups and learn. This is a problem that we have yet to solve.

Another tension that we face is in terms of content. Identifying topics that are familiar to our learners is in tension with the need to avoid stereotyping. Because most of our students are women and the topics we offer are to do with life skills such as parenting, it is easy to see where our critics get their ammunition. And yet in order to recruit you have to offer topics which make sense to the learner. And once you have the learners in a group you can begin to develop both their own self-esteem and the awareness of other opportunities. We make every effort to move learners on to more structured and negotiated learning as soon as their confidence is raised; and in the New Directions workshops we have a mechanism for enabling the decision-making. We are not always successful in moving people on though. Some become addicted to the informal learning process and join group after group, however tangential the course is to their needs. For example, we have had 25-year-old women taking the Planning Retirement course.

Another tension we face is that between continuing to meet the needs of existing learners and continuing the outreach process to involve new learners. Many experimental projects find themselves drawn into changing their provision to meet the changing needs of their current clients rather than continuing to seek new clients. We have tried to overcome this by developing the New Directions pack but this is only in the early stages of use so its effectiveness cannot yet be judged. As resources become more difficult to acquire because of reduced funding, we are forced to be deliberate in our targeting of students and we will move students on to other opportunities more quickly. The danger is that we will move some people too quickly and build them up from success in our groups to failure in the next because their confidence is not sufficiently well developed.

The final tension I will discuss is that involved in pacing the group. Here we have a tension between the individual learning need and the group's need to progress. The support of the group is valuable for the morale of disaffected learners and yet the pressure to get on can be counter productive. Our solution has been to make sure that each student has their own materials and that there is a sufficient gap between meetings for the work to be accomplished.

What will translate elsewhere? The use of well-structured learning materials, the use of groups to support each other and the recognition of success through local presentations are all possible in other areas. The problems of those students disadvantaged by poor reading ability however are compounded by the reliance on resource-based learning and could reinforce failure and increase disaffection. Our approach has not yet solved that problem but we are working on it. Finally, you must make your own judgement about the tension between familiar subject matter and stereotyping.

Conclusion

None of the strategies described above is revolutionary or original. What we have had is the opportunity to apply a range of approaches over ten years and gradually to refine our techniques. The key ingredients seem to be small and achieveable tasks frequently presented to reinforce success and some prestigious recognition of that success. The group seems to be a valuable support to learners so that the benefits gained far outweigh the costs in terms of imposed pace. Finally, we try throughout the process to shift the emphasis from the tutor to the student to reinforce their potential as a learning resource for themselves and others. And we have been working for long enough to have seen large numbers of students move. from disaffection to enthusiasm for learning.

Notes on Contributors

Linda Butler: is a partner in Butler Miles Leigh, and specialises in equality issues in Human Resource Management. She has worked in research, teaching and administration in the education of adults and has written widely on educational guidance for adults and the assessment of prior learning.

Judith Calder: is Head of the Student Research Centre and Deputy Director of the Institute of Educational Technology at the Open University. She is involved in the evaluation of new forms of learning opportunities for adults and has a particular interest in adult learning strategies.

Roger Harrison: is a Lecturer with the School of Education at the Open University. He has worked on a range of courses relating to Adult Life transitions, and is currently Chair of the materials development team for the OU's Enterprise in Higher Education Programme.

Geoff Layer: is Head of the CAPs Unit at Sheffield Hallam University with responsibility for credit accumulation Access links, and South Yorkshire Open College Federation. He is a contributor to conferences and research projects on guidance to adults on entering higher education.

Robert Leach: is National Education Council's Assistant Director for Education. He joined NEC in 1990 after fifteen years teaching and staff development in FE and HE. He is responsible for developing programmes of study and materials for NEC and for learner support. He is also a writer of print and video-based learning materials.

Marian Lever: is the Flexible Access Co-ordinator at James Watt College, Greenock, and was formerly the Project Organiser of the Strathclyde Open Learning Experiment for Strathclyde Regional Council. She has a continued interest in 'enabling' adult returners.

Stina Lyon: is a Principal Lecturer and Head of the Sociology Division at the South Bank University. Her research interests are in the Sociology of Higher Education with particular reference to Equal Opportunities and the relationships between Higher Education and the Labour Market.

Eric Midwinter OBE: Dr Midwinter was the Director of the Centre for Policy on Aging from 1980 to 1991. He is a well known innovator in the field of non formal adult education, with extensive practical experience of adult education in the UK. He holds an honorary doctorate from the Open University.

Peter Raggatt: is the Director of the Centre for Youth and Adult Studies at the Open University. He has been involved in producing staff development materials for improving NVQ's and is directing a research study into the management of assessment for NVQ's and Quality Assessment issues.

Malcolm Tight: Dr Malcolm Tight is Senior Lecturer in the Department of Continuing Education at the University of Warwick. His main research interests are in the philosophy and provision of higher education and in the role of higher education in the lives of adult students.

Colin Titmus: is the former Dean of Adult and Continuing Education at Goldsmiths College, London and External Professor of Adult Education at Leeds University. As one of the leading authorities in the field of comparative adult education, he has written extensively on new ideas and developments in adult education in Europe.

Brenda Walters: was formerly Access Research and Development Officer with Oxfordshire County Council. She is currently lecturing in Social Care at Oxford College of Further Education, and teaching adults with special needs. She has a particular interest in the local use of evaluation and performance indicators.

Roger Webb: Currently responsible as Regional Secretary for administration of support services to Open University students and staff in East Anglia. Professional interests are in the logistics of Student Support Services, specifically the use of information systems.

Alan Woodley: Senior Research Fellow in the Student Research Centre at the Open University. Has written on adult students' progress in distance education, and on outcomes for mature graduates. Is currently carrying out research on equal opportunities and on problems of access to higher education for adults.

Index

Index

Disaffection and Diversity:

Overcoming the Barriers for Adult Learners

Edited by
Judith Calder

A quiet but profound revolution in the design and delivery of learning opportunities for adults and in the accreditation of learning outcomes is taking place. Higher education is expanding at a rate which exceeds even that of the Robbins era; alternative routes for adults into further and higher education and into training are being introduced through the use of Access courses, and through the recognition of competencies acquired in a whole variety of different ways. The structure of the courses and training which adults can now undertake, the methods of teaching those courses and the types of qualifications which are beginning to be awarded reflect the accelerating social, technological and economic changes in the UK.

Judith Calder is Head of the Student Research Centre and Deputy Director of the Institute of Educational Technology at the Open University. She is involved in the evaluation of new forms of learning opportunities for adults and has a particular interest in adult learning strategies.

Cover design by Caroline Archer

ISBN 0-7507-0118-8

9 780750 701181 >

KEY CONCEPTS FOR UNDERSTANDING CURRICULUM

COLIN J MARSH

THE FALMER PRESS TEACHERS' LIBRARY

The Falmer Press

Key Concepts for
Understanding Curriculum

Fundamentals of Educational Research
Gary Anderson, *McGill University, Canada*

Search and Re-Search:
What the Inquiring Teacher Needs to Know
Edited by Rita S. Brause, *Fordham University, USA* and John S. Mayher,
New York University, USA

Doing Qualitative Research:
Circles Within Circles
Margot Ely, *New York University, USA* with Margaret Anzul,
Teri Friedman, Diane Garner and Ann McCormack Steinmetz

Teachers as Researchers:
Qualitative Inquiry as a Path to Empowerment
Joe L. Kincheloe, *Clemson University, USA*

Key Concepts for Understanding Curriculum
Colin Marsh, *Secondary Education Authority, Western Australia*

The Falmer Press Teachers' Library: 5

Key Concepts for Understanding Curriculum

Colin J. Marsh

 The Falmer Press

(A Member of the Taylor & Francis Group)
London • New York • Philadelphia

UK	The Falmer Press, 4 John St, London WC1N 2ET
USA	The Falmer Press, Taylor & Francis Inc., 1900 Frost Road, Suite 101, Bristol, PA 19007

First published 1992

A catalogue record for this book is available from the British Library

Library of Congress Cataloging-in-Publication Data are available on request

ISBN 0-75070-008-4
ISBN 0-75070-009-2 (pbk)

Jacket design by Caroline Archer
Typeset in 10/11.5 Bembo by
Graphicraft Typesetters Ltd, Hong Kong

Printed in Great Britain by Burgess Science Press, Basingstoke on paper which has a specified pH value on final paper manufacture of not less than 7.5 and is therefore 'acid free'.